EX-COMMUNIST WITNESSES

EX-COMMUNIST WITNESSES

FOUR STUDIES IN FACT FINDING

HERBERT L. PACKER

STANFORD UNIVERSITY PRESS
STANFORD, CALIFORNIA · 1962

Stanford University Press
Stanford, California

© 1962 by the Board of Trustees of the
Leland Stanford Junior University

Library of Congress Catalog Card Number: 62-8667

Printed in the United States of America

TO CARL B. SPAETH
forsan et haec olim meminisse iuvabit

PREFACE

These are studies of the public record. The data on which they are based consist of more than 200,000 pages of testimony contained in the transcripts of over one hundred different court trials, administrative hearings, and Congressional investigations, all relating in one way or another to the issue of Communist penetration in the United States and all containing testimony by former members of the Communist movement. The public record is the exclusive source of these studies. In them will be found many statements about people living and dead, about public and private events. Except where the context clearly indicates the contrary, such statements are drawn from the words of the particular witness whose testimony is being analyzed. They are presented here as evidence of what the witness said, not as establishing the truth of what the witness said.

"Public record" may be something of a misnomer as applied to this material. A great deal of it—practically all except for the printed hearings of Congressional investigations—exists only in the form of typescripts, or in microfilms of records that repose in the files of federal courts and administrative agencies. Because of the virtual inaccessibility of so much of this material, I have not thought it useful to provide page references to quoted or cited passages. A complete list of primary sources is given in Appendix B. The principal sources consulted in each of the studies that comprise Chapters 2, 3, 4, and 5 are given at the beginning of the Notes to each respective chapter. The Notes contain references to secondary material and are intended mainly to serve as guides to further reading on some of the matters discussed in the text.

The process of assembling and analyzing the large mass of

primary material is described in Appendix A. In that task, I had substantial help from many persons. Ceceile Murphy Cromwell, my research assistant during a large part of the project, deserves my special thanks, as does Hubert Farris, who completed the Index-Digest described in Appendix A after Mrs. Cromwell's departure. Of the several former students at the Stanford Law School who helped, I am particularly indebted to Paul Freese, who did the research and prepared the first draft for Chapter 5, and to George Norton for his work in helping to devise the Index-Digest. At a later stage I had the benefit of helpful comment from several of my colleagues, particularly John McDonough. I am grateful to my wife for her keen editorial eye, and for much more. My debt for steadfast support in times of trial is acknowledged, though hardly discharged, by the dedication.

The project was supported by a generous grant from the Fund for the Republic, Inc., whose officers and staff were, in the best tradition of philanthropic support, helpful when help was called for but scrupulous in avoiding any intrusion on the independence of the work. Neither they nor anyone else but me is to be charged with liability for the views expressed or for any errors or shortcomings in the analysis.

Chapter 2 was published in somewhat different form under the title *A Tale of Two Typewriters* in the May 1958 issue of the *Stanford Law Review* (Vol. 10, No. 3).

H.L.P.

Stanford, California
March 1962

CONTENTS

1 INTRODUCTION   1

2 CHAMBERS   21

3 BENTLEY   52

4 BUDENZ   121

5 LAUTNER   178

6 CONCLUSION   221

    APPENDIX A   249

    APPENDIX B   252

    NOTES   261

    INDEX   267

EX-COMMUNIST WITNESSES

1 · INTRODUCTION

Social judgments and social action rest on factual data, proven or assumed. The means used to discover and evaluate data are as important a subject of study in the world of governmental action as they are in the world of science. But we tend to take them rather more for granted in the sphere of governmental action. Get the facts, we say, and we will know better how to act. But how good are the processes by which we seek to get the facts? We do not ask that question as consistently as we should. The studies that follow are designed to ask that question about a small area of official fact-finding that has been a subject of great controversy in contemporary American life. Their theme is that fact-finding processes have their strengths and their weaknesses. The focus here is on the weaknesses, the pathology of fact-finding processes.

What we know or believe about the nature, scope and activities of the Communist movement in the United States derives in large part from the testimony of former Communists. The information contributed by these witnesses has covered a wide variety of subjects and has been given on many different occasions. We have had, among other things, descriptions of the organization and objectives of the American Communist Party at various stages in its history, analyses of methods used by Communists to infiltrate policy-making and opinion-making institutions, the identification of individuals as Communists or fellow travelers, and revelations of underground espionage plots engineered by the Communist Party.

The occasions on which ex-Communist witnesses have testified have been equally diverse: investigations by Congressional committees into subjects as varied as the loyalty of State Department officials, Communist proselytizing among Hollywood screen writers, and Soviet espionage in wartime Washington; administrative proceedings before the Subversive Activities Control Board to compel the registration of groups ranging from the Communist Party itself to the Veterans of the Abraham Lincoln Brigade; deportation proceedings before the Immigration and Naturalization Service involving the Communist activities of specific aliens; criminal trials for violations of the Smith Act and for perjury with respect to Communist affiliations, and many others.

What all of these testimonial occasions have in common is that they are working examples of legal processes which, whatever their ultimate purpose, share a common intermediate purpose which is also a common means for achieving their ultimate purpose: they all seek to elicit factual data relevant to the formulation of a conclusion or set of conclusions and to subject these data to tests designed to increase their reliability as premises for judgment. Deferring for the moment a detailed analysis of the functions of the various processes, it can readily be seen that each of them uses and tests factual data in the way just described. The ultimate purpose may be quite open-ended, as in the case of a Congressional committee, or it may be quite circumscribed, as in the case of a court trial. Its nature depends on the nature of the institution that carries on the process.

The purpose of a criminal trial is to determine the guilt or innocence of one or more persons with respect to a specific charge: Did Mr. X lie when he denied under oath being a member of the Communist Party? Did Mr. Y and Mr. Z conspire to teach and advocate the forcible overthrow of the United States Government? These two examples vary greatly in their specificity, but they both pose questions which, at least in theory, can be answered yes or no. By contrast, the purpose of a Congressional inquiry is not usually defined so precisely. It is the difference between "What is the answer to this question?" and "Enlighten us generally about this subject." Yet the two procedures have in common their goal of eliciting and testing factual data. And, in the myriad inquiries into the perplexing subject of the nature and extent of Communist penetration that have so occupied, not to say obsessed, us since the end of World War II, a most important source of raw data has been the testimony of former members of the Communist Party who have placed their knowledge at the disposal of agencies of official inquiry.

There are two general questions that can be asked about the usefulness of these data. The first, and by far the more frequently asked, is: How reliable are the data? The second is: How well adapted to their purposes are the processes used to elicit and test the data? The two questions are to an important extent related, but they are not the same question. The primary focus of this study is on the second question, although the first will necessarily be given some consideration. No very confident answer will be ventured, but it is hoped that a modest increment to our knowledge about the efficacy of official fact-finding processes will emerge from this series of case studies of how the institutions presently at our disposal have gone about the process of eliciting and testing the information about Communist penetration in the United States contributed by former members of the Communist Party.

My object has been to examine the three main procedures by which testimony has been elicited—legislative investigation, court trial, administrative proceeding—with a view to appraising their comparative utility as instruments for eliciting a full development of the facts. My conclusions are set forth in the last chapter of this study.

This emphasis on process seemed a useful approach for several reasons. First, it has not been attempted before, at least in the context of a detailed examination of specific testimony. Second, it offered an opportunity to say something useful about the testimony of these witnesses without attempting to determine who was "right." Finally, and most important, rather than merely to conduct a post-mortem on a series of events that now belong to history, it seemed preferable, if possible, to orient the discussion in a way that might provide useful ideas for future public policy.

The genesis and methodological evolution of the study are described in detail in Appendix A. At this point, some remarks are in order about three subjects: the problems posed by the diversity of witnesses and testimonial occasions relating to the general subject of Communist penetration, the reasons for selecting the testimony of a limited number of ex-Communist witnesses for intensive scrutiny, and the institutional setting of the various kinds of official inquiry whose efficacy we seek to test.

Owing to the *ad hoc* nature of the testimonial occasions in question, the testimony of the typical ex-Communist witness has been a fragmentary, piecemeal affair, sometimes overlapping what the same witness or other witnesses have said on other occasions, sometimes adding to a story already begun, sometimes contributing an entirely new chapter to the history of Communist penetration.

If there existed only one continuous story told by one former member of the Communist Party, there would be no occasion for this particular study, which has its genesis in the diversity of witnesses, of subjects, and of occasions. This diversity has two opposing tendencies. One is the strengthening of testimony by corroboration by other witnesses. The other is the weakening of testimony by contradictions, inconsistencies, and gaps. Thus Whittaker Chambers's testimony about Alger Hiss was strengthened by the subsequent testimony of Hede Massing and Nathaniel Weyl, and Louis Budenz's story about Owen Lattimore was weakened by Earl Browder's denial that a certain meeting in 1937, at which Budenz's testimony placed him, ever occurred. This study is necessarily concerned with these twin results of diversity. It has no preconception about either.

In the Budenz-Browder example cited above, there is obviously no way to determine from the record alone who was right. This question is clearly important, but it will not concern us here. This study, in its fact-finding aspect, performs a much more limited function. It seeks to distinguish those areas where the testimony of a given ex-Communist stands uncontradicted, either by himself or by others, from those areas where, on the face of the record, inconsistencies exist. Likewise, it attempts to distinguish those areas where our knowledge seems reasonably complete from those where there are gaps. Although the need for this type of analysis may seem painfully obvious, the job has never before been done.

As we all know, the record of a witness's testimony consists of questions as well as answers. The completeness of a witness's story, the way it hangs together, has to do at least as much with what questions are and are not asked as it does with the answers themselves. This is particularly true of legislative investigations, where there is no cross-examination and where questions may be dictated by specific political motives that have little to do with getting the whole truth into the record. The successive inquiries by two Senate committees into alleged Communist influence on the formation of State Department policy on China are a case in point. It is fair to say that the first of these, headed by Senator Tydings, tried hard to prove that the Administration had done nothing wrong in China, while the second, headed by Senator McCarran, tried equally hard to prove that the Administration had done everything wrong in China.

Under such circumstances, it becomes highly important to know whether all the questions were asked that should have been asked. This inquiry is made, at least in a preliminary way, in the pages that follow.

Literally scores of ex-Communist witnesses have appeared before scores of official tribunals to give their evidence about Communist goals and activities. From these witnesses it seemed wise to choose a limited number who, by the scope of their testimony and by the reliance that has been placed on it, can be deemed to be of central importance. The criteria of choice were necessarily arbitrary. A limitation in time was the first choice. The focus of attention on the activities of Communist groups in this country has been on the 1930's and early 1940's, when the similarity of goals among the Communists and much more broadly based groups in American society offered great opportunities for infiltration. The problem of dealing with the Depression and with the rise of aggressive totalitarian dictatorships in Europe and Asia afforded the Communists a hand-hold that reached its maximum strength in the common effort to win World War II, after the German attack brought Soviet Russia into the Western Alliance. The suggestions of widespread infiltration and subversion in government agencies brought to the fore a group of ex-Communists who vied with each other for public attention and whose revelations provided most of the raw material for widely prevalent public impressions about the extent and character of Communist penetration.

The serious charges of espionage carried on by clandestine Communists have undoubtedly captured the public imagination to a greater degree than any other aspect of the Communist problem. Accordingly, it seemed relevant to examine the testimony of Whittaker Chambers and that of Elizabeth Bentley, which made the names of Alger Hiss and Harry Dexter White synonymous with subversion in high places.

The name of Louis Budenz came to mind next, partly because

he has been the leading interpreter of Communist theology in the many proceedings in which he has testified, partly because he has been so prolific a source of accusations against persons prominent in American political and intellectual life. In terms of public impact, these three may fairly be regarded as the leading figures among those who have placed their experience in the Communist movement at the disposal of public agencies investigating the role of Communists in American life. To these was added a fourth, John Lautner. Lautner is not well known to the public, but he is an important figure for two reasons. First, his experience spanned an exceptionally long period, from 1932 to 1950. Second, he has been the Government's chief witness in every Smith Act case since his defection from the Communist Party, and his testimony, in so many proceedings involving the same basic issue, appeared to offer an excellent opportunity for comparative analysis. These four, then—Bentley, Budenz, Chambers, and Lautner—are the subjects of these studies.

The picture that emerges from the welter of details contained in the testimony examined is not an easy one to describe. In some ways, to be sure, notably with respect to the objectives of the Communist Party in the United States, it has substantial unity and coherence. The testimony has revealed in circumstantial detail a series of events which cannot but convince a fair-minded reader that the activities of the Communist Party in this country, particularly at the higher levels of the Party hierarchy, were inspired and directed by a dogmatic devotion to the principles of Marxism-Leninism and to the ideal of an international revolutionary movement functioning under the central direction of the Party apparatus in the Soviet Union. Sustained and vigorous cross-examination did not materially shake that testimony, nor did any of the rebuttal testimony adduced. On the basis of the public record, the reality of a Communist conspiracy cannot be doubted.

Beyond this, the ground is less firm. Above all, the record is inconclusive on the two most significant points of controversy: the assertion that certain persons participated in acts of espionage, and the assertion that persons who were not formally identified with the Communist Party nevertheless functioned under its direction and knowingly cooperated in working toward its goals. These two points of controversy are dealt with at length in the four case histories that comprise the body of this study.

II

It seems desirable for the benefit of readers not trained in the law to describe the institutional settings in which the fact-finding processes here described have taken place. Legal scholarship today is increasingly concerned with the institutions that prescribe and apply the rules or norms with which the traditional study of law has usually been occupied, and with the interplay between the rules as they are stated and their effects in practice. What official institutions say about Communist penetration and how they say it cannot be profitably examined without considering the institutions themselves. A major premise of this study is that the functional characteristics of the kinds of institution that are available to do social jobs act as a powerful determinant of how those jobs get done.

While we cannot say anything very definitive in short compass about courts, administrative agencies, and Congressional committees as fact-finders and fact-interpreters, it is necessary to give some attention to what they are set up to do and how they go about doing it in order to provide some anchor in reality for the extensive chronicle of testimony that occupies the next four chapters of this study.

The initial point to be made about judicial proceedings in questions relating to Communist penetration is so obvious as to be a truism, yet it has been strangely ignored by chroniclers of the disturbances of our times. The point is simply this: Courts have a broad and undifferentiated function to perform; they are not set up to undertake historical inquiries; their role is to resolve disputes according to largely predetermined norms. To the extent that they become involved in questions about Communist activities in the United States, they do so only incidentally to some other function assigned to them by our legal order. This truism has a powerful effect on the role courts have played in eliciting and testing the knowledge of ex-Communist witnesses. In particular, it serves to limit in ways often incompatible with the full development of the facts in all their complexity the range of information elicited and its location in the spatial and temporal dimensions of the social context. That is not its function. But when highly charged events come under judicial scrutiny, we often assume that the court has an informing as well as a decision-making function to perform.

That has been notably true in proceedings where Communist penetration is peripherally in issue, as in such *causes célèbres* as the Foley Square trial of the eleven top-ranking leaders of the American Communist Party under the Smith Act and the perjury trials of Alger Hiss and William Remington. There has been a tendency to view such proceedings as primarily directed at providing a kind of official record of contemporary history. Leaving aside the question of official motivation in bringing these proceedings, nothing could be further from an accurate description of their function, which is simply the ascertaining of guilt or innocence on a particular narrowly drawn charge. (Indeed, as we shall see, the more narrowly drawn the charge, the greater the success with which the institution of the criminal trial discharges its distinctive function.) The point becomes clear when we examine the two principal contexts in which data about Communist penetration have been involved in criminal trials: perjury cases and indictments under the Smith Act.

Perjury, under the Federal Criminal Code, is the offense of swearing to facts that the swearer knows or believes to be untrue. The perjury trial has been an important vehicle for the testimony of ex-Communists primarily because of a procedural problem in criminal law, the problem of the statute of limitations. A distinctive feature of our jurisprudence, both civil and criminal, is its reluctance to make determinations based on events which occurred so far in the past that memories have become stale and factual reconstruction difficult. This reluctance is embodied in the statute of limitations, which bars the trial of an alleged offender, even though the evidence of his guilt may be quite clear, after a specified period of time has elapsed since the alleged commission of his offense. In both the Hiss and Remington cases, which are the leading examples of perjury trials in the context of Communist activities, the offense with which the accused were realistically charged was espionage, the unauthorized divulgence of government information to the agents of a foreign power. In both cases, prosecution for the offense of espionage was barred by the statute of limitations. But there was great pressure for prosecution because of the sensational character of the revelations made by ex-Communist witnesses in the context of another kind of official proceeding, the Congressional investigation. Consequently, both Hiss and Remington were interrogated before grand juries about their alleged complicity in Communist activities, and were indicted, not for those activities, but for having falsely denied that they took place. In this way, the bar of the statute of limitations was avoided, since their alleged perjury, not the activities about which they were being questioned, was the event from which the time for commencing prosecution was reckoned.

The use of a perjury indictment, however, limits the ability of a tribunal to elicit the full story of the activity with respect to which the perjury is said to have been committed. The precise assertions that the defendant made under oath become the limiting factor in assessing the relevance, and hence the admissibility, of evidence at the trial. For example, Hiss was not charged with having been engaged in Communist activities over a period of several years. He was charged with having denied two very narrow aspects of the charges made against him by Whittaker Chambers. Consequently, the range of assertions made by Chambers was only peripherally in issue. All that was in question at the trial was whether Hiss had lied when he denied having given Chambers State Department information that Chambers was not authorized to have, and when he denied having seen Chambers after January 1, 1937. All evidence relating to those narrow charges came under the microscope of criminal trial by jury. A microscope is a valuable instrument, but it limits one's field of vision.

Another drawback of the perjury indictment from the standpoint of general fact-finding is that the charge against the defendant must be proved by the testimony of two witnesses, or by the testimony of one witness plus corroborating circumstances. As every prosecutor knows, this rule, designed to protect the perjury defendant from conviction on the basis of unsubstantiated testimony, has the effect of limiting the introduction of otherwise competent evidence which, however probative it might seem, lacks corroboration.

It should be emphasized that none of these distortions can be taken as criticism of the institution carrying on the process. On the contrary, they may be the necessary result of deference to important values that the process is expected to protect. The point is only that the particular process involved—here the trial of a perjury charge by a criminal court—is designed to do a particular job that may not be compatible with the historian's job of fully and faithfully recapturing a complex of past events.

At first glance, the other judicial process involved in this study, the trial of a Smith Act indictment, may seem less open to the historian's objections. Indeed, a detailed chronicle of the Smith Act prosecutions of Communist leaders (which this discussion does not attempt) might suggest that such proceedings pose issues too sprawling and untidy for resolution by the painstaking process of criminal prosecution. The fact is, however, that the criminal process has an inner logic of its own which tends to impose itself on any problem, no matter how unlikely, that is put to it for resolution; it sets in motion a process of channelization and stereotyping, which, however inimical to the kind of historical examination we are postulating as desirable, seems to have saved the Smith Act trials from collapsing completely under the weight of a burden that the criminal process is not capable of bearing. These speculations may have more meaning when considered in the light of a short description of the Smith Act, its purpose, and the history of its use.

The Smith Act must be viewed against the background of the strong tradition against sedition laws in this country. Ever since the notorious Alien and Sedition Law of 1798, which was misused for political purposes by the Federalists against the Republicans, we have had a strong reluctance to use the criminal sanction against utterances deemed by the community to be subversive. The Smith Act, passed in 1940, was the first departure in federal law since 1798 (with the sole exception of the misnamed Espionage Acts of 1917 and 1918) from the view that traitorous deeds, rather than merely traitorous words, should be the target of official intervention. The Act made it unlawful to teach or advocate the overthrow of the Government by force or violence. This individual proscription is extended to group activity (and at the same time made more amenable to prosecution) by application of the general charge of conspiracy, the making of an agreement by two or more persons to commit a crime.

The Smith Act does not mention the Communist Party by name for reasons relating to the constitutionality of a legislative proscription addressed to the activities of named individuals or groups, but there is no doubt that its sponsors had the Communist

Party in mind. The use of the statute by the Department of Justice has been almost entirely a systematic attack against the open activities of the Party by indictment and criminal trial of its leaders. This chapter of American legal history raises many interesting and difficult problems about the use of the criminal sanction to deal with deviant political behavior; we shall not be concerned with these problems in this study, except tangentially. What is more to the point here is a brief description of the processes of a Smith Act prosecution, to enable a reader to view in context the analysis of Smith Act testimony given in subsequent chapters.

The key case in the evolution of the Smith Act was *U.S. v. Dennis*, the prosecution of eleven national leaders of the Communist Party. The theory adopted by the Government in that case was followed in many subsequent prosecutions of so-called "second-string" leaders of the Party in various parts of the country. The theory was based on events following the dissolution of the Communist Party during World War II in the interest of furthering the then common cause of war against the Axis Powers. Following the successful conclusion of the War in 1945, the Party was reconstituted. The Government's theory was that this act of reconstitution signalized the replacement of the Popular Front, with its emphasis on achieving Communist objectives peaceably, by a militant, tightly disciplined, conspiratorial organization emphasizing the incompatibility of communism with other socio-economic systems and the necessity of resorting to violent measures to achieve the ultimate goal of the proletarian revolution. This ideology was said to be based on and illustrated by certain works of Marx, Lenin, and Stalin, often referred to as the Marxist-Leninist classics. These books and pamphlets were read into the record and, as one commentator has pointed out, provided evidence that "was more important to the Government's case than disputed testimony over whether individuals—in most cases Communists other than the defendants—had advocated revolution."

It may then be asked what role the ex-Communist witnesses played in these largely literary proceedings. For the most part, they offered expert testimony on the meaning that the alleged conspirators placed on the Marxist-Leninist classics, and on how those teachings, so interpreted, took form in the activities of the reconstituted Party and its leaders. To a lesser extent, these witnesses also recounted specific incidents designed to show the adherence of the named defendants to the goals of the alleged conspiracy.

In a typical conspiracy trial, the prosecution tries to prove two things: first, the existence of a conspiracy; second, the complicity of the individual defendants in the conspiracy. Nine-tenths of the Government's part of the voluminous trial record in the *Dennis* case (almost 16,000 pages), and in subsequent Smith Act cases, was devoted to proving the first of these two elements, the existence of the conspiracy. Efforts to prove the complicity of the individual defendants were, at least by contrast, perfunctory. The trials, then, while nominally trials of the named individual defendants, were in reality trials of the Communist Party on the charge of being an organization dedicated to the conspiratorial objective of bringing about the forcible overthrow of the Government "as speedily as circumstances would permit" (to use Judge Medina's phrase).

This factor accounts for the depressing sameness that pervades the records of the dozen or so Smith Act prosecutions examined in the course of the research on which this study was based. In each case, the "classics" occupy the center of the stage and the ex-Communists appear in the Talmudic role of glossers on the text. In the *Dennis* case, this role was discharged chiefly by Louis Budenz, whose major contribution was the hotly contested "Aesopian" theory that even when innocent on its face, the language used in Communist texts was understood by the initiate in a different and sinister sense. In later trials, Budenz, who had left the party a few months after the conspiracy was allegedly launched, was replaced in this role by John Lautner, who did not defect until 1950 and who was thereby able to explain in much greater detail than Budenz the interpretation placed on the "classics" in the day-to-day operations of the Party at its lower levels. Budenz has the greater reputation of the two, largely because of his appearance in *Dennis* and other bellwether proceedings and also because of his extra-curricular literary role as denouncer of the conspiracy, but it may be ventured that students of the problem will find the highly detailed testimony of Lautner, as elaborated over a series of Smith Act prosecutions, of considerably more interest. That, at any rate, is the judgment reflected in the choice of areas of these two witnesses' testimony selected for intensive scrutiny in this inquiry.

The *Dennis* case resulted in the conviction of all of the defendants, which was affirmed by the Supreme Court in 1951 in a far-reaching decision upholding the constitutionality of the Smith Act (over the dissent of Justices Black and Douglas). At the same time, trials of the "second-string" leaders were proceeding all over the country, with a prevailing pattern of convictions (although some individual defendants were occasionally acquitted). In 1957 this process was brought to an abrupt halt and the continuing utility of the Smith Act was severely impaired by the Supreme Court's decision in *Yates* v. *U.S.* On review of the conviction of a group of California "second-string" Party leaders, the Court held that the trial in question, which followed the prevalent Smith Act pattern, had not resulted in the drawing of a sufficient distinction between mere "abstract advocacy" of revolutionary doctrines, which the Court found to be constitutionally protected, and incitement to revolution as soon as circumstances permitted. In addition, the Court held that certain of the defendants should be acquitted because under proper instructions a jury could not have found that they had the requisite degree of involvement.

After this decision the Justice Department abandoned this prosecution and discontinued several others in which it was felt that the standards of proof required by the *Yates* case could not be met. At a conservative estimate at least 40,000 pages of testimony and countless man-hours of prosecutorial time went for nought. No new prosecutions have been instituted since *Yates*, and it seems unlikely that any will be. Yet, notwithstanding the *Yates* debacle, it is the opinion of competent observers that the Smith Act prosecutions seriously impeded the efforts of the open Communist Party to gain adherents and to grow in influence. Whether these prosecutions elicited any valuable information on the nature and operation of the Party is a question on which opinions will differ, but which should for our purposes be deferred until consideration of the testimony of John Lautner in Chapter 5.

A second type of proceeding that involves the kind of testimony in which we are interested is the administrative hearing. A few ways in which administrative agencies differ from courts may be noted. In the first place, the administrative agency functions on the basis of its supposed expertness in a particular area. Unlike the criminal trial, where the trier of fact is typically a jury composed of twelve laymen, an *ad hoc* group assembled for this case only, the administrative agency is a continuing expert body whose cumulative competence in a given field is thought to render it particularly capable of making difficult and specialized factual determinations. Since the heyday of the regulatory ideal in the 1930's, there has been some disenchantment with the role of the expert agency, especially in situations where its function is essentially adjudicative (retrospective and individualized), rather than rule-making (prospective and generalized), and is therefore thought to be of much the same character as the function of courts. In the adjudicative context, the agency is thought by some to be at a disadvantage when compared with a court, owing to its lack of independence and its close involvement in the particular problems with which it deals.

However that may be, in 1950 Congress chose to employ the administrative agency device for its most ambitious and far-reaching attack on the American Communists and their allies. The Internal Security Act (popularly known as the McCarran Act) has as its central feature the compulsory registration of "Communist-action" and "Communist-front" organizations. Upon registration, a number of onerous duties and disabilities fall upon an organization: It must file with the Attorney General detailed statements with respect to finances, membership, and other internal affairs; its members are denied public or defense employment, and may not receive or use a passport; literature distributed by the organization must indicate that the source is a "Communist organization." If the organization fails to register, the duty to do so falls upon the individual members. All these duties and disabilities are designed to make it impossible for organizations designated as "Communist-action" or as "Communist-front" to function effectively. One might say that the McCarran Act was designed to play the same role in the repression of subversive organizations as the Smith Act plays in the repression of subversive individuals.

Like the Smith Act, the McCarran Act requires a procedure for determining, on the basis of facts adduced, whether the object of its sanctions corresponds to the statutory prescription. In the case of the Smith Act, as we have seen, that procedure is the criminal trial. Under the McCarran Act, Congress set up an administrative agency, the Subversive Activities Control Board, to hear and determine applications by the Attorney General to compel the registration of organizations pursuant to the Act's provisions. At the risk of considerable oversimplification, it may be said that the Board's task is similar to the task of a jury in a Smith Act case, both being concerned primarily with the objectives of the allegedly conspiratorial organization.

As one might have anticipated, the principal proceeding under the McCarran Act was an application by the Attorney General, filed promptly upon passage of the Act, for an order requiring the Communist Party to register as a "Communist-action" organization. The hearings were matched in verbosity only by the *Dennis* case under the Smith Act. Evidence was taken and documents introduced for over a year, and a record of monumental proportions was compiled. The Government's witnesses included many famous Communists and undercover agents who had joined the Party at the behest of the Federal Bureau of Investigation. Some of their testimony will be dealt with in subsequent chapters of this study. The Board found that the Communist Party was a "Communist-action" organization and on April 20, 1953, entered an order requiring the Party to register as such.

The subsequent vicissitudes of this order need not be described in detail. The vigorous struggle of the Communist Party's attorneys to prevent the order from taking effect lends some point to President Truman's observation, in his unsuccessful veto of the Act, that the registration requirement "is about as practical as requiring thieves to register with the sheriff." The case went to the Supreme Court twice. Not until June 5, 1961, more than eight years after the Board entered its order, did the Supreme Court hold, in a 5-4 decision, that the registration provisions of the Act were constitutional and that the Board did not err in finding on the evidence before it that the Communist Party was a "Communist-action" organization. The Court expressly refused to consider the constitutionality of the requirement that individual members register if the Party itself fails to do so, as it apparently plans to do. At this writing, the practical effect of the registration requirement as applied to the Communist Party remains speculative.

At the same time as these proceedings were under way, the Board was also hearing evidence on applications to compel some twelve groups to register as "Communist-front" organizations. Orders were entered against all these groups, but there was no attempt to enforce them pending the Supreme Court's decision in the proceeding involving the Communist Party.

Whatever the final outcome, it seems doubtful that these proceedings will have any effect other than to place on the record a vast amount of information about the operations of Communist and fellow-traveler organizations on the contemporary American scene. Perhaps the chief purpose of proceedings such as these is the development of useful information. If this is true—and clearly the legislators who voted this ponderous machine into being had other aims in mind—the question arises whether the information so gathered adequately justifies the laborious and expensive process of carrying out these administrative hearings. We shall return to that question later in this study.

If one were designing an official fact-finding proceeding to serve an explicitly informational function, as opposed to a function in which the development of facts is viewed as a basis for official action, should the end product more closely approximate the court trial, the agency hearing, or the Congressional investigation? If the same question is put another way, the answer becomes fairly obvious. Given a choice between an extensive development of facts with the emphasis on readability and an intensive development of facts with the emphasis on reliability, the former is clearly preferable for informational or publicity purposes. A comparative reading of the record of a Congressional hearing on an issue such as the Hiss-Chambers affair, on the one hand, and the record of the perjury trial involving the same affair, on the other, will readily produce empirical verification for the preference.

Its facility of narration is at once the strength and the weakness of a Congressional inquiry, as opposed to the other kinds of fact-finding processes we have been considering. What appears to be a coherent account readily emerges from the testimony of witnesses freed from the confining effect of rules of evidence and, particularly, unscathed by cross-examination. One thing that persons not familiar with legal processes tend to overlook about cross-examination is that this great engine of truth, as Wigmore called it, is usually a slow, unspectacular, foot-slogging way of testing the reliability of what a witness has said. Its cumulative efficacy may be great, but it usually does not make very exciting reading. The absence of cross-examination in Congressional hearings, often deplored on grounds of personal fairness, is at once a boon to the facile narration of complicated facts and a bane to the careful verification of those facts. It is no wonder, then, that in our one official fact-finding process that is almost wholly free of the limitations imposed by the procedures of an adversary system, the most effective and the most irresponsible use has been made of the testimony of ex-Communist witnesses.

Many instances of the operation of Congressional committees and of other fact-finding processes will be reviewed in the chapters that follow. The major concern of this study, implicit throughout and, hopefully, made explicit in the concluding chapter, is the inquiry whether any of the processes just described and about to be exemplified are fully capable of bearing the burden that was thrust on them in the course of proceedings dealing with the issue of Communist penetration.

III

It remains only to say a word about the focus and method of the studies contained in the next four chapters.

The first study examines an aspect of the testimony of Whittaker Chambers. The central fact of the case made by Chambers's testimony against Alger Hiss was the existence of certain documents apparently prepared for espionage purposes and apparently typed on a typewriter owned by Hiss. For reasons explored in detail in this study, not all the possible explanations of the alleged facts were examined at the trials. The study attempts to canvass all the possibilities. From that base, it goes on to examine the larger question of whether or not, espionage apart, Hiss was involved in Communist activities. It considers whether all available evidence was adduced on this question, concludes that it was not, and points out why it was not. It goes on to make suggestions about how such evidence might be obtained. This study serves the function of pointing up, in a highly specific and detailed way, the difficulties involved in arriving at a judgment about the accuracy of the testimony of ex-Communist witnesses, even when the problem is the purely factual one of determining what really happened in a particular instance.

The second study, relating to Elizabeth Bentley, began with an attempt to subject her testimony in the Remington case to the same sort of analysis as was applied to Chambers's testimony in the Hiss case. The attempt proved abortive, principally because of the multiplicity of issues involved in the Remington case. Another difficulty was the fact that whereas the Hiss case involved disagreement over the entire range of the evidence, in the Remington case the common ground between prosecution and defense was substantial, and the differences came down to issues of credibility, to which the available extrinsic evidence bore little relation. Consequently, the study of the Remington case centered on two features: the interplay of testimony and publicity, which resulted in a grand jury situation seriously at odds with proper standards for the administration of justice; and the cross-examination of Bentley, which was the only occasion on which any aspects of her story have been searchingly tested on the witness stand. From both of these aspects of the case there emerge some tentative thoughts about the strengths and weaknesses of the litigation process.

Other aspects of the Bentley testimony canvassed in this study include her remarkable appearance before the House Un-American Activities Committee in 1948, when she revealed for the first time the general outline of her story of espionage in wartime Washington. The course of questioning in that hearing is quite revealing as an instance of how such matters are managed in Congressional hearings. The relationship between what Miss Bentley has testified in public and the unrevealed content of her conversations with the FBI is also examined, as an instance of a particularly important problem in the evaluation of testimony that has not received much critical attention. Finally, as in the case of Chambers, but on a somewhat more systematic basis, an attempt is made to examine the corroboration and contradiction existing in the public record of Bentley's testimony at large, and to assess the gaps in the present record and the reasons for them.

The testimony of the third witness, Louis Budenz, presents very different problems. Where Chambers and Bentley testified essentially to the narrow and specialized roles that they played in the Communist subworld of espionage, Budenz had observed the entire sweep of history from his perch on the *Daily Worker*. He represented himself as an expert on every aspect of United States foreign and domestic policy in which the Communists interested themselves, on all the twists and turns of the Party line, and on the identity and roles of all the people who aided the Party's work in all spheres. That is a large order, and the student of Mr. Budenz's testimony must be prepared either to take a great deal on faith or else to arm himself with an encyclopedic knowledge of current history. Some of Budenz's interrogators took the former course. The others failed, by and large, to prepare themselves adequately to tap this fount of information.

The most striking question raised by Budenz's testimony is what he means by a "Communist." The spectrum of Communist allegiance extends from hard-and-fast Party members through innumerable shadings of collaboration. At some indeterminate point it shades off into conduct that is, at worst, consciously parallel to that of the Communists, without being based on shared ultimate objectives. There is an analogous problem in the field of antitrust law, where "conspiracies" to restrain trade are forbidden. If businessmen behave in identical restrictive fashion, knowing that their rivals are doing likewise, the result may be a restraint of trade. But is there a conspiracy to restrain trade? Does "conscious parallelism," in the jargon of antitrust law, constitute the legal equivalent of "conspiracy"? The Supreme Court has said that conscious parallelism has not entirely read conspiracy out of the antitrust laws. The problem in assessing Mr. Budenz's testimony is to determine whether for him conscious parallelism has replaced conspiracy as the test for determining who is a Communist. At any rate, that is the impression that emerges from a close scrutiny of the confrontation of Louis Budenz and Owen Lattimore, a drama played out in two successive Congressional hearings that arrived at diametrically opposite conclusions. The records of these hearings afford an unmatched basis for comparative observation of the techniques of the Congressional investigation. That is the focus of the third of these four studies.

The fourth study is, again, different in focus from each of the others. Chambers and Bentley captured the public imagination with their dramatic stories of espionage and betrayal of trust. Budenz opined loftily on the theology of American Communism, and made headlines with his denunciation of highly placed persons whom he accused of working with the Communists. Lautner is different; he is the Organization Man. Alone among these witnesses, and indeed among all ex-Communists who have become witnesses in proceedings relating to the issue of Communism in the United States, Lautner trod for over twenty years the path of the Communist functionary. The life of the Party official is epitomized in his testimony as it is nowhere else. And because of the lateness of his break with Communism (1950), he has been in a unique position to testify about the post–World War II activities of the American Communist Party. These valuable attributes have not been lost on the Department of Justice. Lautner has testified in more Smith Act and Subversive Activities Control Board proceedings than any other witness. In each of these proceedings his testimony has covered much the same ground, with only such variations as were necessary to meet the special requirements of the case at hand. In the course of his work he has been subjected to cross-examinations of varying severity. Hence his testimony affords a special opportunity to examine the evolution of a witness's story during the course of many repetitions. That is the focus of the fourth study of this group.

These are studies of the public record. They are not psychological case histories. But to the extent that they describe events as seen through the eyes of witnesses to those events, they cannot avoid taking on the color of biography. Indeed, the processes by which facts are found from the testimony of witnesses must face the challenge of dealing with the highly subjective and individualistic qualities of human recollection and narration. The studies that follow must perforce deal with the interaction of process and personality.

2 · CHAMBERS

As with no other ex-Communist witness, the name of Whittaker Chambers is wholly bound up with the name of one of those whom he accused of Communist complicity. One can think of Louis Budenz without immediately thinking of Owen Lattimore. One can even think of Elizabeth Bentley without immediately thinking of William Remington. But to think of Chambers is at once to think of Alger Hiss. Despite the wide range of Communist activities to which Chambers testified, despite the number of people, some of them very prominent indeed, whom he denounced, Chambers still conjures up Hiss and Hiss Chambers. Accuser and accused, they will go down in history together. Hence it seems particularly appropriate to deal with the testimony of Chambers in the context of the Hiss trial. And if anything new is to be said about that celebrated affair, it also seems appropriate to concentrate attention on an aspect of the case that although not widely known, may be, nevertheless, the fulcrum on which the whole knotted complex of facts, inferences, and doubts remains precariously poised.

I

"The trial . . . is not an investigative, but a demonstrative proceeding." It is up to the parties to supply the information on which a verdict rests. What comes out depends on what goes in.

The truth of this view of the Anglo-American judicial process is nowhere more clearly exemplified than in what a British observer has called "the strange case" of Alger Hiss. After two trials, a jury convicted Hiss of having perjured himself when he swore to a grand jury that he had never passed government documents to Whittaker Chambers. Stripped of its baroque ornamentation, the evidence that the jury must have believed consisted of two things: Chambers's assertion that Hiss had passed documents to him, and the existence of papers concededly prepared for espionage purposes and concededly typed on a typewriter owned by Hiss. Everything else in the case—the prothonotary warbler that Hiss may or may not have told Chambers he saw, the bedroom at 30th Street where Chambers may or may not have slept, the $400 bank withdrawal that may or may not have been given to Chambers by Hiss, the performance of *She Stoops to Conquer* that the Hisses and the Chamberses may or may not have attended together, the red rug that may or may not have been a gift to Hiss from his grateful friends in Russia, the myriad details that made for such fascinated speculation at the time of the trial and that have not, even now, lost their power to prod the imagination—all of them were, finally, peripheral, if not irrelevant. The business of counting inconsistencies—so many for Hiss, so many for Chambers—became, even at the time of the trials, little more than a sideshow in the shadow of the central question: How could documents that were surely intended to be used for espionage have been typed on the typewriter of an innocent man? One might disbelieve Chambers, but how could one disbelieve Chambers plus the typewritten documents?

It was the defense's failure to advance an explanation that sent Alger Hiss to the penitentiary. It was, in the end, a failure of proof. The jury was given no plausible explanation for the existence of the incriminating documents, nothing to crystallize the doubts they must surely have felt about Chambers's largely uncorroborated, often confused and self-contradictory story. From the universe of relevant facts, known and knowable, the defense had not succeeded in extracting and placing before the jury the basis for a reasonable doubt about the central charge of espionage.* Hence

---

* Technically, as we have seen, the charge against Hiss was perjury. He was indicted on two counts for having falsely sworn that he had not passed government documents to Whittaker Chambers and that he had not seen Chambers after January 1, 1937. As a practical matter, the trials were devoted mainly to proving the first count; indeed, much of the evidence tending to support it also supported the second. The dates of the documents passed were such that if the jury believed they went from Hiss to Chambers, they necessari-

it is not surprising that the defense, having failed to convince higher courts that errors of law vitiated Hiss's conviction, was led to reject the fatal concession and to assert for the first time that the incriminating documents had not been typed on the machine owned by Hiss, but had instead been deliberately forged so that all would think they had come from Hiss.

The effort to demonstrate that forgery by typewriter could have taken place and had in fact been committed was, legally, a failure. The motion for a new trial in which it was put forward was denied. That was almost six years ago. Ancient history, one might think, and obscure ancient history at that; for by the time the motion for new trial came on to be argued Hiss had spent almost eighteen months in prison, the public excitement over the case had lapsed, and one may surmise that most of the few people who bothered to learn from their daily papers that Alger Hiss had been denied a new trial had no notion of why the new trial had been sought and what merit, if any, there was in the plea. So it might have remained, a dusty footnote to a famous old case, of interest only to fanatical partisans of one or the other protagonist, had Alger Hiss not chosen to carry his plea to the only forum now open to him.

Lawyer to the last, Hiss has titled his book as a brief would be captioned. But we are no longer in the United States District Court for the Southern District of New York. What we must take to be Alger Hiss's final brief has been filed in the court of public opinion. What does it add to the stacks of pages that have piled up since Chambers made his first public accusation in August 1948?

What the book is not appears more readily on a first reading than what it is. It is not, to begin with the most obvious point, an "inside story." There is little in the book that could not be derived from a close (if biased) reading of the public record and of contemporaneous newspaper accounts of the Congressional hearings and the trials. Very little of Hiss the man comes through, except a kind of stereotype or folk-image of the "smart lawyer"—austere, precise, a little picayune. We get no glimpse of the charm of man-

---

ly also believed that Hiss saw Chambers after January 1, 1937. The essential charge, then, was that Hiss had lied when he said he had not committed espionage (i.e., passed government documents to a person not authorized to receive them). As a matter of substance, the charge being tried was a charge of espionage.

ner or the distinction of mind that won and kept for him so many distinguished friends. Nor is his book the vehicle for sensational new revelations about the facts. Hiss has not, as everyone must now know, either confessed that Chambers told the truth or suggested why Chambers lied. The book is no more sensational in tone than it is in content. This has disappointed many, and has convinced some that Hiss must be guilty, because (so they say) a truly innocent man would be more vociferously indignant. I cannot agree that guilt or innocence is to be measured in decibels, and I find the tone of the book—quiet, reasonable, almost good-tempered—a welcome contrast to much of the sensationalism produced by the case. But *In the Court of Public Opinion* has the defects of its virtues. Its lack of drama and color causes the reader's attention to flag, and this can be fatal to a book whose impact must depend on making the reader pay close and continuous attention to a very complicated narrative.

Of course, the book's quality as literature is not at issue. What we want to know is whether the book sheds any new light on the case. "New light" cannot, after two trials, after conviction, after appeal, mean a rearrangement of subordinate corroborating or impeaching facts. It can only mean something that will clarify for us the ultimate question of guilt or innocence.

"Guilt" or "innocence," in turn, cannot be limited to the precise charges laid in the indictment, because Hiss's defense was not merely that he had not passed State Department papers to Chambers but, more sweepingly, that he had never taken part in underground Communist activities of any kind. It is conceivable that he was not guilty of the precise charges for which he was convicted, and if he was not, a miscarriage of justice certainly occurred. But in view of the position of absolute innocence that Hiss maintained throughout, not many tears will be shed for him if it should appear that he was up to his neck in other Communist activities. Hiss's book is devoted to showing how and why he was wrongly convicted, not to establishing his total innocence. Consequently, any assessment of the book's success must be limited to what Hiss has to say about how he was "framed" by Whittaker Chambers. What he has to say on this score comes down to a restatement of his motion for a new trial, which is thus now for the first time put before a general audience. The essence of his motion for a new trial is the "tale of two typewriters," which is an attempt to demonstrate, as Hiss said just before he was sentenced, "how Whittaker Chambers was able to carry out forgery by typewriter."* In this chapter I shall attempt first to analyze that tale and then to examine the assertion of total innocence and the adequacy of the present record on that issue.

In so limiting this consideration of the questions raised by Hiss's book, I do not mean to suggest that the book contains nothing else of value or of interest. It raises interesting and troubling questions about the interaction of Congressional investigation with criminal prosecution, about the creation of an atmosphere in which fair trial becomes measurably more difficult, and about other aspects of the administration of criminal justice that are not invulnerable to criticism. That these questions are important I would be the last to deny, but they are not unique to the Hiss case and the Hiss case is not unique because of them.

II

The "forged typewriter" theory is a complicated one and cannot be evaluated intelligently without a detailed and, I fear, tedious recital of what the defense did, what questions it asked its experts (as well as what questions it did not ask), and what answers its experts gave (as well as what answers they did not give).

In February 1950, after Hiss's conviction at the second trial, the late Mr. Chester Lane entered the case as counsel of record for Hiss in connection with his appeal, which was briefed by Mr. Lane and Mr. Robert Benjamin and argued by Mr. Benjamin. That

---

* Other grounds relied on in the motion for new trial included impeachments of the credibility of Edith Murray, a government rebuttal witness who had identified the Hisses as visitors at the Chambers residence in Baltimore; evidence tending to show that Chambers had left the Communist Party several weeks before the date of the last State Department document he claimed Hiss had given him as a Communist agent; and the assertion that Lee Pressman's testimony showed that Hiss had not been in a Communist group to which Chambers claimed he belonged. Of these several grounds, perhaps the most troubling is the suggestion that Chambers had withdrawn from the underground Communist movement before he could have received certain documents from Hiss. The matter is not treated adequately in Judge Goddard's opinion denying the motion for new trial. However, the newly proffered evidence was not inconsistent with the possibility that Chambers was readying his retreat to respectability at the same time that he was winding up his work for the Communists. This possibility makes Chambers look a bit less high-minded than he makes himself out to be; but that does not help Hiss.

appeal ended in the affirmance of Hiss's conviction by the Court of Appeals for the Second Circuit and the denial of certiorari by the Supreme Court. At the same time, Mr. Lane began to speculate on the possibility that the defense at the trial had been wrong in conceding that the typewritten State Department documents alleged to have been prepared on the Hiss typewriter and handed to Chambers (the "Baltimore Documents")* had in fact been typed on the same machine as certain letters of Mrs. Hiss (the "Hiss Standards"), which had undoubtedly been typed on a Woodstock typewriter once owned by the Hisses.

The defense's concession was based on the unchallenged assertion by an FBI expert on questioned documents, Ramos C. Feehan, that the Baltimore Documents and the Hiss Standards had been typed on the same machine. Feehan's testimony pointed out the occurrence in the two sets of documents of similar deviations from the norm in ten characters. Mr. Lane speculated that it might be possible to construct a typewriter that would duplicate some or all of the characteristics of another typewriter, that if it were possible to do so, doubt would be cast on Feehan's conclusion that the Baltimore Documents and the Hiss Standards had been typed on the same machine.

In short, the first part of Mr. Lane's theory was that forgery by typewriter could be committed. It would still remain, of course, to show a probability that forgery by typewriter had been committed.

Mr. Lane asked Martin Tytell, a typewriter engineer, whether it would be possible for someone working only from samples typed on a particular machine and without having that machine in his possession, to construct a machine that would produce work sufficiently similar to the original samples to make it likely that the tests applied by Feehan would result in the conclusion that the two sets of samples were produced on the same machine. If Tytell had said no, that would presumably have been the end of the matter, and the case would not have taken its new and interesting turn. But Tytell did not discourage Mr. Lane. On the contrary, he went beyond Mr. Lane's question and said that he could produce

---

* So called because they were proffered by Chambers during a pre-trial deposition held in Baltimore in connection with a libel action brought by Hiss against Chambers.

a typewriter that not only would duplicate *some* of the characteristics of an original sample, but would do work so similar in *all* respects that no expert, even one forewarned about the possibility of
forgery by typewriter, could distinguish the work produced on the
new machine from the original sample. (It should be said at this
point that Tytell did not entirely succeed in making good his
claim.) Encouraged by Tytell's optimism, Mr. Lane commissioned
him to build a typewriter that would effectively "forge" samples
produced on the typewriter introduced into evidence at the trial
as the Hiss machine. (Since there is a question whether that typewriter was in fact the Hiss machine, I shall not refer to it as such,
but instead shall designate it by the serial number it bears, 230099.)

No. 230099 was a Woodstock typewriter which, it appeared,
had originally been owned by Mrs. Hiss's father, Thomas Fansler.
It had been used by Fansler in his business; had been given by him
to the Hisses and used by them; had been given by them to Perry
Catlett, the son of one of their maids, during or after one of their
moves, probably in the winter or spring of 1938; had then passed
through various hands; and had finally, on the eve of the first trial,
been located and purchased by the defense. It was introduced into
evidence at both trials and was considered by all concerned to be
the machine on which both the Hiss Standards and the Baltimore
Documents had been typed. (Indeed, the primary effort of the
defense was to show that the machine had been given to Perry
Catlett before the earliest dates on which the Baltimore Documents could have been typed.) After the second trial, 230099,
together with other defense exhibits, came into Mr. Lane's custody.

Mr. Lane supplied Tytell with specimens of typing done on
230099. Tytell never saw the machine itself. Working entirely
from the specimens, Tytell set out to construct a machine that
would produce work indistinguishable from the specimens. Meanwhile, Mr. Lane attempted to find an examiner of questioned documents who would agree to inspect the results as the work pro-
gressed and suggest improvements where necessary. He encountered great reluctance, apparently motivated either by disbelief
that the experiment could succeed or by fear it might. (The stock-
in-trade of examiners of questioned typescripts is that typewriters
are unique, and a conclusion that their supposedly unique characteristics can be reproduced would have as shattering an effect

on the art of document examination as a discovery that fingerprints can be artificially forged would have on the present police system of identification.) But finally Mr. Lane found a professional, Miss Elizabeth McCarthy, who was willing to break ranks. She aided in the work, compared the product of Tytell's machine with the samples from 230099, and pointed out where the similarities had been achieved and where further refinement was necessary. Finally, after some eighteen months of work (less time would have been needed but for the difficulty in getting expert advice), Tytell produced a machine whose work, Miss McCarthy swears, is so similar to the 230099 samples that, although she herself can still detect differences, "an expert in the field, however highly qualified, would find it difficult if not impossible to distinguish between samples from the two machines."

Mr. Lane then called in another expert, Mrs. Evelyn Ehrlich, to give her opinion whether the product of 230099 was distinguishable from that of the Tytell machine. For some reason that Mr. Lane does not explain, Mrs. Ehrlich was forewarned about the possibility of forgery, and her opinion reiterates in substance the conclusion reached by Miss McCarthy: that she could detect the differences, but only because she had been forewarned, and that an expert who was not forewarned could not have detected differences. Two obvious comments may be made on this opinion of Mrs. Ehrlich's. First, Tytell's claim was not substantiated—an expert who *was* forewarned *could* tell the differences. Second, and more important, the opinion lacks the authority it might have had if Mrs. Ehrlich had not been told in advance that forgery was involved, but had simply been asked to say whether a certain group of documents had all been typed on the same machine. If that procedure had been followed, we might have the opinion of an expert (not forewarned about forgery) that all the documents were typed on the same machine. Such an opinion would be far more convincing proof of the possibility of successful forgery than the opinion we have from Mrs. Ehrlich: that she can tell the difference but that she doesn't think anyone else, unforewarned and applying the conventional tests, could do so. Of course, there is another possibility: Mrs. Ehrlich, unforewarned, might still have succeeded in separating the products of the two typewriters, in which case Mr. Lane would not have had much to show for the

Tytell experiment. As it is, we have only an opinion that it would be possible to forge a typewriter that would fool an expert; we have no proof in the form of an expert who has been fooled.

However, this cavil applies only to the investigative technique followed by Mr. Lane. In fairness to him, it should be pointed out that his experiment was cut short by the necessity of filing the motion for new trial within two years after the final judgment against Hiss. The Tytell machine could have been improved further, Tytell says, and an expert might have been fooled by the similarity between its product and that of 230099. Indeed, the defense submitted samples from the two machines and challenged the Government to have its experts state which documents were typed on which machine, a challenge that the Government ignored (as it was entitled to do on a motion for new trial).

The construction of the Tytell machine certainly suggests at the very least that forgery by typewriter can be committed. But had it been? Let us consider for a moment what would be convincing proof that a forged typewriter had been used to type the Baltimore Documents. We have three pieces of evidence: (a) the Hiss Standards, (b) the Baltimore Documents, and (c) the samples typed on the typewriter in evidence, 230099. We have, let us say, an (unforewarned) examiner of questioned documents whose competence and impartiality are beyond reproach. He examines and compares the documents. What is the range of possible conclusions?

He may, of course, conclude that all three sets of samples were typed on the same typewriter. That, in effect, was the conclusion reached at the trial, a conclusion based in part on mere surmise because there was no comparison of the Hiss Standards and the Baltimore Documents, on the one hand, with samples of typing from 230099, on the other. Or our expert might conclude that each of the three sets was typed on a different machine. Such a conclusion would possibly prove too much, for it is almost inconceivable that the Hiss Standards and the Baltimore Documents were typed on different machines and that neither was typed on 230099. A tale of three typewriters would lead us to think that our expert is being over-refined in his analysis and is spotting differences that are not significant.

Our expert might, then, conclude that the Hiss Standards and the Baltimore Documents were typed on the same machine, but that the machine was not 230099. This would mean that 230099 was not the Hiss typewriter. However, the essence of the case against Hiss was not that 230099 was the Hiss typewriter, but that the Hiss Standards and the Baltimore Documents came from the same typewriter, whatever that typewriter may have been.

The only evidence, then, that at this point in our analysis would seem to substantiate a charge of forgery is evidence that the Hiss Standards and the Baltimore Documents were typed on different machines, and that one of the machines was 230099. Does it matter which set was typed on 230099? I think it does. If our expert were to tell us that the Hiss Standards were typed on 230099 but the Baltimore Documents were not, there would be no difficulty in fixing the provenance of 230099. It would be just what it appears to be: the typewriter which the Hisses owned and used until 1937 or 1938, when they gave it to Perry Catlett, and which then passed through various hands until it was discovered by the defense investigators in the spring of 1949. There would be no question of anyone's having tampered with that particular typewriter in some unexplained way. The forgery would have been committed, as Tytell's work leads us to think it might have been, by someone's constructing a machine from samples of the type work of 230099 and using that machine to type the Baltimore Documents.

But if our expert were to tell us that the Hiss Standards did not come from 230099 but the Baltimore Documents did, a number of troublesome questions would arise. What these questions amount to is this: If 230099 is not the Hiss typewriter, how did it come to be found where the Hiss typewriter should have been? And how did Chambers (if there was forgery and he was the forger) know where the Hiss typewriter could be found? And if, somehow, he knew that, why did he not use the Hiss typewriter itself instead of laboriously constructing a forgery and then planting it in place of the purloined Hiss machine? We shall have to return to these questions at greater length because, as we shall now see, the theory adopted by the defense requires that they be answered.

After making a comparison of the originals of the Hiss Standards, the Baltimore Documents, and samples from 230099 for the first time, Mrs. Ehrlich reached the firm conclusion that the Hiss

Standards had not been typed on 230099. However, she was not able to say definitely whether the Baltimore Documents were typed on 230099, because the grade of paper and the quality of the ribbon used in typing the Baltimore Documents made them unsuitable for comparison. Similarly, she was not able to say definitely that the Baltimore Documents and the Hiss Standards were typed on different machines, and she limited herself to the conclusion that "the observable peculiarities in the type of the Baltimore Documents in my opinion more nearly resemble the peculiarities in the typing from #N230099 than they do the peculiarities in the Hiss Standards which I used for comparison."

Miss McCarthy also examined the originals of the three sets of documents. Her conclusion (not referred to in Hiss's book) is worth quoting *in extenso*:

Without considering the possibility of forgery, I should have concluded, by all standard tests ordinarily applied by questioned document examiners, that all three sets of documents were typed on the same machine. I should not have based this conclusion merely upon an inconsequential number of relatively identical peculiarities, but upon the more convincing fact that I find no substantial consistent deviations in type impressions as among the three sets of documents. However, my own experience has shown me that it is possible, by careful work on a machine, to eliminate almost completely the deviations which would normally have developed between its typing and that of another machine, and therefore, while I cannot say definitely that all three sets of documents were not typed on the same machine, I believe it just as possible, in the light of the observable facts, that the Baltimore Documents were typed on a machine which was not the original Hiss machine used for the standards, but another machine made to type like the original Hiss machine. Since the typing of the Baltimore Documents so closely resembles the typing of the specimens from the so-called Hiss machine, and since Dr. Norman has furnished evidence that that machine is a deliberately fabricated one, I can only conclude that, as between the two possibilities, the forgery of the Baltimore Documents is the more likely. If the Baltimore Documents are forged, the forgery is a good one, but it is no better than I know would be possible with careful workmanship.

This is pretty indecisive evidence. Miss McCarthy admits that had she not been alerted to the possibility of forgery, she would have concluded that all three sets of documents came from the same machine. But, as she herself says, she had been alerted to

that possibility, and further, she had been apprised of the existence of certain other indications (which we shall come to presently) that forgery might have been committed. In this state of
hyperconsciousness, is it entirely unreasonable to suppose that
Miss McCarthy may have looked so hard for signs of divergence
that she found what she was looking for, and that what she was
looking for was, in fact, not there? The examination of questioned
documents is not, after all, an exact science; it is the exercise of
judgment—highly informed, technically competent, but still, in
the end, judgment. If only Mr. Lane had obtained a completely
"blind" expert opinion on the samples from 230099 and the Tytell
machine, we would have a benchmark for assessing what weight,
if any, to assign to the fact that the examination of the crucial
papers (the Baltimore Documents and the Hiss Standards) was
carried on by experts who were alive to the possibility of forgery,
and whose judgment must have been affected by their knowledge.
As it is, we can only surmise, and if there were no other evidence
tending to support a conclusion of forgery, my surmise would be
that Mr. Lane's experts (acting, be it said, in perfect good faith)
had been influenced by their consciousness that forgery might have
been committed into concluding that it had been, when in fact it
had not.

We would be justified, I think, in dismissing the defense theory
if it rested on no more than what I have just described. But as it
happens, there are other considerations suggesting that forgery
may have been committed. Mr. Lane's investigation led him to
conclude, and to offer evidence in support of his conclusions, that
230099 itself, its history and its present condition considered, was
—irrespective of what one might be able to prove about document
comparison—a machine deliberately fabricated to appear to be
what it was not. He asserted (1) that its probable date of manufacture made it in the highest degree unlikely that 230099 could
have been the typewriter Fansler owned and later gave to the
Hisses, and (2) that the type and type bars of 230099 showed un-
mistakable signs of having been altered in ways inconsistent with
the normal processes of manufacture and repair.

Mr. Lane's second point, that the machine showed signs of
having been tampered with, rests on expert opinion: in this instance, that of Daniel P. Norman, president of a firm engaged in

the chemical analysis of metals, papers, and other substances. Like the opinions of Miss McCarthy and Mrs. Ehrlich, and like all expert opinion, Norman's is a matter of judgment, of the assessment of probabilities, and not a matter of airtight certainty. It is sharply contested by experts mustered by the Government. The most that can be said of it is that, if believed, Norman's opinion lends some support to the conclusion that 230099 was deliberately altered for the purpose of committing forgery, but only when that opinion is taken together with other evidence of forgery, if that evidence is believed.

In quite a different category, however, is Mr. Lane's contention that 230099 was manufactured by Woodstock too late to be the Hiss machine. Setting aside for the moment the question of what Mr. Lane was actually able to produce in support of this contention, we can agree that if it could be shown, say, that Fansler owned the "Hiss typewriter" in July of 1929, but that 230099 was not manufactured until August of 1929, then 230099 is not the Hiss typewriter. This is a matter not of probabilities, but of plain historical fact. However, at the risk of wearisome repetition, I must point out that even if this is established as a matter of historical fact, Hiss is not exonerated. All that has been proved is that 230099 is not the machine that the Hisses once owned. That fact is significant only if the Hiss Standards (which we know were typed by Mrs. Hiss on a machine then in the Hisses' possession) and the Baltimore Documents were not typed on the same machine. If they were, the provenance of 230099 is utterly irrelevant. So we are thrown back on Mrs. Ehrlich's opinion, and that opinion as we have seen, did not take a firm position on the crucial question, but only on the question whether the Hiss Standards were typed on 230099.

This puts the matter in the light most unfavorable to Hiss's contention. On the other side, it should be pointed out that the three items of "forgery" evidence—the dissimilarity of the Hiss Standards to 230099, the abnormal alteration of 230099, and the date of manufacture of 230099—are mutually consistent. They all would seem to support the same conclusion: that the Hisses never owned 230099 and that this was the typewriter by which forgery was committed. This may seem obvious, but consider for a moment its significance. As I have shown, the forgery theory can take one of two equally plausible (or implausible) forms: Either (a) the forgery was committed on an unknown machine and the typewriter that turned up (230099) is the Hiss typewriter; or (b) the forgery was committed on 230099 and that machine is not the Hiss typewriter. The former theory, *a priori*, is by far the more likely of the two, because from all the evidence introduced at the trial it seems that 230099 *should* be the Hiss machine. Yet the three pieces of evidence that may in some degree lead to a conclusion that forgery was committed *all* point to the more difficult of the two theories. Each of these pieces of evidence tends to bolster the reliability of each of the other two.

Since two of the three items are matters of expert opinion evidence, with all the limitations of such evidence, the third item— the history of 230099—assumes critical importance. It does not flout the laws of probability that two experts, each approached in a highly tendentious way, could reach mutually consistent conclusions about two separate but complementary propositions and yet be wrong. But by how much is the probability that they are wrong reduced if their conclusions agree with a third connected proposition that is not a matter of opinion at all, but of demonstrable fact?

If Mr. Lane had succeeded in establishing that 230099 was not the Hiss typewriter, an impartial observer could not lightly dismiss the opinion evidence that the Hiss Standards were not typed on 230099 and that 230099 had been deliberately altered. And if these three propositions were accepted as true, even in the absence of a clear-cut opinion that the Hiss Standards and the Baltimore Documents were not typed on the same machine, or that the Baltimore Documents were typed on 230099, or both, it would be an uncritical observer indeed who could resist the conclusion that there had been dirty work at the crossroads. Typewriter A does not turn up in a location and under circumstances suggesting that it is Typewriter B by mere happenstance. (However, as I shall presently show, such a conclusion does not necessarily exonerate Hiss, even of the precise charge against him, let alone of Communist complicity in general.)

The problem is that Mr. Lane, through no fault of his own— indeed, after performing near-miracles of intelligent investigation —was not able to nail the point down. His argument is: (1) The serial numbers and production records of the Woodstock company for the year 1929 indicate that 230099 was not manufactured before July 3 at the very earliest and probably was not manufactured until August or September of that year. (2) Expert examination of letters typed in Fansler's office indicates that Fansler acquired the typewriter that later went to the Hisses sometime between June 20 and July 8, 1929. (3) It is therefore virtually impossible for 230099 to be the Hiss machine. The implied conclusion, of course, is that 230099 was acquired as a reasonable facsimile of the Hiss machine by the forger or forgers, who altered it to conform either to the original Hiss machine or to samples of typing from that machine, used it to produce the Baltimore Documents, and then left it where it would eventually be discovered and mistakenly identified, as it was, as the Hiss typewriter.

Mr. Lane's account of his efforts to establish the impossibility of 230099's having been the Hiss machine reads like one of those melodramas in which the hero is forever just on the verge of making the great discovery that will clear everything up when he is thwarted by some implacable and invisible force, whose identity we do not learn until the last page. The only difference here is that there is no last page. Mr. Lane, like the hero of a penny dreadful, was frustrated in what must have been a heartbreaking way at every turn, but the frustrations were never resolved.

Defense investigators obtained monthly production figures and the approximate serial numbers put on machines made in January 1929, March 1929, and January 1930. Comparison of the figures showed a discrepancy; the difference between the two January serial numbers suggested that 42,000 machines were made in 1929, but the monthly production records showed that only 28,548 were made. It seemed, therefore, that 13,452 serial numbers were skipped during the year. Typewriter 220000 was made some time in March. Assuming that all numbers skipped were skipped before 230099 was manufactured (the assumption most unfavorable to his theory), Mr. Lane reasoned from the production figures that the highest serial number produced in June was 229866, that 230099 would have been produced on July 3 at the earliest, and that it was highly unlikely that Fansler could have used in Philadelphia on July 8 a typewriter made in Woodstock, Illinois, on July 3, especially since the intervening days included both the

Fourth of July and a weekend. Unfortunately, Mr. Lane was working from incomplete figures supplied to his representative by the Woodstock people. Mr. Lane's representative was not given direct access to the figures, the Woodstock people declined to sign an affidavit prepared by his representative, and his representative declined to make an affidavit that he had prepared the affidavit that the Woodstock people wouldn't sign—all apparently for fear of getting mixed up in the Hiss case! As if this weren't bad enough, one of Mr. Lane's associates managed to track down the typewriter salesman who had sold Fansler his Woodstock, only to discover that he had apparently burned all his sales records (which would have contained the most conclusive evidence of when Fansler bought his Woodstock) after an earlier visit from the FBI. Lurking in the background was the interesting suggestion that in the earlier stages of investigation the FBI had been looking for a Woodstock with a serial number lower than 230099. But this was hearsay, since Mr. Lane never managed to get an affidavit from any of those directly involved; and, at any rate, the FBI denied the charge.

Of the three items of forgery evidence, the one relating to the date of manufacture of 230099, although far from conclusive, is the most strongly suggestive. Considered apart from the other two items, it is also the most credible, being based not on the judgment of experts but on data that all are equally competent to assess. One trouble with the Ehrlich and the Norman evidence, aside from its intrinsic ambiguity, is that it was developed *after* there was reason to suppose that 230099 was not the Hiss typewriter and, presumably, with knowledge of this doubt. If an expert knows what he is looking for, the chance that he will find it is increased; to say so is not to impugn the integrity of experts, but only to assert that they are not unlike the rest of us. A conspicuous example of what I mean is to be found in the affidavit of Miss McCarthy quoted earlier. She was inclined to think that the Baltimore Documents had been typed on 230099 *because* of Norman's conclusion that 230099 was a deliberately fabricated machine. To what extent did Mrs. Ehrlich and Norman reach the conclusions they did *because* Mr. Lane had convincingly demonstrated that 230099 was probably not the Hiss typewriter?

In short, Mr. Lane raised interesting and troublesome questions, but he did not demonstrate a high enough probability of forgery by typewriter to enable a judge to say, as he must under the federal standard, that "on a new trial, the newly discovered evidence would probably produce an acquittal." At best, Mr. Lane uncovered leads which, if it had been possible to pursue them, might have resulted in the production of evidence that would exonerate Hiss of the specific charge brought against him; as a matter of law, the motion for a new trial was rightly denied. It does not by any means follow, however, that Hiss's chance of acquittal would not have been greater if the "forged typewriter" theory had been used by the defense at the trial. It is probably easier to create a reasonable doubt in a jury's mind in the first instance, and to secure an acquittal, than it is to persuade a judge after conviction that a given piece of evidence would probably have created such a reasonable doubt, and thereby to secure a new trial. The effect of McCarthy, Ehrlich, Tytell, Norman, *et al.* might well have turned the tide before a jury. But it is still some distance from that possibility, however strong, to the probability that a judge determining a motion for new trial must find.

But the federal rule on new trials is not the rule that prevails in the court of public opinion. So let us speculate a little further. Let us assume that Mr. Lane has succeeded in convincing us that the Hiss Standards were not typed on 230099, and that 230099 was a deliberate fabrication used to type the Baltimore Documents with the design of incriminating Alger Hiss. How and when was this done? Bear in mind that we have now eliminated, by hypothesis, the possibility that the Baltimore Documents were typed on the Hiss typewriter, and that as a result we now have two typewriters to account for.

Mr. Lane theorizes that the forgery probably took place in 1948, after Hiss had filed his libel action against Chambers. Until that time, he points out, Chambers had never asserted that Hiss had committed espionage and, indeed, had denied that espionage was involved. We are invited to infer that in the face of a potentially ruinous suit, against which he had no adequate defense, Chambers forged the Baltimore Documents (perhaps from microfilm or other copies of the underlying papers in his possession) as incontrovertible proof that Hiss had committed espionage, and therefore that Chambers's allegations about Hiss's Communist connections were true.

This aspect of Mr. Lane's theory invites criticism. First, there is the time element. Chambers's initial accusations against Hiss were made in August 1948. The libel suit was filed in September, after Chambers had repeated his accusations in a nonprivileged forum. Chambers produced the incriminating papers in November, during pre-trial examination in the libel suit. Two months is not a very long time in which to fabricate a typewriter (how long would it take just to find a Woodstock of the right vintage?), forge the documents, treat them so that they would not appear to be brand-new, and plant the typewriter where it might be discovered. Second, it is unlikely that such a forgery is a one-man job. It suggests the existence of an efficient and experienced organization. This Chambers presumably did not have in 1948, ten years after breaking with Communism. Third, there is the troubling question of why a fabricated typewriter was used. Either Chambers knew where the real Hiss typewriter was or he did not. It seems almost incredible that he could have known, unless he was in contact with Hiss in 1937 or 1938 when the typewriter was given to Perry Catlett; but that this contact existed is precisely the charge contained in the second count of the indictment, which Hiss denied. I would go so far as to assert that if in August or September of 1948 Chambers knew where to lay his hands on the Hisses' Woodstock typewriter, much of what Hiss said about the extent of his acquaintance with Chambers, and, by easy inference, his denial of any kind of Communist activity, is untrue. Furthermore, if Chambers could lay his hands on the old Hiss Woodstock, why not use it to type the incriminating documents? It is hardly an answer to say that the machine may have been unworkable. No matter how bad its condition, it would surely have been easier to repair the machine than to construct a new one.

On Mr. Lane's hypothesis, it seems far likelier that Chambers did not know where to find the Hiss typewriter—not only likelier but also more compatible with Hiss's own story. Let us imagine, then, a forger equipped with samples of typing from the Hiss machine (hoarded, one must suppose, for well over ten years!) and armed with expert skill in duplicating a typewriter's characteristics from samples of its work. He puts his knowledge to work, alters a Woodstock machine of about the same vintage as the Hiss machine (which he either knows from earlier inspection of that machine or deduces from the samples), and produces the Baltimore Documents. What does he do next?

He gets rid of the fabricated typewriter. He does not "plant" it anywhere. The risks are too great. If he does not know where the original Hiss machine is, he does not dare to plant the fake anywhere, for there is always the risk that the original may turn up. Nor will it do to say that the forger knows that the Hiss machine cannot turn up. He could only know that if he were satisfied that the machine had been destroyed (and the evidence of several witnesses shows that it had not been) or if he had it himself, a possibility which is excluded by the fact that he has constructed a duplicate machine. Furthermore, there is nothing to be gained by planting the fabricated machine. The forger knows that documents are normally identified as coming from the same typewriter by comparison of the documents with each other, not by comparison of the documents with the typewriter. It is enough that the Baltimore Documents are put forward and compared with specimens that necessarily came from the Hiss typewriter (the Hiss Standards). Our forger may be confident that the Standards will turn up (as they did) once the question of comparison becomes important. Not only is it enough to have the two sets of documents without the typewriter, but the physical presence of the fake typewriter is vulnerable to just the sort of attack that the defense (belatedly, it is true) has leveled against it. No one can date a typewriter whose serial number he cannot observe. No one can examine the type bars of a machine that he does not have. In short, it is most unlikely that if the Baltimore Documents had been forged, the typewriter that we know as 230099 would ever have been unearthed. It would have served its purpose and been destroyed. Its very existence goes far to negate the possibility that a forgery took place in 1948.

Suppose, however, that there was forgery and that it took place at some earlier time: Would the same objections still hold? One that would of course be eliminated is the question of time. Had he not been limited to two or three months in the fall of 1948, it is far more probable that the forger would have been able to produce a successful duplication. Also, it is likely that if forgery was committed, it was done when Chambers still had at his beck and call the services of underground Communist operatives, skilled in all the black arts. Finally, if the typewriter was forged at some time during Chambers's days in the Communist movement, it could have been planted *before* the Hisses disposed of it, and the *original*

Hiss machine could have been taken away and used to type the Baltimore Documents. There would then be no problem of two typewriters turning up, for one would be in the hands of the conspirators. However, that one would not be 230099, as has been generally assumed, but would be the Hiss machine. It would presumably be destroyed after it had served its purpose. And the forged typewriter, 230099, would be left to go through the vicissitudes that were described at the trial. The unanswered questions, so damning to the defense's argument, of how and when the fabricated typewriter was planted, evaporate. And the disparity between the Hiss Standards and the samples produced on 230099 becomes perfectly understandable. It seems to me that this theory, which the defense did not adopt, fits the forgery hypothesis far more neatly than does the 1948 theory that the defense advanced in support of the motion for new trial.

If the machine had been fabricated during the mid-1930's, when Chambers was still a member of the Communist Party, the Baltimore Documents must have been typed much later, at a time when Chambers either was in the process of withdrawing from the Communist movement or had already done so. This suggests a possibility not hitherto raised: that the typewriter might originally have been fabricated for a purpose other than that for which Chambers ultimately used it. Perhaps it was originally constructed to produce forgeries that could be used to blackmail Hiss into joining the Communist movement or, what may be more likely, into continuing with the movement and graduating from study groups to espionage. We know from Chambers's own account the doubts that assail even the most devoted of Party members when he is first detailed to go into underground work. Chambers promised his wife he would not do it, but then changed his mind. Perhaps Hiss's scruples were harder to overcome. Perhaps he was then confronted with copies of highly incriminating documents that looked for all the world as if they had come from his own typewriter. Perhaps he was warned that if he refused to cooperate, these might fall into the hands of American counterespionage agents, with the obvious result that his career would be ended. Perhaps, confronted with this evidence of the Party's implacability, he yielded and moved to a less innocent level of activity than the "study group" in which he was placed by the testimony of Chambers and of Nathaniel Weyl. And perhaps, when Chambers finally broke with communism, he tried to use the same means to blackmail Hiss out of the Communist underground as he had used to blackmail him in. And, the ultimate irony, perhaps everything Chambers said about Hiss's involvement with communism was true except for the one act of alleged espionage for which, in effect, Hiss was convicted.

The reader who has stayed with me to this point will no doubt be asking whether I really believe any such wild tale as the one I have just sketched. Of course I have no basis for believing it. But this story, or any one of several variations on it, will fit the defense hypothesis of forgery by typewriter as well as, or better than, the exculpatory argument that the defense makes. In short, there is no reason why the theory of forgery by typewriter is inconsistent with Hiss's guilt, if by "guilt" we mean involvement in clandestine Communist activities. We must not lose sight of the other incriminating evidence in the case. Granted, as the defense argues, that Chambers was just as likely to commit perjury in 1949–50 as he was during his Communist career, it is hard to conclude that his association with Hiss was as casual or as short-lived as Hiss alleged it to be, especially when the testimony of two other witnesses, Hede Massing at the second trial and Nathaniel Weyl subsequently before a Congressional committee, tends to support the conclusion that Hiss was involved to some extent in Communist activities. True, Hiss was technically charged with perjury, not with clandestine Communist activity. But in the light of his consistent assertion of total innocence, it would hardly constitute "vindication" for Hiss to prove that he was wrongly convicted on those two counts by showing that his Communist activities were not of the kind, and did not take place at the time, that Chambers testified to.

Undeniably, the zealous efforts of Mr. Lane and his associates in constructing and supporting their theory of forgery by typewriter raise doubts about the Hiss case. It is far from clear, as I have tried to demonstrate, that those doubts, if they turn out to be well-founded, will necessarily lead to exoneration of Hiss in any but the narrowest and most technical sense.

III

The Hiss case is still a mystery and, in its narrowest aspect, may well remain one. By its narrowest aspect, I mean the question of the documents: Were they the subject of espionage by Alger Hiss? This question necessarily occupied the center of the stage at the trials, for the charge against Hiss, though cast in the form of perjury, was essentially a charge of espionage. If the jury had not been satisfied that Hiss had committed espionage, they would have been obliged to acquit, regardless of what they believed about his other involvements with Communism. The paradox is that those other involvements, peripheral and indeed irrelevant as they were to the charge that Hiss had to face in a court of law, are central to the exoneration that Hiss now seeks in what he calls the court of public opinion.

The public importance of the Hiss case, its symbolic role in the political life of our times, does not relate to whether he was justly convicted of the specific charges of perjury brought against him. It relates to the much broader issue whether or not he was involved in Communist activity during his years of government service. If he was, he told and is still telling lies of a significant magnitude. Indeed, their magnitude is enhanced with every re-telling. If, on the other hand, he was free of Communist involve-ment, then he has been the victim of a miscarriage of justice in a sense that laymen as well as lawyers can comprehend.

Hiss's book sheds little light on this larger aspect of the prob-lem. As we have seen, he is concerned with establishing that he was wrongly convicted of the specific charges for which he was indicted, and to this end he deals at length with the evidence con-cerned with espionage and with the extent and character of his association with Chambers. Other evidence tending to implicate him in Communist activity he all but ignores. Of course, one can say that Communist activity as such is not a crime. But the point that Hiss seems to have missed is that even though it is not a crime, Communist activity is the essence of the real case against him. It is for this reason that his book is so unsatisfactory. Even if one accepts most of the very cogent case he builds against Chambers's veracity, the root question of his own complicity still remains.

On this view of the case I believe that there may be a better prospect for eventual clarification of the facts. If we set aside the question of espionage, accepting *arguendo* the tale of two type-writers or some variation on it, and if we then examine the rest of the evidence, it becomes apparent that there remain a number of loose ends in the case. I hasten to say that these loose ends cannot be simply picked up and tied together on the basis of what the present record shows. What I do suggest is that it may be possible to obtain answers to some questions that the trials left unresolved. It would take another book about the Hiss case to explore these questions exhaustively, and there probably have been too many books already. But in the next few pages I shall summarize four key points about which additional evidence might be obtained, and suggest the means at hand to assemble that evidence.

1. *The Ware Cell.* On a number of occasions Chambers stated that Hiss was a member of a Communist cell headed by Harold Ware that flourished in Washington during the early days of the Roosevelt administration. Chambers made this charge first in 1939 in an interview with Adolf Berle, then Assistant Secretary of State. He repeated it to a State Department security officer in 1945 and 1946. And he asserted it publicly before the House Un-American Activities Committee in 1948. The question received very little attention at the Hiss trials because it related to a period and to activities fairly remote from the charges in the indictment, and because at the time of the trials it was purely a matter of Chambers's word against Hiss's, for reasons presently to be considered.

The composition of the Ware cell, its relation to other Communist groups in Washington, and the nature of the activities it carried on are all matters that are far from clear. Chambers's statements varied from time to time, and even the very full account that he gives in *Witness* leaves some questions unresolved. The main outline of Chambers's story is as follows: In 1933 Harold Ware, a member of a devotedly Communist family, organized a group of bright young government workers in Washington into an underground Communist apparatus. The group's functions included recruiting other government employees into the Communist underground, placing Communists in government posts, and influencing the policies of the Government. The group was headed by a "leading committee," some or all of whose members served as heads of cells. The leading committee included Nathan Witt, Lee Pressman, John Abt, Charles Kramer, Henry H. Collins, Victor Perlo, and, until he was detached for other work, Alger Hiss. This group was in frequent contact with J. Peters, the head of the underground section of the American Communist Party, and Peters's emissary to the group was Whittaker Chambers.

Since the end of the second Hiss trial, the existence of the Ware group has been corroborated by two witnesses. In August 1950, following his break with the American Labor party, Lee Pressman testified that he was recruited into the Communist Party by Harold Ware about 1934, and that he was a member of a Communist group in Washington until he left government service and returned to New York "about the latter part of 1935." He testified that the group was limited to people working at the time in the Agricultural Adjustment Administration and included only four (all of whom had been named by Chambers as members of the larger group that he described): Abt, Kramer, Witt, and Pressman. According to Pressman, the group met once or twice a month to read and discuss Marxist literature, which was brought to them by Ware. Occasionally, according to his recollection, Peters was present at these meetings. He denied having met Whittaker Chambers. He had no firsthand knowledge of Alger Hiss as a Communist, or of any persons other than his colleagues in the AAA whom he named. His account is obviously at variance with Chambers's in important respects.

The second witness who has corroborated the existence of the Ware group is Nathaniel Weyl, who testified in February 1952, during the Senate Internal Security Subcommittee's hearings on the Institute of Pacific Relations. Weyl's story is that Harold Ware recruited him into a Communist group in Washington about the beginning of 1934, when he was working as an economist for the AAA. He named Hiss, Pressman, Kramer, Collins, Abt, Witt, and Perlo as members. During his period of affiliation with the group, about six months, Chambers was not a member. Weyl was not asked why he discontinued participation in the group. Nor was he asked whether he ever saw Pressman and Hiss on the same occasion, a question that might have helped resolve the apparent inconsistency between the testimony of Pressman and that of Chambers. On the vital issue of Hiss's complicity the testimony of Pressman and that of Chambers and Weyl are apparently but not necessarily in conflict. Chambers says that Hiss was detached from the Ware group when he transferred from the AAA to the Nye Committee in the spring of 1934. Pressman states that he was a member of the group starting in early 1934. It is conceivable that by the time Pressman joined the group Hiss had already been detached, although it seems unlikely that Pressman would not have known all the other group members in the AAA. Closer questioning of both Pressman and Weyl might resolve the discrepancy or, on the other hand, might make it clear that it cannot be resolved. The present state of the record on this important phase of the problem is far from satisfactory, and certainly cannot be done justice merely by saying that Pressman said Hiss was not in, but Weyl said he was.

The others named as members of the Ware group have consistently invoked the Fifth Amendment when questioned about Communist affiliations. If their testimony could be compelled, we would be in a fair way to knowing the truth about Chambers's charges that Hiss was a Communist in the early 1930's. Hiss obliquely recognizes the fact of the Ware group's existence, but relies on Pressman's post-trial testimony to establish that he was not a member. Indeed, that testimony was one of the grounds Hiss relied on in his motion for new trial, which was filed just before Weyl testified. Hiss concedes that Weyl's testimony "supplied an offset" to that of Pressman, but implies that Weyl's motive was publicity.

One word more about the Ware group. On two occasions in *Witness*, Chambers hinted broadly that there is still another person, not one of those named as a member of the leading committee, who knows about the Ware group and who knows "the pertinent facts in the Hiss Case." In a striking passage, Chambers said that he would not name the man, but pleaded with him to tell the truth—"for the nation, his honor, my children." It seems a little late for Chambers to have been overcome with scruples about naming names. Who is this man; has he ever been called on to testify; what has he said? These questions can no longer be answered by Chambers.

2. *The Summer at Smithtown.* Chambers testified that in the summer of 1935 he and his wife rented a cottage at Smithtown, Pennsylvania, together with a fellow Communist named Maxim Lieber, and that Mrs. Hiss visited them there for a week or ten days. The Hisses denied it. Chambers's landlord, a Mr. Boucot, and Boucot's sister, both of whom were on terms of great neighborliness with their tenants and lived only a short distance away, testified that they had no recollection of seeing either Mr. or Mrs. Hiss, and that they could not have avoided meeting them had

they been there any length of time. Indeed, Chambers testified that he believed that Mr. Boucot had met both Mr. and Mrs. Hiss. The Hisses might be thought to have had the better of this skirmish. But the matter can hardly be considered settled, in view of the fact that the only other alleged eyewitness, Maxim Lieber, was not called as a witness either by the prosecution or by the defense. In his book Chambers took the bull by the horns and said: "Though he [Lieber] was available, and probably in New York during both Hiss trials, the Hiss defense never called him to the stand." This is gamesmanship at its best. Surely the prosecution must bear predominant responsibility for not having called Lieber. If his testimony had been that the Hisses were there, that would have been better corroboration of Chambers than anything else that was brought forth at the trial. If his testimony had been that they were not there, the prosecution would have been most derelict in suppressing it. Very possibly, of course, the prosecution had determined in advance that Lieber would in all likelihood refuse to testify on fifth amendment grounds.

Lieber's testimony would be a most important piece of evidence, since it would provide proof or disproof in a sharply contested instance of the truth or falsity of Chambers's assertion and Hiss's denial of the continuing close and friendly connection between the two families.

3. *The Rug.* Chambers testified that late in 1936, on the instructions of his superior in the Soviet espionage apparatus, Colonel Bykov, he ordered through Professor Schapiro of New York University, a close friend and an authority on art history, four costly Oriental rugs to be given to Hiss and three others as gifts from "the grateful Soviet people." Chambers directed that the rugs be sent to George Silverman, a fellow Communist in Washington. Chambers then had Silverman take Hiss's rug to a restaurant on the Washington-Baltimore road, where Chambers, who was waiting there with Hiss, transferred it from Silverman's car to Hiss's, without the one seeing the other.

Hiss, on the other hand, testified that he received a rug from Chambers in the *spring* of 1936, more or less as part payment for the rent on Hiss's apartment, where the Chamberses had lived for a few months in 1935. Hiss's version tends to be corroborated by the testimony of his ex-maid, who remembered having seen the rug on the floor of the house in which the Hisses lived in the spring of 1936 and which they vacated on June 15, 1936. Chambers's story is corroborated to some extent by the testimony and records of the rug dealer from whom Schapiro ordered the rugs: The dealer verified that the rugs were ordered sent to Schapiro when Chambers said they were, and Schapiro testified that they were shipped to George Silverman as Chambers said they had been. According to Chambers, the other rugs were given to Silverman, to Harry Dexter White, and to Henry Julian Wadleigh. Silverman was not called to testify at Hiss's trials; White was dead; Wadleigh, who admitted having stolen State Department documents for the Communists, testified that he had received such a rug. Neither the dealer nor Professor Schapiro was, of course, in a position to say what had subsequently become of the rugs.

The question is an important one. If Chambers's story is true, there was certainly close contact, most likely of a conspiratorial nature, between him and Hiss at a time when, according to Hiss, their former casual relationship had long since been broken off. Hiss was charged with perjury for denying that he had seen Chambers after January 1, 1937. The chronology of the rug incident is such that if Chambers is believed, Hiss could not have received the rug before January 1, 1937. If Hiss's story is true on this issue, to which Chambers testified in such circumstantial detail, then Chambers's credibility diminishes to the vanishing point.

Silverman was not produced as a witness and examined about the incident on the Baltimore road. In 1948 Silverman had been named by Elizabeth Bentley as a Communist and a participant in espionage. He had appeared before the House Un-American Activities Committee, had denied the espionage charge, but had refused to answer most questions on fifth amendment grounds. It is a matter for conjecture why the Government did not call him to testify at the Hiss trials. Two other witnesses who might have been expected to invoke the fifth amendment, and who in fact did so, were called. They were William Rosen, the transferee of Hiss's Ford car, and Felix Inslerman, the alleged photographer of the purloined documents. The Hiss rug itself was not produced, and the rug dealer was therefore not given an opportunity to say whether it was the one he had sent to Meyer Schapiro on December 29, 1936, some months after the Hisses insisted they had received it. In his summation, the prosecutor made a great point of the defense's failure to produce the rug for the dealer's inspection, but it seems equally remarkable that the prosecution did not ask the defense to do so. Hiss says that the prosecutor "must have known that he could have had the rug for the asking." That is reasonable enough, as far as it goes, but why did the defense wait for the prosecutor to ask?

4. *Timothy Hobson.* If the relationship between the Hisses and the Chamberses was as close as Chambers said it was, and if it continued as long as he said it did (almost four years), there exists a witness whose testimony is of the greatest importance. That is Timothy Hobson, Mrs. Hiss's son by an earlier marriage. He was eight years old when Hiss and Chambers first met, and twelve when, according to Chambers, the final break came. I do not for a moment suggest that if Hiss and Chambers were engaged in an espionage conspiracy, Timothy would have known about it. But if the Hisses and the Chamberses were such close friends, if they visited back and forth, if they took trips together, and if, finally, Chambers regularly turned up on Hiss's doorstep to receive the documents, it is almost inconceivable that Timothy should not have remembered him, and remembered the frequency of his visits.

Did Timothy Hobson remember? We do not know. The House Un-American Activities Committee would have liked to talk to him at the time Chambers's charges were first made. It became clear that a difficult family situation was involved, and that Hobson, then twenty-two, was to some extent estranged from his stepfather, or, at any rate, was not at his beck and call. The matter was not pursued.

We do not know whether anyone—the Committee, the grand jury, the FBI, the prosecution, the defense—questioned Hobson in private. The public record does not show. Again we lack testimony that could go a long way to convict or to acquit in the court of public opinion.

IV

The four unresolved questions just described bring us back to the proposition with which we started this discussion of the Hiss case: "The trial . . . is not an investigative, but a demonstrative proceeding." For many reasons—reasons of remoteness, reasons of trial tactics, reasons of time and expense—not all of the evidence bearing on the ultimate issue of Alger Hiss's alleged complicity in clandestine Communist activity was brought out at the trials. Underlying these reasons was a more fundamental one: lack of judicial power to compel testimony in the face of a plea of the privilege against self-incrimination. That reason, which existed at the time of the trials, no longer exists. In 1954 Congress passed an Immunity Act, under whose provisions a witness may be compelled to testify about "national security" matters before a Congressional committee as well as before a federal grand jury and in federal litigation, in exchange for immunity from prosecution "for or on account of any transaction, matter, or thing concerning which he is so compelled . . . to testify or produce evidence."

Opinions may and do differ on whether there are any circumstances in which a witness's testimony should be so compelled. Even if the constitutionality of the procedure is eventually vindicated *in toto*, doubts persist as to its wisdom. But it can be argued that if there is any situation that justifies overriding the privilege against self-incrimination in favor of compelling the testimony of reluctant witnesses, the present posture of the Hiss case presents that situation. Here is a *cause célèbre* of the first magnitude, whose political repercussions far transcend the immediate issues determined by Hiss's perjury conviction. Yet supposed facts on the basis of which weighty judgments of public policy have been made remain in doubt. Since the transactions in question occurred twenty-five years ago, the people who know the truth are in no real danger of prosecution, and a grant of immunity could thus scarcely impair the prosecutorial work of the Justice Department. Nor is any legitimate interest of the potential witnesses in jeopardy. They will, it is true, be exposed to infamy if their testimony establishes their former complicity in underground Communist operations. But reputation, as the Supreme Court held in *Ullmann* v. *U.S.*, is not an interest that the fifth amendment protects. Under the circumstances, the privilege against self-incrimination should not legally bar their interrogation. Granted the premise, embodied in the Immunity Act, that there are circumstances in which it is desirable to exchange immunity for testimony, is this not an appropriate occasion for doing so?

Those who believe in the unlimited veracity of Whittaker

Chambers as a witness to acts of betrayal should welcome the opportunity to include in the public record the corroboration of his narrative that has, until now, been lacking. Those who still believe that Alger Hiss was the victim of a miscarriage of justice should be equally glad to see Chambers's story put to the kind of test that it has not yet received. But more than to either of these two committed viewpoints about the Hiss case, a thorough exposure of the still clouded facts of the case should appeal to those who believe that a full and informed awareness of the dangers of the Communist conspiracy, past and present, is not inconsistent with fairness to persons accused of complicity in that conspiracy.

Choosing the proper investigative vehicle for this further inquiry is a difficult matter, which had best be postponed until the concluding chapter.* Let us assume, however, what is not true, namely, that we have in being a tribunal capable of exercising wisely and without oppression the great powers conferred by the Immunity Act. Even so, there may be doubts about the wisdom of proceeding, but for the moment let us suppress those doubts and ask what kind of inquiry such a tribunal should make.

The agenda should include two general topics which I have referred to as "the tale of two typewriters" and the "loose ends." Whatever else may be said about Mr. Lane's motion for a new trial, it has certainly raised questions that deserve more definitive answers than have yet been forthcoming. It may be questionable whether the battle of experts can be expected to yield much more information but the problem of 230099's provenance should certainly be investigated further. The facts that Mr. Lane was unable to secure by voluntary cooperation should be brought out under subpoena. But even if it should be established that 230099 is not the typewriter that Fansler gave to the Hisses, it would be wrong, for the reasons I have suggested, to conclude that Hiss is to be absolved of all complicity in Communist activity. Hence any inquiry should also extend to the loose ends.

Each of the persons named by Chambers as members of the Ware group should be required to tell what he knows. Maxim Lieber should be required to reveal whether either Alger or Pris-

---

* As the act stands, the choice lies between a grand jury and a Congressional committee. Both would have serious drawbacks, so serious that the argument against any further inquiry is almost unanswerable.

cilla Hiss visited the Chamberses at Smithtown. The rug should be ordered produced and every effort made, through the rug dealer who testified at the trial, to determine whether it is one of the rugs ordered on Chambers's behalf by Professor Schapiro. Timothy Hobson should be examined on his recollection of Mr. and Mrs. Chambers and on the extent and duration of their contact with the Hisses. Not until these possibilities, and others, have been exhausted shall we know as much as we would like to know, and as much as society may have a right to know.

Of course, there will be no further inquiry. If that was ever unclear it has ceased to be so now that Chambers is dead. Perhaps it is just as well. Perhaps even if the choice were a real one, we should do better to forgo knowledge in favor of repose. That is a large question and, since in the present circumstances it is a hypothetical one, a question that need not be resolved. But it should be clear that as we now close the books on the Hiss case it must be with the consciousness that we have stopped far short of even so imperfect an approximation of "truth" as the processes of law permit.

3 · BENTLEY

The story of Elizabeth Bentley came to public attention in July 1948, when a series of sensational feature articles in the *New York World-Telegram* revealed that a "red spy queen" had successfully operated an espionage ring in wartime Washington. The first of a long line of highly publicized Congressional hearings soon followed, and it was not long before the name of Elizabeth Bentley became firmly identified as a symbol of widespread betrayal and corruption within the Government. Her story, together with that of Whittaker Chambers, which became public at the same time, constituted the principal evidence for the charge that Communist penetration of the Government had resulted in the transmission of official secrets to Soviet Russia.

In the pages that follow, I shall attempt to assess the manner in which Miss Bentley's story has been put into the public record and to evaluate the present state of that record. I shall first recapitulate the broad outlines of the story and then examine in some detail Miss Bentley's testimony on certain especially significant occasions, notably the hearings held by the House Un-American Activities Committee in 1948, the first occasion on which her general story was made public, and the first perjury trial of William Remington, the only occasion on which she has been subjected to extensive cross-examination. On the basis of this examination, we should be in a position to draw some general conclusions on the extent to which Miss Bentley's story has been either corroborated or contradicted, the efficacy of the various modes in which her story has been developed, and the measures, if any, that might be taken to ascertain information we now lack.

In the course of this inquiry we shall inescapably be faced with

questions about credibility—Miss Bentley's and that of other witnesses. It needs to be repeated at this point that these questions,
while inescapable, are not the main focus of our inquiry. We are
interested in what the public record shows, in how that record was
made, and, most important, in what we can conclude about the
advantages and disadvantages of the various means available to
elicit and evaluate a story such as Miss Bentley's.

By the "common route of genteel poverty, loneliness, and frus-
tration" Elizabeth Bentley found her way into the Communist
Party in 1935. Some thirteen years later she was to emerge a na-
tionally known figure—a notorious "red spy queen" and a leading
ex-Communist government witness.

Born in New Milford, Connecticut, in 1908, Miss Bentley attended Vassar College as an undergraduate and Columbia University as a graduate student, and studied for a year in Italy.
During the two years between her Vassar and Columbia training, she taught languages at the Foxcroft School in Middleburg,
Virginia. While at Vassar she was a mild socialist in political
thought, but in retrospect she testified that her studies there made
her "a complete pushover for communism."

In 1934, shortly after returning from Europe and with Italian
fascism still fresh in her mind, she joined the American League
against War and Fascism. The League was interested, she said,
in her views of Italy. And then, while again attending Columbia
(this time for secretarial training), she became friendly with Mrs.
Lee Fuhr, a militant Communist. Mrs. Fuhr, Miss Bentley tells
us, shamed her into joining the Party. She joined because she believed communism would do away with misery and injustice, and
she felt she was at last "where I had always belonged, with the
people who were fighting for a decent society."

She was attached first to a Communist Party shop unit with
activities centering around Columbia University. Here she worked
with the American League against War and Fascism, acted as
liaison between the Party and unions, and participated in Communist demonstrations and picketing. She was also attached to
the Home Relief shop unit during the period she did social work
for that agency, and to the Macy's shop unit. During 1935 and
1936 she attended the Communist Workers' School, where she took

courses in Marxian political economy. But during the relatively brief period (two and a half years) she was in the open Party, her Communist activity was negligible; she was "just an average run-of-the-mill member."

After working at a number of odd jobs, Miss Bentley in July 1938 become employed as a secretary at the Italian Library of Information in New York City, the American division of the Italian Propaganda Ministry. Upon discovering that the Library was in actuality a fascist propaganda center, she contacted F. Brown (also known as Feruccio Marini), a leading Italian Communist and a Soviet agent in this country at the time, who had an office at Communist Party headquarters. Brown told her to observe activities at the Italian Library that might be of interest to the Party, and to collect all publications, letters, and other documents. He also advised her to disconnect herself from the open Party. She soon became disenchanted with the ensuing lack of interest at Communist headquarters, and in October 1938 Brown made Jacob Golos her contact.

It was at this time that Miss Bentley became a Communist at large, or went underground. She was to be responsible to just one person, and she was not to appear at unit meetings or in any way to continue her contacts with other Communists.

At first Jacob Golos was known to her only as Timmy, she testified; it was some time before she learned of his real role in the Communist apparatus. Golos was in actuality a man of high position in the NKVD, the Russian Secret Police, and a member of the powerful three-man Control Commission of the American Communist Party. His main function, she said, was to make contacts and collect information of value to the Russians. As a front, he ran World Tourists, a travel agency set up by the Party ostensibly to facilitate tourist travel in Russia.

Golos instructed her to remain at the Italian Library of Information. She worked there, under his tutelage ("my amateurish attempts to listen at closed doors and search wastebaskets especially annoyed him"), until the spring of 1939, when her spying came to an abrupt end. The Director of the Library came across an anti-Fascist article she had written for the *Columbia Spectator* a few years before, and she was dismissed.

Miss Bentley then became Golos's assistant. During this period, she also became his mistress—or man and wife, Communist version. Like all true revolutionaries, Golos thought lawful marriage was "bourgeois."

At first, as Golos's assistant, she was a mail-drop and a researcher. She testified that most of the mail she received for him came from Canada and Mexico, but it ceased when Trotsky's chauffeur was shot in Mexico in an aborptive attempt on Trotsky's life. As a researcher, she made a long study of Herbert Hoover, among others, and studies of the Mexican election results. In the summer of 1941 she began to assume a more important role; Golos asked her to serve as the Party's contact for certain United States Government employees who were in positions to furnish information of value to the Russians.

The information that she was to obtain from these informants fell roughly into two categories: nonmilitary, diplomatic information, such as the attitude of American officials toward Russia; and strictly military information, such as production figures on planes and tanks. Some of the informants were contacted in New York, others in Washington. When she met them she collected their dues and brought them Party literature; they, in turn, gave her the information they had collected—either verbally, in documents, or on microfilm.

At the height of her career as a contact and courier, over forty persons were reporting to her, and she was making biweekly trips to Washington to collect the information gathered by her most important sources. Practically every important government agency had someone in it who furnished her, either directly or indirectly, with information. Once, she writes in *Out of Bondage,* when she returned from one of her trips to Washington, her portfolio or knitting bag bursting with papers, Golos asked her what she had brought. She replied, "I think I've brought you the entire Pentagon." "I was not far from wrong," she remembers, "and was rewarded by a glow of appreciation."

In addition to her duties as a courier, Miss Bentley worked at World Tourists. In 1940, Golos, as head of World Tourists, had to register as a foreign agent. In the circumstances, World Tourists could no longer handle passenger and freight traffic between Russia and the United States, and Golos decided to form a new organization for the purpose that would not be branded as Com-

munist. A nonsuspect person with leftish leanings and a good social and business background, John Hazard Reynolds, was found
to head the organization, Miss Bentley was made its vice-president
and secretary, and the United States Service and Shipping Corporation was in business, with funds supplied by Earl Browder.

Miss Bentley continued in her dual role as businesswoman and
Communist agent until November 1943, when Golos died of a
heart attack. After Golos's death, a minor contact introduced her
to Golos's successor, "Bill," to whom she then delivered information
as she had to Golos. After "Bill," she had two more contacts prior
to her defection—"Jack," and Anatoli Gromov, Secretary of the Soviet Embassy. Her work was much the same with these superiors,
but without Golos's protection, she testified, she gradually became
disillusioned with the Communist Party and finally realized its
true function as a fifth column of the Russian Government. In the
fall of 1944, she decided to leave the Party. She also did what she
could to convince her contacts of their error and to persuade them
to abandon their illegal activity.

Although she reached her decision to leave in 1944, it was not
until August 1945 that she reported to the FBI. Breaking with the
Party, she explains, is a long process. Thinking it was safer, she
first went to New Haven, Connecticut, and told her story in a very
general way to the FBI agents there. They, in turn, put her in
contact with the FBI office in New York. At the time of her con-
fession of her espionage activities to the FBI, she was still in contact with members of the Communist underground. She retained
these contacts, at the request of the FBI, until early 1947. She also
continued to work at the United States Service and Shipping Corporation.

In the spring of 1947, Miss Bentley appeared before a federal
grand jury in New York. Shortly thereafter, her story was "leaked"
to the press, and from 1948 until 1953 she was greatly sought after
as a government witness to testify before courts and Congressional committees. Her testimony helped to convict four persons,
and resulted in the termination of government service for many.

Nothing in Miss Bentley's story is more interesting or significant than her description of how she cultivated contacts with underground Communists in government service, obtained from them

a steady flow of secret information, and transmitted this information to her superiors in the Communist espionage apparatus. This
part of her story has consistently drawn the most attention from
Congressional committees, grand juries, official investigators, and
the interested public. Indeed, for all practical purposes, this is
the Bentley story. It cannot be grasped, much less analyzed, without some preliminary identification of the persons who played
roles in Miss Bentley's activities.*

The most important of Miss Bentley's espionage contacts, according to her testimony, was with the group headed by Nathan
Gregory Silvermaster, an economist with the Farm Security Administration (later, during the war, with the Board of Economic
Warfare). Her contact with the group began in July 1941, and
lasted until sometime in 1944. During this period, she would go
to Washington every two weeks or so and pick up the material
assembled for her at the Silvermasters' house. Much of the material was photographed on microfilm on apparatus set up in the
Silvermaster basement and operated at first by William Ludwig
Ullmann, who lived with the Silvermasters. (It should be mentioned at this point that the highly detailed testimony that Miss
Bentley has given on several occasions seems clearly to establish
that she was familiar with the Silvermaster household.) Ullmann
served as an assistant to Harry Dexter White, then Director of
the Division of Monetary Research in the Treasury Department
and subsequently Assistant Secretary of the Department. White
was also a member of the ring, according to Miss Bentley, as were
other employees of the Division, including Solomon Adler, Frank
Coe, Mrs. Sonia Gold, and William Taylor. Other members of
the Silvermaster ring were said to include Lauchlin Currie, one
of President Roosevelt's administrative assistants; Mrs. Gold's husband, Bela, an economist at the Board of Economic Warfare; Irv-

---

* In her various appearances, Miss Bentley identified 43 persons as members of the Communist underground. It would require a separate book to do
justice to all the relevant details about her alleged partners in crime, and
particularly to document the astonishing interrelations among them. Indeed,
the Senate Internal Security Subcommittee has devoted many months and several thousand pages of testimony to examining the "pattern of interlocking
subversion" in government departments. We can do no more here than identify the principal actors as a preface to our analysis of certain aspects of Miss
Bentley's testimony.

ing Kaplan, an employee of the War Production Board; Abraham George Silverman, a statistical economist with the Railroad Retirement Board and later a civilian employee of the Army Air Corps serving in the Pentagon; and Silvermaster's wife, Helen.

Miss Bentley also served as contact for another espionage group, this one headed by Victor Perlo, an economist with the War Production Board. She first met some of the members of this group at the New York apartment of John Abt in March 1944. Unlike the Silvermaster group, the Perlo group sent its information to Miss Bentley in New York, with various members serving as messengers. This group included Edward Fitzgerald of the War Production Board; Harold Glasser, an assistant to Harry Dexter White at the Treasury Department; Charles Kramer, an employee of various Senate committees; Harry Magdoff of the Commerce Department; Allen Rosenberg of the Foreign Economic Administration; and Donald Wheeler of the Office of Strategic Services (OSS).

In addition to these two groups, Miss Bentley had a number of individual contacts in Washington, including several employees of OSS—Maurice Halperin, Bella Joseph, J. Julius Joseph, Duncan Lee, Helen Tenney—and several employees of the Office of the Coordinator of Inter-American Affairs (CIAA)—Joseph Gregg, Robert Miller, Willard Z. Park, and Bernard Redmont. Miss Bentley also maintained a long and fruitful contact with Mary Price, Walter Lippmann's secretary, who supplied information from Lippmann's files on high-level activities within the Government and whose apartment in Washington was a frequent stopping place for Miss Bentley. This relationship also extended to Miss Price's sister Mildred, who worked for the Institute of Pacific Relations in New York and whose apartment served as a meeting place in New York for Miss Bentley and some of her Washington contacts. Finally, there was William Remington of the War Production Board, who by Miss Bentley's account was one of her least fruitful sources of information, but whose case became the major occasion on which any portion of Miss Bentley's story has been subjected to the scrutiny of cross-examination in the judicial process. Aspects of the Remington case are dealt with later in this chapter.

In examining Miss Bentley's story, a problem arises which is familiar to historical scholars (particularly to students of the

Bible), but which we hardly expect to find arising in the analysis of nearly contemporary events. That is the problem of separating the genuine from the apocryphal, of determining what is to be taken as representing Miss Bentley's considered version of the facts—the problem, in short, of fixing the Bentley canon.

Clearly, we are to regard anything to which Miss Bentley has testified under oath as representing the truth as she remembers it. Her testimony on eight occasions before Congressional committees and in four trials forms the body of material in which we are interested. But the problem is complicated by the existence of a remarkable book, *Out of Bondage*, which Miss Bentley published in 1951 and which purports to be a connected account of her life as a member of the Communist underground.

Perhaps the major difficulty about accepting *Out of Bondage* as a useful adjunct to Miss Bentley's formal testimony lies in its use of dialogue. Direct quotations make up about half the book, and, as one reviewer remarked, "It is inconceivable that Miss Bentley can have remembered, word for word, hundreds of conversations ranging from 1934 onward." Miss Bentley's tendency to bolster a story by the elaboration of detail, in this case through the use of dialogue, raises questions about both the accuracy of her recollection and her sincerity, questions that persist throughout her testimony and make reliance on her book as a summation of her testimony rather difficult. The flavor of the book cannot be described; it must be experienced. The following passage may give some idea of the difficulty. Miss Bentley and Earl Browder are discussing the proposal, which she resists, that the Silvermaster ring be put directly in touch with Russian espionage agents:

The next day, as I faced Earl across his desk, he refused to look me in the eye.

"I've told our friends that they can have Greg," he said.

"But why did you do it, Earl?" I cried out. "You know what the Russians are like. They'll ruin Greg."

He shrugged his shoulders and carefully looked at the wall.

"Don't be naive," he said cynically. "You know that when the cards are down, I have to take my orders from them. I just hoped I could sidetrack them in this particular matter, but it didn't work out."

"But Greg's an old friend of yours," I said accusingly.

"So what?" he replied. "He's expendable."

Blindly I stumbled out of his office. Once in the street, I walked aimlessly, unaware even that it was a very hot day and that the sweat was dripping down me. I tried to comprehend what had happened.

Why had Earl behaved like that? Why, knowing how ruthless Bill was, had he permitted his old friend Greg to be turned over to him? All along he had backed me up in my determination to protect our American comrades and now, suddenly, he didn't seem to care any more—indeed, he was completely cynical about their fate.

Two points about this extract. First, quoting directly in 1951 a conversation that occurred in 1944, is, to put it moderately, questionable. Second, the tone is the tone of a pulp magazine. The extract is not unrepresentative of the book as a whole. Taken together with other indications, this sort of thing raises doubts about whether the book is solely Miss Bentley's work and whether it is a reliable account of her experiences.

On May 17, 1954, Miss Bentley's deposition was taken in connection with a libel proceeding by William H. Taylor, one of the persons she had named as a member of the Silvermaster ring, against a Washington newspaper. One of the attorneys who participated in the deposition made an affidavit the same day that when Miss Bentley was taxed with certain things she had written in *Out of Bondage,* she said, "I don't see why reference is being made to my book, that's fiction"—or words to that effect. Miss Bentley later denied that she had ever said any such thing, but, as we shall see, on at least one other occasion she has tried to defend an inconsistency on the ground that a writer is entitled to a certain amount of license. The question, of course, is whether and to what extent Miss Bentley has availed herself of that asserted license.

For present purposes, we shall assume that *Out of Bondage* is a genuine account, but in the case of inconsistencies between statements made in it and statements made in her testimony under oath, we shall prefer the latter.

II

On July 31, 1948, Miss Bentley appeared before the House Un-American Activities Committee and inaugurated the hearings before that Committee on Communist espionage in the United States. Three days later she was followed to the witness stand by Whittaker Chambers. As the Bentley and Chambers stories unfolded and as a parade of witnesses, some reluctant, some not, followed them to the stand and attempted to justify their own positions, there took place what is undoubtedly the most dramatic set of legislative hearings dealing with the problem of Communist penetration. We are concerned less with the drama of these hearings than with their efficiency as an instrument for putting Miss Bentley's story into the public record.

The interrogation of Miss Bentley was conducted principally by Mr. Robert E. Stripling, Chief Investigator of the Committee. At various points in her testimony, she was questioned in turn by each member of the Committee who desired to put questions to her. And Mr. Stripling's interrogation was interrupted from time to time by questions from Committee members. As we shall see, some of these questions had little or no relevance to Miss Bentley's story, but are explicable only as serving the political interest of various Committee members. By the same token, the questioning on points that should have been of genuine interest tended to be rather desultory and often stopped short of eliciting adequate responses.

Miss Bentley was first allowed to sketch in very general terms her career in the Communist movement. She testified that in June or July of 1941 she was asked by Golos to serve as a contact for government employees who were in a position to supply information. At that point she was asked how this espionage organization was set up and there began the process of identifying the "individuals and groups" who comprised it, a process that occupied the bulk of her subsequent testimony. She first identified Silvermaster. Then she began naming the people who were members of the Silvermaster ring. After naming Helen Silvermaster and Ullmann, making it clear that she knew them personally, she produced the names of two others, Solomon Adler and William Taylor. She was not asked whether she knew either of them personally. Her statement that Adler was in China while she had charge of the group might be interpreted as an admission that she did not know him personally, although the point was not directly raised. But her identification of Taylor suggested that she did know him:

MR. STRIPLING   Are there any other persons who were employed in the Government at that time who were members of this espionage group?
MISS BENTLEY   Yes. William Taylor.
MR. STRIPLING   Where was he employed?
MISS BENTLEY   William was in the Treasury.

The point is an interesting one because Taylor is the one person accused by Miss Bentley who has been finally cleared of the charges against him. It was not until over two years later, in testimony before another Congressional committee, that Miss Bentley was asked point-blank whether she knew William Taylor. The answer was "No."

Miss Bentley was then asked for other names in the Silvermaster group and she came up with that of Harry Dexter White. Once again, she was not asked whether she knew him personally. It later developed that she did not.

The questioning next turned to the identification of other groups. Miss Bentley testified that beginning about March 1944 she had also handled a group headed by Victor Perlo. She proceeded to identify members of this group, again without any differentiation between what she knew of her own knowledge and what she had been told by others. During this part of the interrogation the following exchange occurred:

MR. STRIPLING   Did you ever collect any dues from Mr. Magdoff?

MISS BENTLEY   The dues were brought to me by whichever member of the group came to New York City, and Mr. Magdoff's dues were among them; yes.

MR. STRIPLING   What did you do with his dues when they were turned over to you?

MISS BENTLEY   I turned them over to Mr. Golos during his lifetime.

Miss Bentley was not asked during this hearing when Mr. Golos died, but her testimony on other occasions has established that he died in November 1943. Only a few minutes earlier Miss Bentley had testified that she had her first contact with the Perlo group in March 1944. If that was right, she must have been mistaken in thinking that she had turned over dues from this group during his lifetime. But the point passed unnoticed, and has apparently not been raised in any subsequent interrogation of Miss Bentley.

After a brief diversion caused by the interest of two Committee members from the South in the fact that one member of the Perlo ring had been employed by Senator Pepper of Florida, the questioning returned to the subject of the Silvermaster ring and its members. Miss Bentley identified George Silverman and Frank Coe. Again she was not asked whether she knew them personally. It began to be clear, however, that she probably did not, as the following exchange suggests:

MR. STRIPLING   Before we go on with what was furnished, would you tell the committee whether or not there is anyone else in this group that you have not named?

MISS BENTLEY   Frank Coe.

MR. STRIPLING   Where was he employed?

MISS BENTLEY   In the Treasury.

MR. STRIPLING   Do you know what his position was?

MISS BENTLEY   No; I am sorry. All these people Mr. Silvermaster took care of, and I simply knew that they had important jobs in the Treasury; but I couldn't tell you what it was.

MR. STRIPLING   He was a member of the Communist Party, according to your information?

MISS BENTLEY   According to my understanding; yes.

The questioning continued, and she identified "William Gold" and his wife Sonia. Gold's name was in fact Bela; he testified a few days later that he had never used the name William and that he had never known Elizabeth Bentley. Her testimony, once more, had not specified whether or not she knew him.

Not until much later in her testimony did it finally become clear that Miss Bentley probably did not know most of the persons whose names she associated with the Silvermaster ring. Characteristically, this point did not emerge in response to a direct question, but instead must be inferred from the answer to a question dealing with quite another subject.

MR. STRIPLING   At any time when you were at Mr. Silvermaster's home here in Washington did you meet an individual by the name of George Silverman?

MISS BENTLEY   I would hardly call it meeting. I was sitting in the kitchen, Mr. Silverman had come in the front door with some material and was leaving by the kitchen door, and he went past very hurriedly. I was introduced by some name, I do not recall, as being a friend of Mrs. Helen Silvermaster, and he went out the kitchen door.

MR. STRIPLING   Did any discussion ensue among the Silvermasters and yourself regarding Mr. Silverman's visit and what his business was?

MISS BENTLEY   Yes. They said that as usual he had come to bring material and they were quite upset that I was there. Usually, you see, they kept their house clear the night I was coming there because they didn't want me to meet other members of the group, and particularly George Silverman was extremely nervous and they said if he realized who I was, he would probably fall to pieces—I believe was the expression they used.

Therefore, they felt that if he had to see me in the kitchen, it was better to pass me off as a friend of Helen Silvermaster's and gloss over the situation.

From her testimony on this and other occasions and from the testimony of others it is deducible that Miss Bentley had no personal knowledge of any members of the Silvermaster ring other than Mr. and Mrs. Silvermaster, Ullmann, and marginally, Silverman. Surely it is remarkable that never in the course of her interrogation on this occasion—or, indeed, on the seven other occasions when she testified before Congressional committees—was this point made clear.

As the questioning continued, it became apparent that members of the Committee were interested in what Miss Bentley had to say at least as much because of its relevance to their own political concerns as for any other reason. Consider, for example, the following exchange:

MR. STRIPLING   Do you know John Abt?
MISS BENTLEY   Yes.
MR. STRIPLING   Was he a member of either group?
MISS BENTLEY   John Abt was the man who took charge of the Perlo group before I had it.
MR. STRIPLING   Do you know whether John Abt was employed in the Government?
MISS BENTLEY   No; I know very little about him except I believe he was with the PAC at one time. Or the PCA*
MR. STRIPLING   He is with Mr. Wallace now.
MR. RANKIN   Get that PAC. That is very important. You mean the CIO-PAC? Is that what you are talking about?
MISS BENTLEY   Yes.

And again, at a later point, when the Chairman of the Committee, Mr. Thomas, felt that he had to defend himself against Mr. Rankin's charge that the Committee was suppressing references to the Remington case (which was simultaneously being investigated by a Senate committee), he did so in the following terms:

THE CHAIRMAN   Mr. Rankin, you and I have served on this committee for a long time. We have had our disagreements, and we have agreed on many things. You know, Mr. Rankin, well down deep in your heart that this committee is not going to whitewash anybody

---

* The CIO's Political Action Committee (PAC) under the chairmanship of Sidney Hillman, was formed in 1943 to promote policies and work for political candidates favorable to organized labor; it was influential on behalf of President Truman in the 1948 elections. The PCA (Progressive Citizens of America), formed in 1946, made up the nucleus of the Progressive Party on whose ticket Henry Wallace ran for President in 1948.

or anything, and you also know that this committee has done a very
big job—a very big job—and especially a big job in the last 2 years.
We have been unearthing your New Dealers for 2 years, and for 8
years before that.

MR. RANKIN   I know the Senate is busy now nagging the white people
of the South, and all of the FEPC, and all this communistic bunk.

Obviously, much more was at stake in these hearings than testing the validity of Miss Bentley's story. It is no wonder that the
Committee proceedings show so little concern with bridging the
gap between accusations and proof.

In the rush to get Miss Bentley's charges on the record, perfectly preposterous statements were allowed to go unchallenged:

MR. HEBERT   You say you know very little about the American Government?

MISS BENTLEY   Yes.

MR. HEBERT   Did they not have courses in Columbia?

MISS BENTLEY   No; they did not teach it.

And when an occasional searching question was put, the weakness
of the answer was overlooked as the conversation turned to more
metaphysical things:

MR. HEBERT   What did you think these people wanted this information
for about our Air Force? Did it not occur to you as a normal individual, with more than normal education, that Russia was supposedly our ally in this war, and they did not have to resort to these
means to get secret information?

MISS BENTLEY   It never occurred to me that way because I think the
mistake you make when you look at communism is that you take it
as an intellectual process. It is not. It is almost a religion and it
gets you so strongly that you take orders blindly. You believe it
blindly. That accounts for the fact that no real Communist is re-
ligious, nor has any religion.

MR. HEBERT   You say "you" take it. You do not mean to infer that the
members of this committee take it that way. We recognize it for
what it is, and that is what we are trying to combat. We do believe
it is a religion, and a godless religion.

MISS BENTLEY   That is correct, but in the process your intellectual
faculties cease to function in a critical sense.

The superficiality of the Committee's questioning was matched
only by its lack of concern for the effect of largely hearsay testimony on the lives and reputations of those accused. The one ex-

ception confirms the general point. Miss Bentley had earlier identified Lauchlin Currie, a member of President Roosevelt's staff, as one who furnished information through the Silvermaster ring. Mr. Rankin began to have some doubts about the weight to be accorded Miss Bentley's evidence on this score, and the following dialogue occurred:

MR. RANKIN   You say that you never met Mr. Currie?

MISS BENTLEY   Not personally; no.

MR. RANKIN   You never saw him?

MISS BENTLEY   No.

MR. RANKIN   You would not know him if you saw him?

MISS BENTLEY   I think I have seen his picture in the papers, but I do not know if I would recognize him.

MR. RANKIN   Now, this information that came to you through a man named Silverman—

MISS BENTLEY   That is right.

MR. RANKIN   (continuing). Was passed on to a man named Silvermaster.

MISS BENTLEY   Or Mr. Ullmann, depending on the situation.

MR. RANKIN   It came to you third hand?

MISS BENTLEY   Correct.

MR. RANKIN   Now, Silverman, you say, is a Communist?

MISS BENTLEY   Yes.

MR. RANKIN   And no Communist has any regard for the truth, has he?

MISS BENTLEY   It depends on the situation.

MR. RANKIN   That is what I say. They have no regard for the truth. When it suits their purpose to lie they just as soon lie as tell the truth; is that not right?

MISS BENTLEY   That is correct.

MR. RANKIN   Now, the thing that disturbs me is that you take the testimony, the statement of two men, Silverman and Silvermaster, relayed from one to the other, about what this Scotchman in the White House, Mr. Currie, said about communism.

Did you ever investigate to find out whether or not Silverman or Silvermaster were telling the truth?

MISS BENTLEY   Well, for one thing, in espionage rings you cannot investigate. They are built up on this particular type of flimsy connection.

MR. RANKIN   Well, here we have gone on all day—here is what is disturbing me—I would not know Mr. Currie; I am fairly familiar with the incumbents of the White House and have been for the last 15 or 20 years. I do not know him. I know Mr. McIntyre and Steve Early, and all those gentlemen, but the thing that disturbs me is that here we are voting by a vote of 3 to 2 to keep from inquiring about one man, and yet we have put this committee—we have put in the whole day accepting from an ex-Communist, which you admit you are, testimony relayed through two Communists as to what this man Currie in the White House is supposed to have said.

Now, that looks to me as if we are going pretty far afield when we take that kind of testimony and charge all this up to Mr. Currie. When I glance over the list I see several that seem to me who would be more likely to have given that information than Currie, who occupied similar positions. But here we put in a whole day, a whole day, smearing Currie by remote control through two Communists, either one of whom you admit would swear to a lie just as soon as he would swear to the truth if it suited his purposes, and relayed to you, who at that time was a member of the Communist Party. We have come in here and put in a whole day with that kind of testimony about a man who happened to occupy a rather responsible position in the White House, and yet we shy around and we are denied the opportunity or the right to ask a question about this man Remington, who is still on the payroll.

MISS BENTLEY Might I say just one thing in that respect? It is quite true that Communists lie to the outside world. It is not true that they lie within the party, particularly to the person whom they regard as their superior. They do not do that. That was what was told me by Mr. Silvermaster. I have every reason to believe that he was telling me the truth. I have no desire to smear anyone. I have simply told the facts as they were told to me. It is up to the committee to decide whether or not that is credible or not.

MR. RANKIN You certainly have an unlimited credibility. If you would take the word of any Communist, Silverman or Silvermaster, or both of them, and I believe you named another one, whom you relayed it through, who was also a Communist, if you take that testimony as to what this man Currie, as I said, a Scotchman, has said about the Communists—it just looks to me as if we have gone pretty far afield here to smear this man by remote control, instead of getting some-one who heard him or who knew that he had made any statement.

It is perhaps worth remarking that this expression of solicitude seems to have been voiced in part because of Mr. Rankin's pique at being barred from asking questions about the Remington case, and in part because Mr. Currie was fortunate enough to be a "Scotchman."

After what we may call Miss Bentley's examination in chief, on July 31, 1948, she remained at the Committee's disposal and testified briefly on subsequent days as several of those whom she had accused appeared before the Committee, either voluntarily or under subpoena. This phase of the hearing will be discussed below, as part of the evaluation of corroborative and contradictive factors relating to Miss Bentley's testimony.

The hearing, as these examples have suggested, was not a particularly meritorious example of its kind. But even if it had been, there are limits to the utility of the committee procedure, however well conducted. The chief such limitation is well illustrated by the following example:

MR. COE   Mr. Chairman, I have a request to make. If Miss Bentley is here, I would like to ask her some questions.

MR. MUNDT   The position of this committee has been—and you explained it very clearly in your statement—that we are not functioning as a court, don't have the power, unfortunately, that a court does have, and so we have not made it a policy to cross-examine witnesses or to permit counsel to do so.

Had we the full authority of a court, certainly it would be easier to get down into the disputed evidence in this particular case. Since we do not have, we cannot adapt ourselves to part of the rules of the court without having the authority that goes with being a court. Unfortunately, we cannot accept your request.

MR. COE   Mr. Chairman, may I ask you to reconsider that on these grounds? My name was brought into this by Miss Bentley. She made a very distinct allegation about me. Perhaps she was the reason why over several years not only myself but my friends have been interrogated, and now she is certainly the reason for the very harmful publicity which I have received.

It seems to me only fair, since I believe the committee can adopt any procedures, that you allow me to ask her a few simple questions bearing on what I may have done or what she knows I did relating to any of the groups that she asserts she handled.

MR. MUNDT   Is that the extent of your renewed request?

MR. COE   Yes, sir.

MR. MUNDT   The Chair will have to rule the same way due to the unfortunate fact that while we can adopt rules of procedure, we cannot arrogate to ourselves the power of the court, since we do not have the authority of the court, in order to get the proper decorum and the proper rules of evidence and rules of perjury and the rules of contempt which go with court procedure. Certainly, we cannot adopt part of the procedure without having the authority which is essential if we are going to do that.

The witness is excused.

III

The timing of Miss Bentley's revelations to the FBI and the Bureau's participation in her final contacts with Soviet espionage agents are important elements in the effort to find corroboration in the public record for Miss Bentley's story. At first glance, that corroboration appears to be amply provided. Briefly, it seems to be established that Miss Bentley received $2,000 from a Soviet espionage agent and turned it over to the FBI while acting under the Bureau's instructions and surveillance. And the Director of the FBI has unequivocally stated that Miss Bentley's story has been carefully checked and found to be true in all respects in which it was susceptible of being checked. This would appear to be one such instance. Yet, on a closer examination, certain discrepancies emerge which call, at the very least, for further explanation.

In her initial public appearances, Miss Bentley testified that she had first gone to the FBI in New Haven on August 21 or 22, 1945, and had at that time given the essence of her story. She further suggested that it had taken her perhaps three or four months to give the FBI all the details. The initial impression, then, is of fairly sustained and continuous contact with the FBI from August 21 or 22 on. The impression is also that the FBI knew from the first, at least in general outline, about Miss Bentley's underground Communist activities.

At the same time, Miss Bentley testified that she received $2,000 in twenty-dollar bills from her espionage contact "Al," later identified as Anatoli Gromov, first Secretary of the Soviet Embassy. This transaction occurred in New York on or about October 17, 1945. Miss Bentley's testimony is very explicit that she was then acting under the instructions of the FBI.

MISS BENTLEY   Well, it rather dates back quite a time before that, because from January and February 1944 on my Russian contacts—either Bill or Jack, or later Al— had been trying to pay me off—I guess is the expression—and had been persistently chasing me to take a salary as a member of the organization. I had refused and then they temporarily sidetracked onto trying to give me a fur coat, and an air-conditioning machine, and then, with the advent of Al, had tried, as I suppose, to bribe me with the Red Star.

But a few months after the Red Star, Al again had started asking me to the effect that I must be a traitor, that there was something wrong with me, because I would not accept my salary, and he told me that this salary, although I refused it, was piling up in Moscow on my behalf.

At the time I received the money he had been fairly persistent in the last few meetings, and at this meeting I met him on the corner of Twenty-third Street and Eighth Avenue, near that Bickford's cafeteria there, and he immediately took me on a long trek toward the docks in a very deserted region of New York.

The day previously I had spoken to the FBI agent I was in contact with, had informed him I was meeting this Russian agent, and had asked for instructions. He said, "Keep in contact with him; don't let him know that you are suspicious, and do anything which is necessary to keep in touch with us so that we can continue with the job we are doing." Neither he nor I knew that Al would turn up with $2,000.

We walked along the waterfront; I was quite upset, because I assumed, and I am quite sure I am correct, that I did have some of the FBI agents behind to protect me, but nevertheless it was deserted, and I was terribly upset by being alone with him there. He kept pressing me and told me that unless I accepted the money that he had in his pocket that he would consider me a traitor, and I knew what that meant.

Finally, I got him away from the dock region, as far as Tenth Street and Fourth Street, and he gave me the money. I gave him a receipt for it.

MR. STRIPLING   What kind of a receipt did you give him?

MISS BENTLEY   He had brought it to me in one of these envelopes, No. 10 envelopes, and I tore off one corner of it, wrote the date, "received $2,000," and signed it "Mary."

MR. STRIPLING   What denomination of bills was this money?

MISS BENTLEY   Twenty-dollar bills.

MR. STRIPLING   Do you know whether or not the FBI agents observed this transaction?

MISS BENTLEY   I have every reason to believe they did. They have not told me so, but they have not told me lots of other things, of course.

MR. STRIPLING   What happened after you received the $2,000?

MISS BENTLEY   After I received the $2,000, I put it in the safe at my office, and then turned it over to the FBI.

MR. STRIPLING   Did you turn it over to two agents?

MISS BENTLEY   I turned it over to two agents who transferred it into a separate envelope, and countersigned their names on it.

· · ·

MR. HEBERT   Miss Bentley, you received this money from the Russian agent?

MISS BENTLEY   That is correct; yes.

MR. HEBERT   At that time, you were acting under instructions and in full cooperation with the Federal Bureau of Investigation?

MISS BENTLEY   Yes; that is right. In fact, that was the only consideration under which I would have taken the money.

MR. HEBERT   In other words, you received your instructions on how to conduct yourself in your continuous contacts with the Russian agents from the FBI.

MISS BENTLEY   Yes; that is correct.

MR. HEBERT   And in meeting the agent, why, you were carrying out the instructions of the FBI.

MISS BENTLEY   That is correct; yes.

MR. HEBERT   In other words, to give the FBI an opportunity to establish contact and tangible evidence.

MISS BENTLEY   That is correct. I worked for them over a year and a half after that in an attempt to do something about this matter.

MR. HEBERT   Now, where is the $2,000, so far as you know?

MISS BENTLEY   As far as I know it is in the hands of the Government.

MR. HEBERT   It has never been returned to you?

MISS BENTLEY   It has never been returned to me; no.

MR. HEBERT   That is all.

MR. MUNDT   That is all.

MR. MUNDT   Mr. Chairman, I have one other question. In view of the fact that some of the witnesses have endeavored to cast doubt upon the credibility of Miss Bentley's testimony, I think it is tremendously important to recognize that we now have something tangible in which everybody concerned can set his teeth. Two thousand dollars is a tangible sum of money. It either has been handed by Miss Bentley to the FBI or it has not. That is a matter of record.

I am not going to ask you to name the agents to whom you handed this money, Miss Bentley, because I realize that the FBI agents operate without benefit of the spotlight of publicity.

I will ask you this, however: Would you be able, if necessary, to name the two agents to whom you handed—the two agents of the FBI—to whom you handed the $2,000?

MISS BENTLEY   Yes; I would be able to do that.

MR. MUNDT   You would be able to do that?

MISS BENTLEY   Yes; I would.

MR. MUNDT   So that we can confirm that definitely and specifically?

MISS BENTLEY   Yes; I think if you will get in contact with the FBI, I think they can confirm that entire story; yes.

MR. MUNDT   Thank you.

THE CHAIRMAN   Right on that point, the Chair would like to say that he has absolute confirmation that Miss Bentley took the $2,000 and the $2,000 were handed over to the FBI.

There would be no reason to question this sequence of events were it not for official statements of the Attorney General of the United States and of the Director of the FBI. On November 6, 1953, Attorney General Brownell made a speech in which he accused former President Truman of having retained Harry Dexter

White in an important public position with knowledge that serious charges of espionage activities had been made against White. On November 17, 1953, Mr. Brownell appeared before the Senate Internal Security Subcommittee and documented his charges in some detail. The documentation consisted essentially of declassified FBI reports that went to the White House beginning in November 1945, warning of espionage activities being conducted by White and others. The first of these is a letter from J. Edgar Hoover to the President's Military Aide, General Vaughan, dated November 8, 1945, stating that as a result of information "recently developed from a highly confidential source" it appeared that certain named persons including White, were engaged in espionage activities. The list of names strongly suggests that the "highly confidential source" was Miss Bentley, and the fact that it was she has since been confirmed.

A further and more detailed report was prepared by the FBI under date of November 27, 1945. That report has not been made public in its entirety, but one passage relating to the Silvermaster ring is reprinted in the Senate Subcommittee hearings. It reads as follows, in relevant part:

N. Gregory Silvermaster, with aliases. *This case first came to the attention of the Bureau on November 8, 1945,* when Elizabeth Bentley, an official of the United States Service and Shipping, Inc., New York City, came in to the New York office of the Bureau and stated for the past 11 years she had been actively engaged in Communist activity and Soviet espionage.*

At the same time, Mr. Hoover offered his testimonial to Miss Bentley's reliability. It is worth quoting at length:

In connection with the sources, I would like to mention one in particular, Miss Elizabeth Bentley. From the very outset, we established that she had been in a position to report the facts relative to Soviet espionage which she had done. We knew she was in contact with a top-ranking Soviet espionage agent, Anatoli Gromov, the first secretary of the Soviet Embassy in Washington, D.C., as late as November 21, 1945, in New York City. At a previous meeting on October 17, 1945, Gromov had given her $2,000 to carry forth her work as an espionage agent.

All information furnished by Miss Bentley, which was susceptible to check, has proven to be correct. She had been subjected to the most searching of cross-examinations; her testimony has been evaluated by juries and reviewed by the courts and has been found to be accurate.

---

* Italics mine.

It should be noted that whereas Mr. Hoover does state that the FBI "knew" that Miss Bentley was in contact with Gromov as late as November 21, 1945, he does not state that they knew at the time of Miss Bentley's meeting with Gromov on October 17, when she received the $2,000. This passage does not appear to offer clear corroboration of Miss Bentley's statement that she met Gromov on October 17 pursuant to instructions from the FBI. Some explanation seems to be called for, since all the other evidence supplied by Brownell and Hoover appears to suggest that Miss Bentley did not tell the FBI her story about the Silvermaster ring and Harry Dexter White's complicity in it until November 7, 1945.

Of course, this evidence is far from conclusive. Even if we had no other corroboration for Miss Bentley's version, it would still be possible that she was in contact with the FBI and acting under its instructions when she met Gromov on October 17, 1945. It may be that her initial account to the FBI on August 21 or 22 was so general that she did not give them the names of those who were involved in her espionage activities, although it does seem a bit doubtful that the FBI would have been interested enough to assign agents to work with Miss Bentley in October if they did not know then at least the broad outlines of her story. And it seems rather unlikely that she could have given even the broadest outline without mentioning the name of Nathan Gregory Silvermaster. Yet the indication seems to be that Miss Bentley did not give the FBI his name until November 7, 1945.

It becomes important, then, to know something about the nature and frequency of Miss Bentley's contacts with the FBI from August 21 or 22, 1945, when she first went to the New Haven office, to November 7, 1945, which the Brownell-Hoover testimony seems to fix as the date her story became known to the authorities. Definitive information would have to come from the FBI itself. Since we do not have the FBI's account, it is necessary to piece together what we can from other scraps of evidence. The primary source of that evidence is Miss Bentley's cross-examination in the first perjury trial of William Remington. That examination is quoted from and discussed in some detail later in this chapter. Here I shall merely summarize what it has to say about the question at hand.

In brief, it appears that Miss Bentley went to the FBI in August at least in part because of her connection with one Peter Heller, whom she suspected of falsely impersonating a government officer.

There is no evidence that Miss Bentley was in contact with the FBI again until some time in October. On October 8, 1945, the New York office of the FBI sent her a letter that was introduced into evidence at the first Remington trial. The letter asked her to make an appointment to be interviewed at the New York office "in connection with the investigation of one Peter Heller who may be impersonating an officer of the United States Government." It was addressed to Miss Bentley at Old Lyme, Connecticut, where she had gone to think things over before going to see the FBI in August. Apparently that was the address she gave the FBI agent who interviewed her in New Haven. She testified that this letter took "two or three" weeks to reach her, since she was no longer in Old Lyme. There is no suggestion that she was in contact with the FBI at any time between August 21 or 22 and her receipt of the letter of October 8, which by her own account was not until October 22 at the earliest. Therefore, it would not have been possible for her to be in touch with the FBI on the day before her meeting with Gromov on October 17, as she testified she was at the 1948 hearings. Indeed, the chronology suggested by her Remington testimony seems to fit in fairly well with an appointment to see the FBI in New York on November 7, 1945, the date referred to in one of the FBI reports as the "first" occasion on which Miss Bentley brought the Silvermaster case to the Bureau's attention. We may be sure that counsel for Remington would have given his eyeteeth to have had the facts about the November 7 chronology at his disposal when he cross-examined Miss Bentley. But that cross-examination took place in January 1951, and the data about the timing of the FBI reports on the Silvermaster ring were not released until November 1953.

There may well be explanations for these apparent discrepancies. It may be that Miss Bentley was mistaken about either the date she received the Bureau's letter asking her to come in or the date she met Gromov and was paid the $2,000. It may be that the reference to Peter Heller in the October 8 letter was just a cover, and that she was already in contact with the FBI about her story of espionage. It may be that agents of the FBI did have firsthand knowledge of her receipt of the $2,000.

All this needs further elucidation. Unlike so many other aspects of Miss Bentley's story, these discrepancies should not be difficult to explain, since the other party to the transactions in question was not one of her co-conspirators in the Communist underground, but an investigative agency of the United States Government. Surely the veil of secrecy that was partially lifted by Mr. Brownell in 1953 could without impropriety be lifted a little further to provide answers to the following questions:

1. Did Miss Bentley begin telling her espionage story to the FBI in August 1945, as she has testified she did?

2. Did Miss Bentley meet Gromov on or about October 17, 1945, under instructions from the FBI, as she has testified she did?

3. Did agents of the FBI have Miss Bentley under surveillance when she met Gromov?

4. If not, how long after her meeting with Gromov did she turn the $2,000 over to the FBI?

IV

The case of William Remington presented obvious parallels in the public imagination to that of Alger Hiss. Both Hiss and Remington were bright young men of good family who distinguished themselves academically in the Ivy League. Both rose to responsible positions in government service. Both were accused in Congressional hearings by ex-Communists (Hiss by Chambers, Remington by Miss Bentley) of having been secret Communists and of having transmitted classified government documents to unauthorized persons. Both were indicted by federal grand juries, not for criminal offenses arising out of the conduct with which they were charged, but for perjury in denying allegations that they had so conducted themselves. Both underwent two trials; both were finally convicted; both went to the penitentiary. Both served as convenient symbols of what Alistair Cooke has called "A Generation on Trial."

These parallels have been allowed to obscure a very basic distinction between the two cases, viewed either as exercises in the proof of facts or, more specifically, as testing-grounds for the credibility of former members of the Communist Party. What the distinction comes down to is this: Chambers and Hiss disagreed on almost every point, Bentley and Remington on almost nothing. Almost the only point of agreement between Chambers and Hiss was that they had once been acquainted. Consequently, the corroboration of Chambers's story had to come almost entirely from documents, notably the typewritten documents that Hiss was alleged to have passed to Chambers. And the effort to impeach Chambers proceeded primarily with reference to the story he had to tell about Hiss.

By contrast, Miss Bentley and Remington agreed on most of the facts about their relationship, the principal point of difference being whether Remington knew that Miss Bentley was a Communist agent. Consequently, the corroboration of Miss Bentley's story had to be supplied largely by reference to other incidents and relationships tending to show Communist involvement on Remington's part. And the effort to impeach Miss Bentley, in order to be successful, had to proceed primarily with reference to her general credibility. This distinction, which has been overlooked, is basic to an evaluation of the significance of the Remington case as a vindication of Miss Bentley's position and as an example of the use of the testimony of an ex-Communist witness. In the pages that follow, I shall undertake such an evaluation. First, however, it is necessary to sketch in brief the story of the Remington case.

The substance of Miss Bentley's general allegations has already been recounted. As a result of her references to his role as a supplier of information in 1942–44, Remington was interrogated by a grand jury in April 1947 and again in September 1947. Immediately after the revelation of Miss Bentley's story in the *New York World-Telegram* series, she was summoned to testify before the Investigations Subcommittee of the Senate Committee on Expenditures in the Executive Departments. The story she told at that time was that she had been introduced to Remington as a fellow Communist by Golos at a meeting in a Schrafft's Restaurant in New York, attended also by Mrs. Remington. Golos told Remington, who had previously been supplying information through Joe North, the editor of *New Masses*, that henceforth Miss Bentley, who was identified to him only as "Helen," would be his contact. She would visit him in Washington, where he was employed by the War Production Board; she would bring the Remingtons Communist literature, receive whatever secret government information they had, and collect their Party dues. This she did over a period of about two years, visiting Remington fifteen or thirty times. In the course of their relationship, Remington supplied her with much secret information, including figures on aircraft production and a formula for turning garbage into rubber. Remington eventually ceased to be a useful contact, partly because he did not have access to much helpful information and partly because he became increasingly difficult to deal with. Their contacts became less frequent, ceasing altogether sometime before Remington's entry into the Navy in 1944.

Remington appeared before the Subcommittee on the same day and gave his version of the relationship. He had indeed known Miss Bentley and had given her information, but under circumstances very different from those she had related. He had been introduced to Golos by Joe North, a friend of his mother-in-law. The introduction had been arranged as an outgrowth of arguments he had been having with North about whether American industry was doing an adequate job of mobilizing for the war effort. North was following the then prevalent Communist Party line of depreciating the effort. Remington defended it and appeared to be shaking North's view. North urged Remington to give his views to North's friend Golos. Remington suspected that Golos was a Communist, but did not know definitely. At their first meeting, Golos appeared highly interested in what Remington had to say. At a subsequent meeting (the Schrafft's encounter), Golos introduced Miss Bentley to the Remingtons as "Helen Johnson," a free-lance researcher doing work for him and for various newspapers, including *PM*.* Golos asked if "Miss Johnson" might call on Remington in Washington and get his version of what was going on in the defense effort. Remington enthusiastically acceded, because of his interest in convincing left-wing doubting Thomases that American industry's contribution to the war effort was a real one.

"Miss Johnson" did call him from time to time. He always asked her to come to his office, but she always had some reason why it was more convenient to meet him elsewhere. He obliged, and they met at street corners, or park benches, or restaurants. He gave her information, including data about aircraft production

---

* A New York City daily newspaper, now defunct, well known for its espousal of "liberal" positions.

and the "crackpot" scheme to make rubber out of garbage. None of the information he gave was classified, and it was all information of the type that he and others were constantly giving to other newspapermen and writers. Occasionally "Miss Johnson" would bring him copies of the *Daily Worker* and *PM* and would ask him to comment on specific items appearing in them. He did not want to take any gifts from her and so always paid her for the papers. Once he gave her on behalf of his wife and himself a contribution of $25 or $35 for the Joint Anti-Fascist Refugee Committee. He never knew that she was a Communist but began to be suspicious of her, particularly after he found out that no one named Helen Johnson worked for *PM*. He became reluctant to see her, and eventually their contacts ceased.

These two versions of the Bentley-Remington relationship are strikingly similar in external details. The principals did meet through Joe North and Golos. Remington did give Miss Bentley information. He did pay her money. They did meet at places away from his office. The difference was neatly summed up in a colloquy between Remington and the Subcommittee's counsel, William P. Rogers (later Attorney General of the United States):

MR. ROGERS   As I understand the substance of your testimony, you admit everything she says, except you say she misunderstood your motives; is not that about it?

MR. REMINGTON   That is one way of putting it, sir; I would put it much stronger.

Miss Bentley's charges against Remington resulted in his suspension from government employment while a Loyalty Board examined the allegations against him. Shortly before the Board reached its decision, Miss Bentley repeated her charges over the radio, thereby exposing herself to a libel action, which Remington promptly brought. On Setember 28, 1948, the Loyalty Board found against Remington. He appealed to the Loyalty Review Board, which sought to obtain the appearance of Miss Bentley. Since the Board had no subpoena power, it had to rely on the voluntary cooperation of witnesses. In this case that cooperation was not forthcoming; Miss Bentley failed to appear. On February 10, 1949, the Loyalty Review Board reversed the determination of the Loyalty Board, holding that on the basis of the evidence before them it could not be said that Remington was disloyal. Approximately one year later, presumably because of this finding, the libel case against Miss Bentley was settled by her co-defendants, the radio network and the program sponsor. Remington received $9,000 and gave all the defendants, including Miss Bentley, a general release.

Impetus to reopen the Remington case came in May 1950, when two self-confessed former Communists testified before the House Un-American Activities Committee that they had known Remington as a Communist when he worked for the Tennessee Valley Authority in Knoxville in 1936–37. Remington was then summoned before another grand jury, which also heard testimony from his former wife, Ann Moos Remington, as well as from Miss Bentley and the new witnesses against him. As a consequence of its inquiry, the grand jury indicted Remington on one count of perjury for having falsely sworn before it that he had never been a member of the Communist Party.

The trial of this indictment commenced before Judge Noonan of the United States District Court for the Southern District of New York on December 20, 1950, and took about a month and a half. The principal witnesses against Remington were Miss Bentley and Remington's former wife, who substantially corroborated Miss Bentley's account of the relationship. There was also much testimony about Remington's alleged Communist involvement while a student at Dartmouth and during his employment with the Tennessee Valley Authority. On February 7, 1951, the jury found Remington guilty, and the next day he was sentenced to five years' imprisonment and fined $2,000. This conviction was reversed by the United States Court of Appeals for the Second Circuit on the ground that the judge's charge did not instruct the jury that they had to agree on an act or acts evidencing Remington's belief that he had been a member of the Communist Party. Because of this failure, it was impossible to tell whether the federal rule of proof requiring that perjury be established by the testimony of two witnesses, or by the testimony of one witness and corroborating circumstances, had been complied with. The Court did not reach the contention, vigorously pressed by counsel for Remington, that irregularities in the grand jury process which had led to Remington's indictment required that the indictment be quashed. These alleged irregularities raise important issues about the use of testimony such as Miss Bentley's, and will be discussed after this brief recapitulation of the history of the Remington case.

Remington applied to the Supreme Court for a writ of certiorari, contending that the Court of Appeals had erred in failing to quash the indictment. Thereupon, on October 21, 1951, the Government took the unusual step of causing a fresh indictment to be returned, charging Remington with five counts of perjury alleged to have been committed during his testimony at the first trial. The Government then asked the Supreme Court for permission to seek leave from the District Court to dismiss the first indictment. The purpose of this maneuver, presumably, was to cause the issue of irregularities in the grand jury process with respect to the first indictment to become moot, thereby forestalling Supreme Court review of the question. On December 11, 1951, the Supreme Court denied the Government's motion. On March 24, 1951, the Court denied Remington's petition for certiorari, two justices dissenting, and a third, Mr. Justice Frankfurter, reiterating his often expressed admonition that denial of a petition for certiorari is not to be taken as an expression of opinion about the merits of the case.

On January 13, 1953, the trial of the second indictment commenced, and on January 27 the jury found Remington guilty under two counts of the new indictment. They found that he had lied under oath when he denied at the first trial (1) that he had ever given Miss Bentley information to which she was not entitled, and (2) that he had known of the existence of the Young Communist League when he was a student at Dartmouth. The jury acquitted him of perjury in denying that he had ever asked anyone to join the Communist Party. And the jury failed to agree on counts charging perjury in denying that he had ever knowingly attended Communist meetings or paid Communist dues. Remington was sentenced to three years' imprisonment on the counts on which he was convicted. He appealed on the sole ground that the improprieties in procuring the first indictment were so gross as to vitiate all subsequent proceedings. His conviction was affirmed, one judge dissenting. Shortly before the completion of his term of imprisonment, Remington was killed by a fellow inmate at the penitentiary.

Four triers-of-fact have considered the case of William Remington and have assessed the charges brought against him by Elizabeth Bentley. They are the Loyalty Board which in 1948 found a reasonable doubt as to his loyalty; the Loyalty Review Board, which in 1949, after a *de novo* hearing, cleared him; the jury which in 1951 convicted him of perjury in denying that he had ever been a member of the Communist Party; and the jury which in 1953 convicted him of perjury in denying that he had known of the existence of the Young Communist League while at Dartmouth and that he had given Miss Bentley information to which she was not entitled. What do these verdicts contribute to an evaluation of Miss Bentley's account of her activities?

We do not know the basis for the Loyalty Board's finding against Remington or for the Loyalty Review Board's finding in his favor. We do not know what evidence was before either Board. The Boards were presumably acquainted with the public testimony of Remington and of Miss Bentley, as well as with testimony given before the Senate Subcommittee in executive session, which was not made public until the renewed accusations against Remington in 1950. And we may probably assume that the Boards had some access to material from the files of the FBI. Whether that material consisted of "raw data"—verbatim transcripts given to the FBI by Miss Bentley, transcripts of interviews with her, and the like—or whether it consisted of summaries or evaluations of her testimony, we do not know. Of course, neither Board had before it the testimony later supplied by Mrs. Remington. It may be fairly inferable that Miss Bentley's failure to submit to examination by the Loyalty Review Board contributed to its finding.

A finding that a reasonable doubt as to Remington's loyalty did not exist was not necessarily a finding that Miss Bentley's story was untrue. The finding was one of present loyalty based on past conduct: the Board might conceivably have credited Miss Bentley's version of the relationship, or at any rate thought the truth was nearer her version than Remington's, and still viewed Remington, in the total perspective of his life and work, as a loyal citizen. There is a vast difference between a proceeding designed to establish the truth or falsity of a given proposition and a proceeding that is an unrestricted inquiry into the beliefs, attitudes, and associations of an individual. A loyalty proceeding is of this second kind. It is the trial not of a charge, but of a man. That aspect is usually thought to bear on its unfairness to the individual accused of disloyalty. But it also bears on the weight that can be attributed to its general conclusion when it comes to assessing the truth or falsity of any given proposition of fact. In short, the verdict of the loyalty proceeding, even if it had not been followed by the development of new evidence and the two perjury trials, tells us nothing about the weight that should be accorded to Miss Bentley's story of Remington's Communist involvement.

The significance of the verdict in the first perjury trial is our next inquiry. That verdict was deprived of legal effect by the Court of Appeals' reversal of the conviction, but this does not necessarily deprive the verdict of significance. If the verdict had been that Remington lied when he denied knowing Miss Bentley as a Communist and the reversal had been predicated on, say, the admission of evidence obtained by an illegal search of Remington's house, we would still have the considered opinion of twelve jurors that Remington had lied and Miss Bentley had told the truth in a crucial regard. But the verdict was much more general than that. It was that Remington had lied in denying that he had ever been a member of the Communist Party. And the reason for the Court's reversal is, significantly, also the reason why the verdict has no significance in evaluating Miss Bentley's charges against Remington. The Court of Appeals reversed because the trial judge failed to isolate for the jury the overt acts which might evidence Remington's belief that he had been a member of the Communist Party. The testimony at the trial ranged over Remington's entire life, including at least three other episodes of alleged Communist involvement. The jury might well have pinned its verdict on one of those other episodes, particularly Remington's labor movement activities when he was working for the Tennessee Valley Authority in Knoxville. Or, what is more likely, some of the jurors might have been impressed by that episode, with which Miss Bentley had nothing to do, while others were taken with her story. The Government persistently refused to specify the act or acts that evidenced Remington's perjury in denying Party membership. In consequence, we have no way of knowing whether or not the jury believed Miss Bentley's story. Since the development and corroboration of her story occupied a major part of the trial, we might well surmise that the jury did believe her; but that would be nothing more than surmise.

The verdict in the second perjury trial was more specific. The jury found that Remington had lied when he denied knowing of the existence of the Young Communist League when he was a student at Dartmouth and when he denied having given Miss Bentley information to which she was not entitled. The first of these had nothing to do with Miss Bentley's story; the second did. But again, it is not precisely on point. Remington himself admitted having given Miss Bentley a wide range of miscellaneous information. He denied that any of the information was classified, i.e., that it was information to which any unauthorized person, Communist or not, was to be denied access. The Government attempted to show that this information was classified, i.e., that Remington was not entitled to transmit it to anyone, Communist or not. It is technically consistent with the jury's verdict that they believed Remington when he denied being a Communist and denied knowing that Miss Bentley was one, or at any rate that they did not believe Miss Bentley beyond a reasonable doubt. Indeed, it may be more than technically consistent, given the jury's failure to agree on the only count that put directly in issue the basic controversy between Remington and Miss Bentley. That count, it will be recalled, charged Remington with having falsely denied that he paid Communist dues to Miss Bentley. A verdict of guilty on that count would clearly have established the trier-of-fact's view that the truth lay with Miss Bentley rather than with Remington. The guilty verdict on the count relating to giving information did not perform the same office. Of course, common sense may suggest that a jury would probably not subject a defendant to the penalties for perjury if they did not believe, not merely that he had lied under oath, but that the gravamen of the charge against him was true. But that, again, is surmise.

To say all this is not to say that Remington told the truth and that Miss Bentley lied. A reading of the evidence as a whole would not tend, I believe, to support that conclusion. It is to say that the jury verdict cannot be taken as vindication for Miss Bentley, even in the limited sense in which the verdict in the Hiss case represents vindication for Whittaker Chambers. No one is to blame for this. It does not reflect discredit on Miss Bentley. Nor does it reflect discredit on the Government's attorneys who drew the charges against Remington. It was not their job to shape the case in a way that made it a clear contest between Miss Bentley and

Remington. When they combed the record of the first trial for statements by Remington that could be made the basis for a successful perjury indictment, they were not trying to vindicate Miss Bentley. They were just trying to put together a winning case. In this they succeeded. But the price of their success in *United States* v. *Remington* was the continued presence of a question mark in the case of Bentley v. Remington.

The circumstances under which the first indictment against Remington was returned merit detailed examination, for they raise important issues about the uses made of testimony such as Miss Bentley's. As previously mentioned, the first official public cognizance of Miss Bentley's charges came hard on the heels of a series of sensational stories in the *New York World-Telegram* about the activities of this "blonde spy queen." Those stories were produced pursuant to an arrangement by which Miss Bentley profited financially. After her testimony before the Senate and House committees in July 1948, Miss Bentley supported herself by lecturing and writing about her career in the Communist underground. At the very time the indictment was returned against Remington, she was working on a book about her experiences, later published as *Out of Bondage*. In addition to the interest that any person normally has in being regarded as a truth-teller, Miss Bentley had a strong financial interest in the success of her book, to which she referred during the course of the first Remington trial as her "livelihood."

In retrospect, it appears that the period between her first public appearance as a witness and the return of the indictment against Remington (July 1948 to June 1950) was a difficult one for Miss Bentley. Her charges against Remington appeared to have foundered when the Loyalty Review Board cleared him. None of the other persons whom she named as participants in her espionage activities were prosecuted. And Remington's libel suit against her was compromised by a cash settlement in his favor. It may not be an overstatement to suggest that Miss Bentley's financial future depended upon bringing her story before the public once again in a dramatic way.

In the spring of 1950 Miss Bentley began negotiating with the publishing firm of Devin-Adair for the publication of her book. The president of the firm, Devin Garrity, arranged for her to receive literary and editorial assistance from John Brunini. There was testimony at the trial that Brunini was to share in the proceeds of the book and that a contract mentioning him by name and identifying his financial interest was drawn up. There was also testimony that this contract was destroyed and a new one prepared, omitting any reference to Brunini, and that this second contract was executed early in June 1950, at or about the time the grand jury returned its indictment against Remington. All this would be very irrelevant, were it not for the fact that Brunini was foreman of the grand jury that indicted Remington. And his role in the proceedings that culminated in the return of the indictment was, as we shall see, crucial.

Counsel for the Government knew the basic facts about the Bentley-Brunini relationship at the time the indictment was returned. The United States Attorney who prosecuted the case stated that he had discussed the problem with the Attorney General of the United States and with some judges of the District Court. He did not, however, call the matter to the attention of the defense. It came to light during the trial, when an ex-employee of Devin-Adair, who knew the facts about the relationship, came forward with information. This witness, Mrs. Collins, and another former employee of Devin-Adair, Miss Sefa, appeared as witnesses for the defense. It appears that they were completely disinterested witnesses. The substance of their testimony was that Brunini was to collaborate with Miss Bentley in preparing her manuscript and that a contract was drawn up pursuant to which Brunini was to receive a portion of the proceeds of the book. Miss Sefa testified that she had typed this earlier contract and was told that it had been destroyed. She asked Miss Bentley why it had been necessary to destroy the old contract and draw up another, and Miss Bentley told her that there was no special reason for it.

This information became available to the defense just before Miss Bentley took the stand for the prosecution, and on cross-examination she was questioned about her relationship with Brunini. Her testimony in this respect may fairly be characterized as evasive. At first she denied that Brunini had done any work on her book, but then she admitted that he had done editorial work on it. She denied that he had a financial interest in it and that there had been an earlier contract which explicitly recognized such an interest. This testimony, it should be noted, was given before Miss Sefa and Mrs. Collins took the stand.

The Government attempted to impeach the testimony of Miss Sefa and Mrs. Collins, going so far as to characterize them in the jury's presence as liars. However, counsel for the Government successfully resisted the efforts of the defense to obtain disclosure of a narrative statement in the Government's possession which purported to contain the truth about these incidents. My residual impression after examining the very complicated portion of the record dealing with this affair is as follows: Brunini and Miss Bentley had a joint interest, probably of a financial nature; Miss Bentley was uncandid in her testimony about this interest; the Government did all in its power to prevent disclosure of the incident.

The defense moved promptly for dismissal of the indictment on the ground that gross improprieties had occurred in the grand jury process. This motion was denied. They also moved for inspection of the grand jury minutes; this motion was also denied. The trial judge did, however, grant a defense motion to seal the minutes and have them made a part of the record on appeal. As a consequence of that action, we are in a position to appraise the significance of Brunini's interest, although defense counsel were not in a position to do so at the trial.

The Court of Appeals did not find it necessary to reach the question of the grand jury process in deciding the case, since they reversed on the error in the judge's charge, thereby sending the case back for a new trial. However, the Court did rule that on a retrial, if one occurred, the defense should have an opportunity to inspect the grand jury minutes and to make its case, if it could, that the indictment should be quashed. As previously related, the Government then took the novel step of causing a fresh indictment to be returned, this time charging perjury in Remington's testimony at the first trial. The prospect that this kind of practice opens, of a series of perjury indictments, one hanging onto the coattails of another, until finally a verdict of guilty is reached and upheld, has seemed to many a dangerous inroad on the principle underlying the constitutional prohibition against double jeopardy. One need not reach that question, however, to see in the Government's action in procuring a fresh indictment clear recognition of the improprieties involved in the return of the first one. The Court of Appeals had left open the possibility that the first indictment might be quashed; as one member of the Court later said, "It was to escape this risk that the indictment was abandoned."

On the appeal from the conviction under the new indictment, the defense had to argue not only that the first indictment was improper but that the impropriety vitiated the subsequent proceedings, thereby requiring reversal of the second conviction. In this they were unsuccessful. A majority of the Court of Appeals held that the impropriety of the first indictment, even if assumed to be such as to warrant quashing that indictment, did not give the defendant license to lie with impunity at the trial of that indictment. The Court's view is probably one that would be accepted by most tribunals, but we need not stop to examine the question. The point that concerns us here is that there was never a judicial examination of the merits of the defense's contention that what occurred in the grand jury room should have caused the indictment to be dismissed.

What did happen in the grand jury room? We have two sources of information on that. One is the brief filed in the Court of Appeals by Remington's counsel on the appeal from the second conviction. It refers to but does not quote from the examination of Remington's wife before the grand jury. If believed, it would indicate that Mrs. Remington was browbeaten into changing her story by the combined efforts of Brunini and the Government attorney who presented the case to the grand jury, Mr. Thomas J. Donegan. We need not, however, attempt to weigh this second-hand paraphrase from an interested party, for the crucial portion of the grand jury minutes is reprinted in the opinion of the dissenting judge in the Court of Appeals. It shows that at a critical moment, when Mrs. Remington was being pressed to admit that her husband had told her that he was making payments of dues to the Communist Party, Brunini himself had administered the *coup de grace* of threatening her with contempt proceedings by implying, falsely, that she had no privilege to withhold the information. The description of the incident in Judge Learned Hand's dissenting opinion cannot be improved upon by paraphrase:

For myself the examination went beyond what I deem permissible. Pages on pages of lecturing repeatedly preceded a question; statements of what the prosecution already knew, and of how idle it was for the witness to hold back what she could contribute; occasional reminders that she could be punished for perjury; all were scattered throughout. Still she withstood the examiners, until, being much tried and worn, she said: "I am getting fuzzy. I haven't eaten since a long time ago and I don't think I am going to be very coherent from now on. I would like to postpone the hearings. * * * I want to consult my lawyers and see how deep I am getting in." This was denied, and the questioning kept on until she finally refused to answer, excusing herself because she was "tired" and "would like to get something to eat. * * * Is this the third degree, waiting until I get hungry, now?" Still the examiners persisted, disregarding this further protest: "I would like to get something to eat. But couldn't we continue another day? Or do I have to come back?" Thereupon there took place what I quote in the margin,[1] and what

---

[1] *"By Mr. Donegan.* Q. Well, do we have to go through all this background? We are right down to the issue right now, after all this time we have just reached the question now. Why not answer that question and then we'll postpone it for another day; if you answer that question, we'll postpone it for another day. That isn't going to involve you, is it? It couldn't involve you. All you have to do is say yes or no as to whether that money was for the Communist Party. And your yes or no isn't going to decide the issue, I'll tell you that; it's something else that exists. You know that I wouldn't ask you questions—you can't accuse me of fishing in here. I haven't learned anything yet.

"A. Well, I don't want to answer.

"By the Foreman [Brunini]. Q. Mrs. Remington, I think that we have been very kind and considerate. We haven't raised our voices and we haven't shown our teeth, have we? Maybe you don't know about our teeth. A witness before a Grand Jury hasn't the privilege of refusing to answer a question. You see, we haven't told you that, so far. You have been asked a question. You must answer it. If a witness doesn't answer a question, the Grand Jury has rather unusual powers along that line. We are, to a certain extent, what you might call a judicial body. We can't act, ourselves. Our procedure is, when we get a witness who is contemptuous, who refuses to answer questions, to take them before a Judge. Now, at that point there will be a private proceeding. He will instruct the witness to answer the question. Then we come back here and put the question again. If the witness refuses to answer the question, we take him back to court and the judge will find him in contempt to Court and sentence him to jail until he has purged himself. 'Purging,' in that case, is answering the question. Now, I have already pointed out to you that you have a question from the Special Assistant to the Attorney General: Did your husband or did he not give this money to the Communist Party? You have no privilege to refuse to answer the question. I don't want at this time to—I said 'showing teeth.' I don't want them to bite you. But I do want you to know that. And remember, you have a very sympathetic body here. We want to avoid anything like that. I didn't mention, of course, the second proceeding before a jury is of course a public hearing. And I mention that to you in fairness because I do know that you have a certain grave concern about what your obligations are, and I think in fairness to you we should tell you that. And in view of the time and, I think, the empty stomachs of all the

proved to be the *coup de grâce,* after which she made a full disclosure
of what she knew: a very large part of it what Remington had told her
during their marriage and before they separated in January 1947.

. . .

. . . I shall assume for argument that, had there been nothing more than
I have mentioned, the indictment might have stood up. It is the added
circumstance that, as I have already said, a very large part of Ann Remington's testimony consisted of confidential communications from her
husband to her, that satisfies any doubts I might otherwise have had.
That was testimony as much privileged in a federal court, as in a state
court; moreover, the privilege extends to a proceeding before a grand
jury. Although I have found no federal decisions, I accept it also as the
law that her later separation and divorce from Remington did not open
the witness's mouth; indeed, any other view would be completely inconsistent with the theory of the privilege. It will have been observed
how important a part this played in the result, for in his final admonition
that effected her breakdown, Brunini not only threatened her with contempt proceedings, but expressly told her that she had no privilege.
His language is worth repeating: "Now, I have already pointed out to
you that you have a question from the Special Assistant to the Attorney
General: Did your husband or did he not give this money to the Communist Party? *You have no privilege to refuse to answer the question.*"
Read literally, that was true; but, read as the witness must have understood it—that is, whether her husband had not told her so—it was
altogether false. I do not intimate that Brunini, a layman, thought it
false; but Donegan was present, and he did not intervene to correct the
mistake.

It is interesting that Judge Hand's view did not take into account that Brunini, who brought all this about, was an interested
party. When that factor is added to those discussed by Judge
Hand, it is hard to see how the Government could have avoided
dismissal of the first indictment, had any court chosen to rule
squarely on the issue of its propriety.

The significance of this incident for the administration of criminal justice generally is obvious. The processes of the law should
seem, as well as be, impartial. In this case, whatever they in fact

---

Jurors—I know mine is very empty—I think we can very quickly dispose of
things if you will just proceed now. I think you have in your heart answered
the questions as to what your procedure should be. (To Mr. Donegan) Do
you want to put the question again?

"Q. Can you find that question, Mr. Reporter?

"A. My answer is yes."

may have been, they did not seem to be impartial. Whether Remington was guilty or innocent of the crime with which he was charged, he was brought to book in a way that does not reflect credit on the administration of justice. That this was so resulted proximately from the inconsistent roles played by Miss Bentley: as a pathetic witness to acts of betrayal, and as the commercial exploiter of her own story.

Since the first Remington trial was the only public occasion on which Miss Bentley was subjected to extensive cross-examination, it may be of some interest to consider certain aspects of it, both for the light they shed on her demeanor as a witness and, more important, for what they tell us about the extent to which the judicial process can be helpful in unraveling the complexities of a story such as hers.

Miss Bentley's examination occupies almost 400 pages in the typewritten transcript of the Remington trial. She was on the witness stand for the better part of three days, most of this time under cross-examination by Mr. William Chanler, counsel for Remington. One might suppose that so protracted an examination would have afforded an opportunity to canvass most of the significant aspects of her story. But it did not. The reasons were several. One is the cumbersome nature of the trial process, particularly when a stubbornly fought battle takes place between counsel who do not credit each other with even an adversary's good faith. From an inspection of the record, one concludes that the trial was conducted by its chief protagonists, Mr. Chanler for the defense, and Mr. Irving Saypol, then United States Attorney for the Southern District of New York, in an atmosphere of bitter mutual hostility and distrust going far beyond the normal combativeness of the litigation process. Whether this occurred because of the temper of the times, personal incompatibility, or a combination of these factors, is impossible to determine from the record. But it is clear that extended colloquies between counsel, often in the presence of the jury, prevented the orderly examination of the witness. By a rough count, almost one third of the time Miss Bentley was on the stand was consumed in interchanges between counsel that, to put it mildly, did not advance consideration of the issues.

A second factor that militated against an extensive examination of Miss Bentley's story was defense counsel's apparent decision not to question her veracity in broad outline. In his opening statement to the jury, Mr. Chanler implicitly accepted her story of espionage activity with the Silvermaster ring. A third factor, which undoubtedly explains the tactical decision involved in the second, is that defense counsel did not have at hand the materials to construct a generally impeaching cross-examination. This was partly because in 1951, when the trial took place, much information that later became available was unknown, including, most importantly, the information disclosed by Attorney General Brownell in November 1953, which tends to raise questions about Miss Bentley's account of her transactions with the FBI.

Still, the examination was a penetrating one, and it raised a certain amount of doubt about the extent to which Miss Bentley has tended to substitute imagination for recollection. Nothing in the transcript seriously shakes the main outline of her story, but a number of passages suggest tendencies that it is rather disturbing to find in a witness whose veracity has been as heavily relied on as Miss Bentley's has.

Some of the instances are trivial. For example, Miss Bentley testified on cross-examination that her lover, Golos, was unmarried. It was brought out that she had given the same testimony in the Brothman trial. But in her 1948 testimony before the House Un-American Activities Committee, she had testified that Golos had a wife and son, whom Silvermaster knew. The apparent discrepancy was resolved by her pointing out that Golos and his first "wife" were not legally married, and that their relationship was, in fact, the same as the later relationship between Golos and herself. Perhaps Miss Bentley was a little disingenuous in not volunteering that Golos had family ties at the time he took up with her, but her testimony in this regard cannot be viewed as substantially contradictory.

Somewhat more serious is a colloquy that occurred with reference to Miss Bentley's knowledge of Mrs. Remington's first name. Under questioning about the dinner at Schrafft's when she and Golos met the Remingtons, she testified that Mrs. Remington was introduced as "Ann." She was thereupon taxed with her testimony before the Senate Committtee in 1948 that she had not known Mrs. Remington's real name but had only known her by the nickname

"Bing." The point itself is a trivial one. There was no argument about the fact that the dinner had taken place and that Golos, Bentley, and the Remingtons had been there. What is somewhat disturbing is Miss Bentley's explanation for her lapse of memory.

Q. How then do you now remember in 1951 that Mr. Golos introduced her as Ann Remington when in 1948 you said you did not know her real name?

A. Because little by little, Mr. Chanler, I remember facts; in fact, sometimes when I think back over things, I remember a number of things that I did not remember before.

This suggestion that her own unaided recollection summoned up Mrs. Remington's name has a disingenuous ring. In 1948, when Mrs. Remington was not involved in the effort to determine the truth as between Remington and Miss Bentley, Miss Bentley did not know Mrs. Remington's first name. In 1951, when Mrs. Remington was very much involved, Miss Bentley did know the name. It would be incredible if Miss Bentley had not come across Mrs. Remington's first name by the time of this examination. If she did not read it in the papers, she probably heard it from one of her associates. That is perfectly innocent. But pretending to an all-encompassing personal recollection is not.

One of the most impressive aspects of Miss Bentley's testimony is its detail. But every once in a while, the elaboration of detail boomerangs, and we are left with a disturbed feeling about her respect for accuracy. The following instance is an illustration. On direct examination, Miss Bentley testified as follows:

During dinner Mr. Golos and Mr. Remington talked together and Mrs. Remington and I chatted together about casual things. We sat for a while after we had finished the actual meal and then, as we were going out and putting our coats on, Mr. Golos turned to both the Remingtons and said that he himself could not make trips to Washington to contact them and hence that in the future I would be considered their new Communist contact, that I would go down and collect their dues, Communist Party dues, that I would bring them Communist Party literature as it came out, and that I would collect from Mr. Remington any information he had been able to obtain in Washington.

On cross-examination this passage was read to her and she was pressed about how she reconciled this conversation with her testimony about the Communist underground's passion for secrecy.

Q. Isn't it a very extraordinary thing that here you were meeting a new
contact, Mr. Redmont,* for the first time—
A. I was, but not Mr. Golos.
Q. You were, and you met them at Schrafft's restaurant and then you
started having a conversation while you were putting on your coats
in front of the coat girl, I assume, on the way out, in which I think
you three times mentioned the Communist Party. I will withdraw
the three times until I check the record.
MR. SAYPOL   Will you take the coat girl out too because I don't recall
she was there?
Q. Is there a coat girl at Schrafft's?
A. Not at the hour and not at the Schrafft's. It is about one of the most
deserted places you can find at that hour, or at least it was in those
days.

In rebuttal to this testimony, the defense subsequently called
as a witness Mrs. Mildred Shelhorse, the manager of the Schrafft's
restaurant in question, who was also manager at the time of the
Golos-Bentley-Remington dinner. She testified that during the
dinner hour there were three employees of the restaurant constantly on duty within easy earshot of customers who were putting
on their coats to leave. If believed, and this was a disinterested
witness, Mrs. Shelhorse's testimony pretty well negated Miss Bentley's attempt to explain how it could have been safe to talk so
freely about Communist activity in a public place.

Again the point is not a crucial one. Miss Bentley may have
been mistaken about the precise time the conversation about Communist activity took place. It may have been outside the restaurant. Or she may have been mistaken in remembering so circum-
stantially that she did not hear what Remington and Golos were
saying to each other at the table. But she had claimed to remember that; and so her description of the alleged conversations about
Communist activities may have seemed, consciously or unconsciously, to strengthen her story by showing how she knew at
first hand that the Remingtons understood they were involved in
Communist activities—knew this not just from something Golos
told her later, but from something that she said in the Remingtons' presence. But surely extreme doubt is cast on the accuracy
of her recollection by this incident.

---

* This appears to be either an error in transcription or a slip by the
examiner. The passage clearly refers to Remington.

This is not an isolated example of Miss Bentley's tendency to use detail in her narrative, to have the detail challenged, to add extra detail in an effort to extricate herself from a difficult situation, and then to find herself mired deeper than ever. Here is another example, growing out of the one just mentioned.

In an effort to impeach her testimony about the conversation defining the Remingtons' knowledge that they were getting themselves into Communist activities, Mr. Chanler read to Miss Bentley from her 1948 testimony before the Senate Subcommittee.

Q. Do you remember being asked the following questions and giving the following answers at page 29?

"*Senator Ferguson.* Tell us exactly what happened when you got to Washington. As I understand it, you do not know of the conversations between Golos and Remington as to the actual delivery of the material?

"*Miss Bentley.* No."

A. That is quite correct, they did. I testified that they talked together at the table.

Q. You don't know of any arrangements between Mr. Golos and Mr. Remington, if there were any, as to the actual delivery of the material?

A. I don't know the rest of that. I think we were talking about the conversation at the table at that point. You are taking things out of context. I don't know what comes before it. I haven't reread that testimony. I haven't the slightest idea.

Now it will be observed that the passage quoted from the Senate testimony is not precisely contradictory to what Miss Bentley testified was said as they were leaving the restaurant. It only concerned what she heard at the table, and she had consistently testified that she did not hear what Golos and Remington said to each other at the table. The point that Mr. Chanler was attempting to bring out was that in her Senate testimony Miss Bentley had not mentioned the conversation about Communist activity when they were putting on their coats. But in her desire to avoid the implication that she had embroidered her testimony after realizing that her 1948 Senate testimony was incomplete, Miss Bentley fell into a neatly laid trap. Here is what happened next:

Q. You haven't read this testimony at all in recent months?
A. I certainly have not.
Q. Haven't you published an article published last December in which you said you had been reading your prior testimony?

A. Not that particular testimony.

Q. What testimony did you refer to that you had been reading in the article that was published last December?

A. I don't offhand remember, Mr. Chanler. One volume that was around I was looking back to see how I had characterized communism because that article was intended to give an idea of communism and that is what I was searching for.

Q. Did you testify before the Senate at any time or times except the time we have been talking about in 1948 before the Ferguson Committee and then once in 1949 before the Committee on Immigration?

A. Not that I recall, no.

Q. This is the article that you wrote. It was published last December (*handing*).

A. You know, it is very odd but this is the first time I have seen it. They forgot to send me a copy.

Q. You wrote the article, didn't you?

A. Yes, certainly.

Q. And didn't you state there on the second page: "Anyone who reads a verbatim transcript of what he said under emotional stress, as I have read this record of my Senate Committee testimony, will have mixed reactions," and so forth? The first sentence of that paragraph (*handing*).

A. I am afraid it is merely a literary device, Mr. Chanler.

Q. You mean that when you wrote this—

A. I mean that I did not reread the testimony and I put that in there as sheerly a literary device, that is all.

In order to extricate herself from the difficulty in which she found herself, Miss Bentley suggested that this was not an occasion on which strict accuracy was important.

Q. When you are writing articles about your own life and your own activities and adventures, don't you make any effort to stick to the facts?

A. I definitely do, where facts are important, but where you put in local color like that, I suppose any writer is going to use a device like that.

Whereupon Mr. Chanler closed the trap the rest of the way:

Q. In that paragraph that I just showed you the first sentence of—I think I will read the paragraph, if I may, and ask you if you remember writing it: "Anyone who reads a verbatim transcript of what he said under emotional stress, as I have read this record of my Senate Committee testimony, will have mixed reactions. He will wonder why he said this and why he said that rather than something else, wonder why he did not put things more neatly. I have not been the exception. Analyzing what I said under oath I will again swear that each word and phrase was sincere but I do know that I have given the most sketchy types of answers even if, since there were no further questions, those had apparently satisfied the Committee." You wrote that even though really you had not read it at all?

Miss Bentley could only reply rather lamely: "I have glanced through it, yes, but I have not reread it."

And so Miss Bentley found herself in a dilemma. Either she was in error when she asserted so positively that she had not reread her Senate testimony or she was in error when she wrote that she had reread it, in a context where it certainly made a difference whether she had or not. The reader must judge for himself whether her explanation was satisfactory.

The important role of Miss Bentley's Remington testimony in the general question of the time and circumstances of her revelations to the FBI has already been discussed in some detail. I have referred several times to the difficulties of using the *ad hoc* occasion of a given criminal trial as a vehicle for exploring a story such as Miss Bentley's. The point can be graphically illustrated by considering the version of the affair developed in the trial, and comparing its fragmentary nature with what we have been able to piece together in the light of such knowledge as we now possess.

The pertinent extracts from Miss Bentley's testimony follow. The reader's attention is particularly invited to the italicized passages.

Q. Now will you tell us again just what it was that motivated you to go to the FBI in August of 1945 with your story?
A. Good old-fashioned New England conscience, I think.
Q. When did your conscience begin troubling you?
A. It began troubling me from the moment I discovered that communism was not what I thought it was.
Q. So what did you do?
A. I went to the FBI.
Q. Where?
A. In the New Haven office because I thought it was safer.
Q. What did you do when you got there?
A. I told the man there that I was working for a firm dealing with Russia, that I was mixed up with undercover activities, and he said, "Go on back home, we will get in touch with you."
Q. You did not tell him then—you did not give him in New Haven any details of your activities?
A. I gave him broad things, and he said to go on home and they would get in touch with me, which they did.

Q. And what is the next thing that happened?

A. The next thing that happened was that I got word from the Bureau to come to the New York office.

Q. How soon was that?

A. Well, it is difficult. I was in New Haven there; the letter was sent by mistake to New Haven and it was forwarded on to two places *and by the time it got to me I would say it was possibly two weeks or three weeks;* I am not clear on that.

Q. And what did that letter say?

A. That letter asked me to call up and make an appointment to come in to the New York office. I have forgotten the name of the agent who was mentioned.

Q. And you went in?

A. Yes, I did.

Q. What happened then? Did you start telling your story?

A. Yes, I talked to the man there and he said he wasn't the expert on communism, and would I come in again and speak to the men who knew more about it than he did.

Q. Did you then start talking to the experts on communism?

A. Yes, I started talking to the experts on communism.

Q. About when did you start doing that?

A. I don't know. I am trying to place the exact date. I don't recall exactly. It was not too long after that.

Q. And then you set to work and started to tell this whole story from start to finish, what you have told here, and more, of what you knew?

A. Yes, that is correct, yes.

Q. Did you make a written statement for the FBI at that time?

A. It seems to me I made a written one covering the major points. I do not think it included the entire business, the written one, I don't know. They took so many notes and so many things went down, I just don't know.

Q. Did you sign several statements, do you think?

A. That I don't know.

Q. I think you have testified before that it was not until January or February that you finally had finished telling your story, is that right?

A. Again I can't place the exact date. It may have been the end of that year; it may have been in January or towards February; it was along in there sometime.

Q. And you went there solely because your conscience drove you to it?

A. Yes.

Q. And that is what you have always said, of course, to the Senate and the House, isn't it?

A. If it was mentioned I said that.

Q. When you said why you went.

A. Well, if they asked me that is what I said. I don't remember whether they asked me or not.

Q. Now, Miss Bentley, I suggest to you that when you went to New

Haven in 1945 in August you went there only for the purpose of asking the FBI to tell you about a man named Captain Peter Heller?

A. Was he a captain?

Q. Or was he a lieutenant at that time?

A. I seem to recall he was a lieutenant. Yes, I asked them about him while I was there, yes.

Q. Isn't that what you went up there about?

A. No, that was completely a side issue. Since I was there I thought I would ask them about him.

Q. And when you received a letter from the New York office, didn't that letter refer solely—didn't it say at the top "In the matter of Peter Heller"?

A. That I don't recall, what was in the letter, I am sorry.

Q. Have you still got that letter?

A. No, inasmuch as I was still dealing with the Gay Pay U [GPU, the Soviet secret police] I destroyed it immediately. I didn't want to have it on the premises.

Q. You destroyed it immediately?

A. Yes.

Q. You sure nobody has ever seen it?

A. Not my copy of the letter, no. I don't know about anybody else's copy of the letter.

Q. And who was Lieutenant Peter Heller?

A. I don't know exactly what his position was. He was a man that I had met in the spring of 1945.

Q. And where had you met him? In the lobby of the St. George Hotel, wasn't it?

A. Yes, I met him at the St. George Hotel.

Q. And you saw him there several times?

A. Yes. Not there. He would take me to dinner, he would take me to the movies, I think he took me once dancing.

Q. And you got to know him quite well, didn't you?

A. I don't know as I would say too well. He was a very nice person. He was a person I went out with at that time.

. . .

Q. Now you had some conversations with Lieutenant Heller about your Communist activities, didn't you?

A. Not that I recall, no.

Q. Didn't you tell him that you had been mixed up with the Communists in some way?

A. Not that I recall, no.

Q. Well, why then did you ask the FBI about him?

A. Because although I didn't realize it, in trying to sort of build himself up to me he had claimed to be an undercover government agent.

Q. How did the coversation as to being an undercover government agent come up?

A. That I have forgotten, how he happend to tell me that. He said he was an undercover government agent. His implication was that he was doing some super hush-hush business for the Government.

Q. And isn't it a fact the sole purpose of your going to the FBI in August the first time you went was to ask them whether or not Heller was in fact a government agent?

A. My sole purpose in going to the FBI was to give them the information I had. I also asked them about Lieutenant or Captain Heller at the same time.

Q. And isn't it a fact that when the FBI sent for you to come to New York the only questions they asked you about at that time related to Lieutenant Heller?

A. On the contrary, they asked me about communism.

Q. Right away?

A. Yes.

MR. CHANLER *I ask the Government to produce a copy of a letter signed, I think, by Mr. Conroy of the FBI addressed to Miss Bentley sometime after the 21st of August within, say, six or eight weeks of the 21st of August, 1945.*

MR. SAYPOL I never heard of it, I never saw it, I consider it immaterial. I object to the request and ask that the Court not allow it. If the Court does allow it, I shall make an effort to find it and bring it here to submit to the Court.

THE COURT I suggest that you look for it first. Then we will see if it is relevant or material.

MR. SAYPOL It is your Honor's desire that I do it now or may I do it after the session?

MR. CHANLER Oh, after the session.

MR. SAYPOL May we have the date?

MR. CHANLER I don't know the exact date. It is, I believe, the first letter written from the New York office of the FBI to Miss Bentley, the one that asks her to come in.

THE WITNESS It is the only letter, Mr. Chanler.

Q. It is the only letter you received?

A. I think it is the only letter, yes.

Q. Now I suggest to you, Miss Bentley, that the only subject that you discussed with the FBI during August, September, and until certainly the middle of October, related to Lieutenant Heller and had nothing to do with your own Communist activities.

. . .

Q. Did you tell them anything about your own activities as a spy before the 8th of October of 1945?

A. I am sorry, I can't remember dates, Mr. Chanler.

Q. The 8th of October I think was the date when Mr. Budenz announced publicly that he had renounced communism.

A. It seems to me that I had already made up my mind in talking to them before that came out, but again I wouldn't swear to that, Mr. Chanler.

Q. Isn't it a fact that when you read in the paper that Mr. Budenz, who knew all about your activities, had renounced communism you then decided you had better tell your story?

A. Mr. Budenz knew absolutely nothing about my activities except the small part he was mixed up in, and there was nothing in Mr. Budenz's relationship with me, in the material he was giving me, that would in any way have endangered us. Moreover, I had already dropped Mr. Budenz on orders of the Gay Pay U in June, I believe, of 1944 as a contact because they said that his sympathies were changing.

The next day Mr. Saypol produced the letter, and at his request the following colloquy took place at the bench, out of the hearing of the jury:

MR. SAYPOL   In accordance with your Honor's direction last night, I have a letter from the files of the Federal Bureau of Investigation pertaining to the matter Mr. Chanler has talked about. As a general proposition, I consider that it is hearsay, a letter written to the witness, not written by her, and thereby not binding upon her.

I submit further that it is a matter from within the files of the prosecution in relation to the investigation of the charge, which because of its character is not available to my adversary. I suggest, if the Court nevertheless requires its production, that the Court first examine it before making it available.

In conjunction with it, if that should be the Court's disposition, I have the preceding communication on the basis of which this letter was sent, which contains matters that are directly material, assuming that this is. I should want parts of that, although not all of it, made available and made part of the record in conjunction with the letter which counsel for the defendant has sought.

It would unduly prejudice the prosecution, aside from the privileged character of the communication and its status as a secondarily or tertiarily removed document from the witness, to allow only that part to be used without the related matters in the preceding communication from the New Haven office of the Federal Bureau of Investigation. It should be quite obvious, as a matter of fairness in the pursuit of matters relating to espionage, that ordinarily documents which may fall into the hands of others are not admissible, certainly not a letter requesting a witness to call at an office.

MR. CHANLER   Your Honor understands our position. We are attempting to show that this witness was not being entirely frank when she says she went and told the FBI solely on account of her conscience. She went to find out about this matter when [man whom] she met at the St. George Hotel. Our information is that for quite a number of weeks, if not more, that was the only subject which she and the

FBI discussed, and that she did not begin telling her story about the espionage ring until sometime probably in November. I think that is a material variance from her story that she has always told.

MR. SAYPOL   Would you be satisfied if we submitted the material to the Court and rested on the Court's ruling?

MR. CHANLER   Certainly it is up to the Court.

MR. SAYPOL   I direct your Honor's attention to the reference (*handing to the Court*).

THE COURT   What is this, the early one (*indicating*)?

MR. SAYPOL   This followed on it.

MR. CHANLER   That is the only one we have asked for, the one that went to the witness.

THE COURT   Well, I think I will let them see this letter; that is, the second one you have handed me dated *October 8, 1945,* from Mr. Conroy to the witness Bentley.

MR. SAYPOL   May I interrupt. Will your Honor allow me to then refer to the preceding communication even in the face of objection by the defense?

THE COURT   Well, that would depend entirely on what she answered in response to the questions concerning this letter of October 8, 1945, I should judge.

. . .

THE COURT   I think the immediate question is whether or not this letter should be made available, and I will rule that it should be; that is, this letter of October 8, 1945, and see what you want to do on cross-examination with the other.

Then Mr. Chanler resumed his questioning of Miss Bentley. At the outset, the following exchange occurred:

Q. Miss Bentley, you said yesterday that you remembered that sometime after your visit to New Haven you received a letter from the FBI asking you to call at their office and I think you said you only received one letter, didn't you, yesterday?

A. To the best of my recollection, yes.

Q. I ask you if this refreshes your recollection as to the letter that you received (*handing*).

A. It could be; it could not be. I am sorry, it is so long since I had the letter I don't recall.

Q. You did receive a letter?

A. I received a letter asking me to call their office. That is the only thing I recall about it.

Q. And then you did call at their office as requested?

A. I did ring up the office and I did make the appointment.

The rest of the cross-examination on this point took Miss Bentley over substantially the same ground she had been over before the FBI letter was produced. Mr. Chanler tried to show that she had gone to the FBI in New Haven in August only because she was worried about her contacts with Peter Heller, and that she did not start describing her role in the Communist underground until after Louis Budenz's defection from communism was publicly announced, the obvious implication being that she went to the FBI not, as she had said, from motives of patriotism and conscience, but simply to save her own skin. Mr. Chanler's effort thus to impeach Miss Bentley can only be regarded as inconclusive. She continued to maintain that she had talked about her Communist involvement from the start, and Mr. Chanler was unable to refute her version.

It is ironical, though, that the testimony evoked by this cross-examination, which probably did not justify the amount of courtroom time that was devoted to it, tends, when combined with bits and pieces drawn from elsewhere, to raise an interesting and important unsolved problem about Miss Bentley's story. As we have seen, it seems difficult to reconcile the asserted timing of Miss Bentley's receipt of the $2,000 from Anatoli Gromov on October 17, 1945, with her assertion that she was at that very time in contact with the FBI and acting under their instructions. It is the evidence unwittingly drawn from her lips by Mr. Chanler in 1951—that she started talking to the FBI in New York about her underground activities some two or three weeks after October 8, 1945—that appears to warrant some further inquiry into this aspect of her story, particularly when combined with Attorney General Brownell's revelations in 1953 about the apparent timing of Miss Bentley's conversations with the FBI.

The truth of this matter cannot be determined from the public record. The solution of this and other riddles lies in the files of the FBI and also, perhaps, in the many secret transcripts of testimony by Miss Bentley and others. The chances are that these riddles will remain unsolved.

V

We next inquire to what extent Miss Bentley's story has been corroborated by the testimony of others and to what extent it still rests on her own uncorroborated assertions. In this inquiry, we shall be concerned also with contradictions of her account and with gaps in her story that might possibly be filled by available but hitherto unelicited testimony.

The most detailed and circumstantial corroboration of any aspect of Miss Bentley's story comes from the testimony of Ann Remington, as given at Remington's first trial for perjury. That testimony substantiates Miss Bentley's in every material respect. In addition, it supplies background information on the circumstances of Remington's initial affiliation with the Communist movement which was not available to Miss Bentley but which tends to strengthen the probability that Remington's contact with her was maintained with full knowledge of her position as a Communist courier. Mrs. Remington confirmed Miss Bentley's account of her initial meeting with the Remingtons and her conclusion that Remington understood her role and the destination of the material that he was to transmit to her. Mrs. Remington's testimony also established the receipt of Communist literature from Miss Bentley and the payment of money to her, although she proved to be somewhat vague in her conception of Communist Party dues. If believed and taken as a whole, Mrs. Remington's testimony adds materially to Miss Bentley's credibility. If we had similar corroboration for the larger and more important aspects of Miss Bentley's story, we could assert with confidence that the facts are what she has represented them to be.

Miss Bentley's accusations against Harry Dexter White call urgently for corroboration. White was perhaps the most distinguished civil servant implicated in espionage activities. He shared with Lord Keynes the distinction of being the chief architect of the International Monetary Fund, on which he eventually served as the representative of the United States. He rose through the ranks in the Treasury Department to become Assistant Secretary of the Treasury. Surely accusations against such a man ought not to be accepted lightly, particularly accusations that are essentially hearsay. It will be recalled that Miss Bentley claimed no personal contact with White. He was said to be a member of the Silvermaster ring who gave information through that apparatus and whom Miss Bentley never met. Is there, then, any corroboration for Miss Bentley's charge?

We find corroboration in the testimony of Whittaker Chambers, who stated that White, while perhaps not a member of the

Communist Party, was a willing collaborator during the years when Chambers served as a Communist courier in Washington. Specifically, White was in frequent conspiratorial contact with Chambers, gave him much information about policy matters affecting the Treasury, and received one of the famous rugs which Chambers's superior in the espionage apparatus directed him to give to four of his contacts as a gift from the grateful Soviet people. (Miss Bentley has stated that the Silvermasters once noticed the rug on visiting White. It would be interesting to know whether she told that to the FBI before Chambers's story was made public.) Chambers also produced some physical evidence of his contact with White: four sheets of foolscap covered with notes in White's handwriting, which Chambers asserts was the form in which he received material from White for transmission to Russia. How these sheets came into Chambers's possession and what their significance is are matters on which we have only the word of Whittaker Chambers. But it cannot be denied that their existence in his possession requires some explanation. That explanation cannot, of course, come from White. He died of a heart attack two weeks after his appearance before the House Un-American Activities Committee in the summer of 1948.

Further corroboration of White's alleged complicity comes from the fact that Chambers mentioned him as a source of information in interviews with the FBI in 1942 and with a State Department security officer in 1945, all before Miss Bentley went to the FBI with her story. That sequence of events appears to rule out the possibility that Chambers fabricated his account after learning of Miss Bentley's. It does not rule out the possibility that Miss Bentley fabricated her account after learning of Chambers's. But in order seriously to entertain that possibility, we would have to assume that she was led by the FBI to name White, on the strength of their existing suspicions about him. That could not be believable unless the FBI is to be accused of incredibly sloppy investigative techniques, or worse. It seems most reasonable to assume that what probably happened was what appears to have happened, namely, that Miss Bentley and Chambers, independently and without knowledge of each other's stories, accused Harry Dexter White of complicity in espionage activity at two different times. And that is corroboration of a kind that cannot lightly be dismissed.

Chambers also serves as an important corroborative source for Miss Bentley's identification of certain members of the so-called Perlo ring. Miss Bentley named Victor Perlo and Charles Kramer, and stated that she was first introduced to them at a meeting arranged in John Abt's apartment on Central Park West in New York. Chambers named Perlo, Kramer, and Abt as members of the so-called Ware group, with whom he was in conspiratorial contact in 1934. That testimony was further corroborated by Nathaniel Weyl, who testified that he also was a member of the group for some time.

Louis Budenz has corroborated Miss Bentley's account of the position of Jacob Golos in the Communist hierarchy and her assertion that Golos was engaged in directing espionage activities. He also had some peripheral contact with Miss Bentley herself, although he was not in a position to corroborate her account of the activities in which she engaged.

Finally, Miss Bentley's testimony has been to some extent corroborated by the testimony of persons whom she accused of being part of her circle of informants. In addition to Remington's account, we have the testimony of Bernard Redmont, Robert Miller, and Duncan Lee that they knew Miss Bentley, although all have claimed that the relationship was an innocent one.

Redmont was introduced to Miss Bentley by the Remingtons. He testified that he knew Miss Bentley as a researcher who was interested in Latin American problems. He was at that time working for the Office of the Coordinator of Inter-American Affairs. It appears to be common ground that Redmont did not give Miss Bentley any restricted information; but there is a dispute over whether he knew her as a Communist. He denied that he knew her as a Communist; Miss Bentley asserted that he did; and her account is corroborated by Mrs. Remington, who testified that she and her husband put the Redmonts in touch with Miss Bentley only after ascertaining that they were Communists and that they were eager to help in the effort to secure information that would be helpful to Russia.

Robert Miller, who, like Redmont, was a newspaperman working for the CIAA, presented a story that has striking parallels to Redmont's and Remington's. He first met Miss Bentley through Golos, whom he knew, not as a Communist, but as a man who shared his interest in Latin America. (Golos, apparently, was a man of many faces.) Golos introduced Miss Bentley to Miller under the name of Helen Johns and she thereafter called on him a number of times in Washington. Like Remington, Miller testified that he thought she was a researcher. Like Remington, he gave her information that he came across in his professional activities. Like Remington, he met her, by request, at places other than his office. Like Remington, he finally tired of the association and stopped seeing her, although he adds the fillip that she was under nervous tension and appeared to be drinking too much. Miller's wife, he said, had been with him on some of the occasions when he saw Miss Bentley. His wife was not called to testify. The only real difference between Miller's story and Remington's is that no testimony has been adduced to corroborate or contradict the accounts given by the two protagonists. And, once again, the difference between the stories told by accuser and accused is narrow but crucial: whether or not the accused knew what the accuser was up to.

Duncan Lee's story is much the same. He and his wife first met Elizabeth Bentley, this time as Helen Grant, at the apartment of Mary Price in Washington. (It will be recalled that Mary Price was identified by Miss Bentley as one of her important espionage contacts.) They were attracted to her and she to them. She subsequently called on them at their apartment and a warm friendship developed. They met Golos, this time as a refugee writer, in her company. Lee denied ever giving Miss Bentley any information of any kind. This of course is a variance from the accounts given by Redmont, Remington, and Miller, all of whom testified that they furnished Miss Bentley with some information but denied that it was secret. Lee's story is also different in that he described the relationship as a purely social one, which the others did not. Assuming for the moment that Miss Bentley's account is the true version of their relationship, it is easy to see the reason for these departures in pattern. Lee was an employee of the Office of Strategic Services. Unlike the others, he had no nonsecret information to furnish. If he were fabricating a story that admitted the fact of acquaintance with Miss Bentley but denied its import, he could not have said, as did the others, that he knew her as a researcher to whom he gave only such information as she was entitled to have. Lee stated that he did not know that Miss Bentley was a Communist, nor did he know that Mary Price was one. His wife did not testify. Neither did Mary Price.

At the very least, the testimony of Redmont, Remington, Miller, and Lee serves to establish that Miss Bentley was indeed busily engaged in making and sustaining contacts with government officials in wartime Washington. It also establishes that she used different aliases with different people and that she had a propensity for clandestine meetings. All of this is perfectly consistent with, and goes a long way toward confirming Miss Bentley's own account of what she was doing. She plainly thought that she was in the espionage business. But the crucial question is what they thought. And this is placed squarely in issue by the testimony of those who admitted knowing Miss Bentley.

If the corroborative testimony of witnesses is inconclusive, what other evidence is there? We enter here the realm of guilt by association. In the absence of direct evidence, we can only inquire into a suspect's record of affiliation with Communist organizations and activities, of attitudes and beliefs that favor the Communist cause. To be sure, evidence of Communist affiliation or of views favorable to communism is not evidence of espionage, but this can be acknowledged without conceding that evidence of affiliation has no probative value at all. The problem is one of assessing probabilities. If X is a member of the Communist Party, he is more likely to be willing to commit espionage for the benefit of the Soviet Union than he would be if he were not a member of the Party. Thus stated, the proposition is a truism, but it is a truism that cannot be ignored. Absent other evidence, a charge of espionage activity carries more weight if coupled with evidence of Communist affiliation than it would if there were no such evidence.

The phrase "guilt by association" has rightly acquired an invidious connotation. But we must be clear on what we mean by it, or it will stultify thought. Properly delimited, the content of the phrase incorporates two important general principles of our legal and ethical system. One is that social control through legal sanctions ought to be directed not against thoughts, but against acts. The other principle, corollary to the first, is that democratic pluralism requires the broadest possible latitude for people to enter voluntarily into associations with others; it implies that im-

portant values are menaced by any attempt to control associations
or to inflict sanctions because of them. When we declare against
"guilt by association," all we properly mean is that before we use
the fact of association as a predicate for inflicting sanctions, formal
or informal, there must clearly be a rational connection between
the particular association under scrutiny and the likelihood that
antisocial acts will be generated by the association.

We would not convict a man of bank robbery merely on evidence that he consorted with bank robbers. Much less would we
convict him of bank robbery merely on evidence that he consorted
with undesirable characters. But if such evidence were ancillary
to evidence identifying him as one of the bank robbers, we would
tend to be somewhat swayed by it. And our consciences would
not be much troubled by an accusation that we were indulging in
"guilt by association." So, here, the question is not whether it is
proper to take into account evidence of Communist activity in
evaluating a charge like Miss Bentley's. Rather the question is
how much weight to ascribe to such evidence.

There seems to be little doubt that at least some of the persons
accused by Miss Bentley have been engaged in Communist activity. In some cases, this conclusion results from testimony about
their activities. Silvermaster, for example, is said to have been
active in Communist activities ever since 1920. A further difficulty arises here because of our inability to evaluate the evidence
supporting this conclusion. The conclusion is embodied in government investigative reports stemming from sources other than
Miss Bentley. As early as 1942, the Civil Service Commission had
compiled a dossier on Silvermaster which led those who had access
to it to conclude that he was, and had been for many years, an
important Communist functionary in the United States. That is
merely conclusory, of course, so far as the public record is concerned. But in the absence of denial or explanation (a point we
will shortly consider), the suggestion that Silvermaster was a Communist adds some credence to the Bentley charge. Similar evidence exists about many but not all of the others accused by Miss
Bentley. Unfortunately, this evidence is rarely assessable. It usually consists of excerpts from investigative reports of various intelligence agencies read into the record of Congressional hearings.
The evidence underlying the conclusions stated in these reports is
not produced; the witnesses who gave the evidence are identified

only as "informants." In a sense, this takes us back to where we were with Miss Bentley's evidence. We at least know who she is, but what would we make of her story if it were put before us, for example, in the form of the FBI's first report to the White House, on November 8, 1945, about the existence of the Silvermaster ring?

This brings us to the difficult and delicate subject of what weight we can ascribe, in this evaluation of the public record, to information whose evidentiary basis is contained in dossiers to which the public has no access. What we have are conclusions, broadly and blandly stated in a way that entitles us to give no more weight to them than we are willing to give to the judgment or good faith of those who state them. The classic instance is J. Edgar Hoover's assertion that such of Miss Bentley's testimony as is susceptible of being checked has been found to be accurate. That raises two questions: How much of her testimony has been checked? What is the corroborative evidence? It is helpful to know that Mr. Hoover is satisfied. It is even helpful to know that Mr. Hoover's satisfaction has satisfied others. But all that is no substitute for having the evidence made public, so that it can be scrutinized and assigned its due weight by any one sufficiently interested to want to appraise it.

There remains another body of corroborative evidence whose probative value must be assessed. That is the continued refusal of many of those accused by Miss Bentley to testify in response to her charges. To put the matter another way, the question is what weight ought to be assigned to invocation of the Fifth Amendment. Those who have consistently invoked the Fifth Amendment before Congressional committees in response to Miss Bentley's charges include Silvermaster, Ullmann, Perlo, Glasser, Magdoff, Fitzgerald, Joseph, Halperin, Kramer, Abt, Silverman, Rosenberg, and Wheeler.

For some, the question presents no difficulty. Invocation of the Fifth Amendment means that a truthful answer would incriminate. Or, put more summarily, invocation equals guilt. That attitude is consistently reflected in the reports and hearings of Congressional committees that have given attention to the subject. One may go so far as to say that it is the "official" atitude. Consider, for example, the remarks of Attorney General Brownell, in pointing out the accuracy of the information contained in the FBI's report to the White House dated November 27, 1945:

It is interesting to note how accurate this information was that the FBI supplied at that time. Following is a list of White's close associates referred to in the FBI reports who were members of the espionage ring who have claimed their privilege not to answer questions on the grounds that it would incriminate them: Silvermaster, Perlo, Glasser, Coe, Ullmann, Silverman, Halperin, and Kaplan.

How offhand this is! There is not the slightest suggestion that there are any additional links in the logical chain between invocation and guilt. If these men invoked the Fifth Amendent in response to questions about espionage, it follows ineluctably, so says Mr. Brownell, that they must have been involved in espionage. But does it? In order for us to conclude that it does, or even that it probably does, we would have to be satisfied, first, that the protection of the Fifth Amendment can be invoked only when a truthful answer to a particular question would tend to show that the witness had committed a crime, and second, that the protection of the Amendment is invoked properly more often than it is invoked improperly. The first of these propositions is plainly false; the second is probably also false.

The error of the first proposition lies in its disregard of the highly complex and unsettled question of waiver. It has often been held that the protection afforded by the Fifth Amendment's privilege against self-incrimination may be waived. One way it may be waived is for the witness to answer certain questions that bear some relation to other, further questions with respect to which he may wish to invoke the privilege. Great uncertainty attends the determination of the circumstances under which an answer to question A will be held a waiver of the privilege with respect to question B, many lawyers familiar with the problem take the position that it is utterly unsafe to predict what will or will not be held to constitute a waiver. Consequently, they advise their clients to claim the privilege whenever they are in doubt. A concrete example may make the application of this principle clear. Imagine a witness who has been at some time in the past a member of the Communist Party. Rightly or wrongly, he believes that the circumstances of his membership were such as to expose him to possible criminal liability. He is asked whether he has ever committed espionage. Or, perhaps, he is merely asked whether he knew Elizabeth Bentley. The truthful answer is that he has not committed espionage or that he does not know Elizabeth Bentley. However, the witness fears that if he answers the question he will be compelled to answer other questions, including the question of Party membership; and he believes that a truthful answer to this question will incriminate him. So he declines to answer the question about espionage on the ground of possible self-incrimination. There is little doubt that this constitutes a proper invocation of the Fifth Amendment as a means of avoiding waiver of its protection.

Our witness in the example just given may be guilty of something, even though a truthful response to the question he has declined to answer will not incriminate him. Is it possible for a witness to decline to answer even though he will not be incriminated by any truthful answer he might give? That issue has been extensively debated, but usually in terms of whether the privilege may properly be invoked under such circumstances. That question need not detain us. The fact is that the Fifth Amendment has often been invoked under circumstances which make it very doubtful that the invocation is a proper one. The motive may often be nothing more than the desire to be let alone. Or it may be the desire to avoid a perjury prosecution based on a conflict between what the witness believes to be a truthful answer and contradictory statements made by someone like Miss Bentley. Invocation of the Fifth Amendment is likely to represent, among other things, a way of asserting that the questions asked are none of the questioner's business, without exposing the witness to the normal consequences of that assertion. In short, a witness who invokes the Fifth Amendment may be guilty of contempt of Congress (because of the improper invocation) rather than of whatever substantive offense he is being questioned about.

This kind of reaction on the part of witnesses tends to be encouraged by the attitude of their interrogators. Time and time again in Congressional hearings relating to the issue of communism, the object of the questioning seems to be to get witnesses to invoke the Fifth Amendment in response to as many questions as possible. These invocations then become the basis for the claim that the witness is guilty of all the things he has refused to talk about. Of course, he may well be guilty. But once it is recognized that the privilege may be invoked improperly, the inference that the witness would be incriminated by a truthful answer to the question becomes very weak indeed.

It would be interesting to compare the testimony of, say, five witnesses accused by Miss Bentley who testified under the compulsion of the Immunity Act, with the inferences drawn from their previous invocation of the Fifth Amendment. We do not have the material for performing this exercise, because the Immunity Act has been used only to compel testimony before grand juries, whose proceedings take place in secret. If such a comparison were possible, however, we would probably be led to conclude either that the witnesses had invoked the Fifth Amendment improperly in their earlier appearances or that their testimony before the grand jury was perjured.

I am led, therefore, to conclude that little or no corroboration is afforded Miss Bentley's story by the fact that some of those whom she has accused of complicity in espionage activities have invoked the Fifth Amendment in response to questioning before Congressional committees. It may be noted that one such witness, Frank Coe, after having previously refused to answer questions about espionage, has subsequently testified before a Congressional committee that he did not engage in espionage activities; and that another witness, William L. Ullmann, after long invoking the Fifth Amendment, has categorically denied to a grand jury that he participated in the activities of which he was accused by Miss Bentley. Obviously, we cannot conclude that these witnesses are telling the truth. They may now be committing perjury. But it should be clear that their about-face adds strength to the conclusion that we ought to be wary of relying on the invocation of the Fifth Amendment as proof of the truth of Miss Bentley's testimony.

Finally, there is the general endorsement of Miss Bentley's testimony by the Director of the FBI. This statement has been referred to before, but the authoritative character of its source requires that we consider it further before drawing any general conclusions about the extent to which Miss Bentley's story has been corroborated. According to Mr. Hoover, "All information furnished by Miss Bentley, which was susceptible to check, has proven to be correct. She had been subjected to the most searching of cross-examinations; her testimony has been evaluated by juries and reviewed by the courts and has been found to be accurate."

There are two separate thoughts involved in these two senten-
ces. The first is that the FBI is satisfied on the basis of its investigations that Miss Bentley's story is true. The second is that courts and
juries have found her testimony to be accurate. We are in a better
position to evaluate the second than the first, but we ought to look
at both.

I have already analyzed the ambiguities in Miss Bentley's
account of how she went to the FBI in 1945 and how her collaboration with the FBI dovetailed with her final contacts with Soviet
espionage agents. Mr. Hoover's statement suggests that there are
adequate answers to the questions I have raised. This is a matter
which was clearly "susceptible to check." It would be interesting
to know the data on which his conclusion rests. Beyond that, it
would be interesting to know whether there was any FBI surveillance of Golos, Miss Bentley, and their contacts in the Government
during the period of her operations. Miss Bentley has stated that
she is sure there was. The fact of such surveillance and the conclusions drawn from it would make an important addition to the
public record.

Mr. Hoover's second statement—that Miss Bentley's story "has
been found to be accurate" by courts and juries—is an overstatement. The main outlines of her story have never been put in
issue in a court trial. We have already seen how little the verdicts
in the Remington case contribute to an evaluation of the Bentley
story, and how inadequate a cross-examination was possible at that
time. Miss Bentley has appeared as a witness in only two other
trials. One of these, the trial of Abraham Brothman for attempting
to obstruct the administration of justice, did not even involve the
truth or falsity of Miss Bentley's substantive allegations against
Brothman, but concerned only the question of whether he attempted to cover his tracks by inducing a co-conspirator to tell a
grand jury an agreed-upon story. Even taking the verdict in the
Brothman case for more than it necessarily stands for, it does no
more than show that Miss Bentley did receive documents from
Brothman, an engineer with a private firm in New York. It has
even less to do with the main outlines of Miss Bentley's espionage
story than does the Remington case. Miss Bentley's other courtroom appearance was in the Rosenberg case, where her role was
even more marginal. She testified that she had received several

telephone calls from one "Julius." She did not even know Julius.
The testimony was admissible only as corroboration for the testimony of two of the Rosenbergs' co-conspirators that Julius Rosenberg had mentioned to them that Miss Bentley probably knew him.
In both the Brothman case and the Rosenberg case, Miss Bentley
was allowed to testify at some length about her general experiences
in the Communist underground and the extent to which the work
she was doing was subject to Soviet control. In neither case was
she cross-examined at any length about these matters.

In summary, the suggestion that Miss Bentley's story has been
reviewed and found accurate by operation of the judicial process
is unwarranted. The fact is that she has never been involved in a
confrontation comparable to that between Chambers and Hiss. The
very limited issues of fact that can be taken as settled by her court
appearances constitute no more than a makeweight in the assessment of the extent to which her story has been corroborated and
accepted.

We turn now to a consideration of the extent to which Miss
Bentley's story has been contradicted. Direct, external contradiction has come only from interested witnesses: those whom she has
accused who have been willing to risk the possibility of perjury
indictments by denying the truth of her testimony under oath.
These have included both alleged members of the Silvermaster
ring—Currie, Coe, the Golds, Harry Dexter White, and William H.
Taylor—and alleged independent contacts—Remington, Duncan
Lee, Robert Miller, Bernard Redmont. It is noteworthy that all
those in this second group have admitted personal acquaintance
with Miss Bentley, while no one in the first group is accused of having known her personally.

With the exception of Remington's, none of these denials has
been subjected to judicial scrutiny. We have already noted the in-
conclusiveness of the verdict in that case. It is equally true, of
course, that Miss Bentley's story cannot be regarded as having been
shaken by any of these other denials, untested as they are. Nor can
we conclude, as some have urged, that the Government's failure to
bring perjury indictments against any of the others who have
denied involvement with Miss Bentley is evidence of the weakness
of her charges. That contention evaporates entirely when the peculiar requirements of proof in perjury cases are considered. The

federal courts follow the so-called "two witness" rule, according to which a case of perjury is legally insufficient unless the perjury is proved by the direct testimony of two witnesses or by the direct testimony of one witness plus corroborating circumstances. In the Remington case, there were two witnesses—Miss Bentley and Mrs. Remington. In the Hiss case, there was one witness—Chambers—plus corroborating circumstances—the documents typed on the Hiss typewriter. The obvious reason why no perjury indictments have been returned against Lee, Miller, and Redmont is the unavailability of corroboration. Lack of corroboration is far from being the same thing as contradiction, and it is contradiction that we are now trying to assess. The failure of the Government to indict these men for perjury is no more a contradiction of Miss Bentley's story than the failure of the accused to sue for libel is a corroboration.

One case requires separate comment. It is the case of William H. Taylor. Taylor, a Treasury Department monetary expert, was one of those named as a member of the Silvermaster ring by Miss Bentley in her first appearance before the House Un-American Activities Committee. Her reference to him by his first name suggested that she knew him. It was not until over five years later that she was asked the direct question whether she did know Taylor, and her answer at that time was that she did not. Taylor consistently denied that he had ever been a Communist or participated in espionage. He was subjected to a round of inquisitions by grand juries and Congressional committees. And, as the last surviving member in public service of the alleged Silvermaster ring, he was subjected to an all-out effort to force him out of office. Fortunately for him, he was an employee of an international organization, the International Monetary Fund, which was somewhat hardier than domestic agencies about withstanding attacks on the loyalty of its employees during the early 1950's. Taylor's case was finally adjudicated by an agency set up to handle loyalty problems of American citizens working for international agencies, the International Organizations Employees Loyalty Board.

Ably represented by counsel, Taylor did what no other person accused by Miss Bentley has done. He did not content himself with attempting to show that she was mistaken about his identification with the Silvermaster ring. He went further and launched an all-out attack on her general credibility, in a remarkable brief filed with the Board in March 1955. The Board's initial decision was adverse. But Taylor sought and secured a rehearing, which resulted in his clearance by the Board in December 1955. If we could be sure that the Board's decision was based on its acceptance of Taylor's effort to impeach Miss Bentley's credibility, we would have a clear-cut instance of an official determination adverse to her position. And this would constitute a kind of contradiction of her story that would far outweigh the very limited and qualified endorsement of it which might be thought to result from the outcome of the Remington case.

Unfortunately, the situation is not that clear-cut. Not only is there no indication that the Board believed Miss Bentley to be a liar, but the evidence is that it probably did not. The Board had before it all the material relating to Miss Bentley's credibility that Taylor could produce when it decided, in July 1955, that there was a reasonable doubt as to his loyalty. The rehearing was based on a very convincing demonstration by Taylor's counsel that certain evidence against Taylor had been manufactured. This evidence was a purported letter to Taylor from William Ludwig Ullmann, the Silvermasters' friend and house guest, which tended to suggest that Taylor was appointed to his position at the Treasury as the result of a White-Ullmann plot to get a fellow conspirator into a strategic position, this as against Taylor's assertion that he had no previous acquaintance with White or Ullmann. It would take us far afield from our consideration of Miss Bentley's story to recount in detail the development of this incident. For present purposes it is enough to relate the denouement. Taylor adduced persuasive evidence that he had never received such a letter and that the letter was, in fact, a fabrication. His clearance followed. It must be attributed in major part to the Board's conviction that it was dealing with a case of manufactured evidence. It is no wonder that under these circumstances it reversed its initial determination. To say this much is not to say that Taylor was either innocent or guilty of the charges against him. If we take the Board's determination as a general verdict, Taylor's position was vindicated. But the circumstances were such that we cannot say with any degree of assurance that his vindication constitutes a repudiation of Miss Bentley's position. Much more will have to be known before we can either affirm or deny that Miss Bentley was a truthful witness.

Some of the internal inconsistencies in Miss Bentley's story have already been cited. Chief among them, I think, both in significance and possibility of eventual clarification, is the question of her activities during August–November 1945. Other inconsistencies appear to result mainly from her tendency to add details in order to add an air of verisimilitude to her story. These instances do not bulk large in the total context of her story. They do not suggest that she is lying. All they do, along with everything else that we have discussed, is point toward a need for more information than we now possess.

We may conclude this attempt to strike a kind of trial balance by considering the gaps, remediable and irremediable, that the present record reveals. The chief irremediable gap is the total absence of any of the fruits of Miss Bentley's years in the espionage business. Unlike Whittaker Chambers, she failed to take out insurance by reserving a few choice morsels for later use. This is particularly unfortunate because she has been consistently vague about the precise nature of the material that was transmitted through her. A chance to obtain some real evidence of her espionage activities apparently did present itself after she went to the FBI, when she met several of her old contacts while under surveillance. However, she did not avail herself of the opportunity, and the record therefore remains barren on this issue.

The remediable gap is the potential testimony of a number of persons accused of complicity in her operations who have never been called on to testify. Some of the gaps are really surprising. Mary Price, who is one of the most important figures in the Bentley story, has apparently never been called on for public testimony. Miss Price is charged with having ransacked Walter Lippmann's files while she was his secretary in order to produce information for Miss Bentley. She was also accused of having brought Miss Bentley into contact with Duncan Lee for the express purpose of recruiting Lee into espionage work. Her Washington apartment served as a base of operations for Miss Bentley, and the apartment that she shared with her sister Mildred in New York was used as a meeting place for Miss Bentley and members of the Perlo group.

When Miss Bentley's accusations were made in public, in July 1948, Miss Price was chairman of the North Carolina Progressive

Party, and its nominee for Governor. She was quoted in the press as admitting that she had known Miss Bentley, but denounced the accusations as "fantastic." It is curious that a potential witness who was apparently willing to admit knowing Miss Bentley was not called upon to testify, but Miss Price was never brought before any of the Congressional committees that investigated aspects of Miss Bentley's story. After the passage of the Immunity Act she was summoned before a grand jury, but the substance of her testimony has never been made public.

It is likewise surprising that Mrs. Helen Silvermaster was never called to testify, although there are intimations that she, like her husband, invoked the Fifth Amendment in executive session before the beginning of the public hearings at which Miss Bentley's charges were aired. The circumstantial detail in which Miss Bentley testified about the Silvermaster household makes it reasonably clear that there was some contact. Perhaps further questioning would shed some light on what the nature of the contact was.

Ullmann testified, apparently freely, before a grand jury in 1956. He is another person with whom Miss Bentley has claimed to have had personal contact. For some reason, no Congressional committee has been sufficiently interested in pursuing the problem to obtain the substance of Ullmann's testimony so that it might be spread on the public record.

It is also surprising that Earl Browder has not been summoned to testify about Miss Bentley's efforts to link him to espionage activities. Browder did testify during the Tydings Committee hearings in 1950 that he had known Miss Bentley as a secretarial worker at Communist Party headquarters, but he was not pressed about her detailed account of how information that she had acquired for transmission to Russia was shown to him whenever it was of possible interest to the American Communist Party.

Another remediable gap that is decisive in its importance is the information locked in the files of the FBI. We have already referred to Miss Bentley's closing contact with Soviet espionage agents. It would be invaluable in assessing her story to have available all written records of her conversations with members of the FBI. One has the feeling in reviewing the testimony she has given in public that her story was pretty well planned before she ever reached the witness stand. What did she first tell the FBI agents who interviewed her? What questions did they ask her? How did they go about testing her memory, perception, and sincerity? Did they catch her in any slips that she was later able to repair? Were names ever suggested to her, or did she bring them all forward spontaneously? A complete and accurate account of the Bentley story would have to get the answers to questions such as these. I stated that this gap is remediable. It is, but only in the sense that the evidence is in being. High reasons of investigative policy, Mr. Hoover has said again and again, preclude any sweeping inspection of the FBI files. That policy appears to have strength and solidity approximating a constitutional provision. It took a national crisis occasioned by Senator McCarthy's charge that the Department of State was harboring subversives to cause President Truman to permit four Senators to inspect material in the FBI files on persons accused by the Senator. And even then, it was not the raw files themselves, but only summaries of them, that the Senators were allowed to inspect. It is hardly likely that, lacking some such immediate and overwhelming compulsion, even so limited a degree of access would be afforded. It is even less likely that the Executive Branch would go further and permit the raw data in the FBI files to be released to any person or group, even to a committee of the Congress. Nevertheless, there may be compelling reasons why on certain occasions and under strict safeguards such a step ought to be taken. If it ever were, the circumstances surrounding the exposition and development of Miss Bentley's story would be a highly appropriate study.

Finally, there is a body of information that could perhaps be released without danger of revealing official secrets. Miss Bentley has said time and time again that she is certain she was under FBI surveillance, not just in 1945, when she had already gone to the Bureau with her story and was engaged in breaking off her conspiratorial relationships, but much earlier, when she was actively carrying on her espionage activities. A detailed enumeration of the occasions on which she did come under surveillance, the persons with whom she was in contact on those occasions, and the circumstances of the contacts might lend important corroborative weight to her story.

If any or all of these gaps could be filled, a much more substantial record than is now available could be constructed. If such action is thought desirable with respect to the story of Whittaker Chambers, who enjoyed the silent corroboration of the documents he saved from his days of espionage, how much more desirable it is that a similar process be undertaken with respect to the important, tantalizing, still unresolved account rendered by Elizabeth Bentley.

4 · BUDENZ

Louis Francis Budenz was born in Indianapolis on July 17, 1891. Born and raised a Catholic, he was educated in parochial schools, and received his law training at Indianapolis Law School. He was admitted to the Indiana Bar about 1913, but practiced law only briefly, engaging in "some activities against loan sharks" in Indianapolis. He then devoted all his energies to the labor movement, and continued to do so until, at the age of 44, he joined the Communist Party.

In the latter part of 1913 he became affiliated with *The Carpenter*, the official organ of the Carpenters' Union, United Brotherhood of Carpenters and Joiners. From the early 1920's until approximately 1933, he edited *Labor Age*, a radical socialist magazine that eventually became pro-Communist in tone. During this time, he also engaged in labor organizing and publicity. He was arrested 21 times on picket lines, but was always acquitted. In 1932 *Labor Age* and the Brookwood Labor College, which had been condemned by the AFL, joined forces to form the Conference for Progressive Labor Action, a socialist group bent on organizing the unemployed. The Conference worked with the Communists, although it was not directly connected with the Party. Soon after the organization was formed, Budenz became its Secretary. The Conference was succeeded by the American Workers' Party, also known as the Musteites after its founder, A. J. Muste; this party, in turn, joined the Trotskyites in the fall of 1934. Budenz opposed the merger and broke with the party. The reason he later gave was that the Trotskyites advocated the overthrow of the United States Government by force and violence, whereas in his view socialism could be attained in this country by constitutional amendment.

In August 1935, following a prolonged illness, Budenz joined the Communist Party. His decision was by no means a hasty or emotional one. He had read the works of Marx, Engels, Lenin, and Stalin, had read the *Daily Worker* fairly regularly, had worked in united front activities, and was acquainted with many Party leaders, among others Jack Stachel, Clarence Hathaway, and Alexander Trachtenberg. According to Budenz, Dimitrov's report to the Seventh World Congress of the Communist International was crucial to his decision to join the Party. This report espoused the People's Front policy, emphasized communism on a local level, and led Budenz to believe that the Communists would champion democracy. He has referred to himself when he first joined as a "People's Front Communist." However, he has stated that soon after he became a member, J. Peters, allegedly liaison officer between the Soviet secret police and the Communist International, told him of the "true" conspiratorial nature of the Communist Party.

From August until October, 1935, Budenz was a secret member of the Party. Then, with the approval of Stachel and Earl Browder, he became an open member; on October 2, 1935, a public statement of his affiliation with the Party was published in the *Daily Worker*. He remained an open member until he left the Party.

On the day of his public avowal of Party membership, Budenz became a staff member of the *Daily Worker*. This was to be his major endeavor during his years as a Communist. A few months later, Earl Browder appointed him labor editor of the newspaper. He continued in this position until November 1937, when Stachel informed him that the Politburo of the National Committee of the Party had decided that he should go to Chicago to head the *Midwest Daily Record*, a "Communist-controlled, organized, and financed newspaper . . . the Communist gift to the people's front." Budenz organized the staff, conducted fund-raising campaigns, and got the paper started in February 1938. He remained as editor until February 1940, when the *Record* ceased publication.

Returning to New York, he resumed work on the *Daily Worker*. He also became president of Freedom of the Press, Inc., a dummy corporation set up "in large measure" to get around the McCormick Act, which required foreign agents to register with the Secretary of State. In 1941 he was appointed managing editor of the *Daily Worker*, after serving in essentially that capacity (he claims) since his return to the newspaper. He continued as managing editor until he broke with the Party.

Apart from his work for the Communist press, Budenz was active in various Party endeavors. He was a member of the Illinois State Committee of the Communist Party while in Chicago, and of the New York State Committee. He participated in the work of both the New York State Trade Union Commission and the National Trade Union Commission in 1936 and 1937. These commissions were composed of Communist trade unionists who met and discussed Communist infiltration of trade unions. He was also a member of the National Committee, which governed the American Communist Party between conventions, from 1936 on, but not publicly after 1940 because of his position as president of Freedom of the Press, Inc. And although he was not actually a member of the Politburo, which really directed the Party, he did attend meetings irregularly, both in Chicago and in New York.

In addition to these activities, Budenz taught labor history at the Workers' School in New York and courses at a functionary school in Chicago.

Budenz's first and most important brush with espionage work came early in his Communist career, while he was still labor editor of the *Daily Worker*. Through Jacob Golos, then chairman of the Control Commission of the Communist Party, Budenz was put in touch with several Russians who were seeking information regarding Trotskyites and their movements, purportedly to thwart any possible Trotskyite plot against Stalin. They also sought introductions to Stalinists who were penetrating the Trotskyite circles or who would be useful in doing so. Budenz put Ruby Weil, among others, in contact with the Russians; and she in turn was instrumental in introducing Sylvia Ageloff to Frank Jacson, the eventual assassin of Leon Trotsky. Golos also attempted to have Budenz contact William Ullmann, who was then working with the OSS in Washington, but Budenz demurred because of his work on the *Daily Worker*.

On October 11, 1945, Budenz left the *Daily Worker* and the Communist Party; 48 hours later he was a professor at Notre Dame. In January of that year he had decided to return to the Catholic

Church, and in June to leave the Party; in October his decisions were carried out. His disillusionment with communism was based on the Soviet enslavement of people, the recognition that Catholicism and communism were irreconcilable, and his awarenes that all Communists were subservient to the Soviet dictatorship. He arrived gradually at his decision to leave the Party, since, as he explains, "Leaving the Communist Party is not a matter that you just decide to do . . . one day and do it the next. It is a struggle." His final leave-taking, however, was carefully thought out and executed. He had arranged for his job at Notre Dame two weeks prior to his defection, had asked for his *Daily Worker* check in advance for the week he resigned, and together with his family, was received back into the Church by Monsignor Fulton Sheen. The Party learned of Budenz's break from the radio and the press. They were so completely surprised that on the day the newspapers were reporting his break, his name was still carried on the masthead of the *Daily Worker*. Budenz chose this surreptitious method in order to forestall a smear campaign against him by his former comrades.

Arriving at Notre Dame, Budenz began his "year of silence"; he made no public appearance until he appeared on a radio broadcast in October 1946. He did, however, spend two weeks with the FBI, furnishing them with information, approximately four months after he arrived at the college. During the year he taught economics and journalism.

From October 1946 until recently, Budenz has testified on 33 separate occasions in Congressional hearings and court and administrative proceedings. His testimony has shed light on Communist penetration in almost every field and has included information bearing on the suitability of people to teach, to operate a radio station, or to remain in the Foreign Service. In addition to testifying, Budenz has written four books and numerous articles, has taught courses at Fordham University and Seton Hall College, and has lectured throughout the country on the subject of communism. In 1953, Budenz claimed he had received gross earnings of $70,000 from his activities as a former Communist.

On February 13, 1957, Budenz suffered a severe heart attack while lecturing in Newport, Rhode Island. Because of his heart condition, he has not been called upon by the Government to testify during recent years.

II

The confrontation of Louis Budenz and Owen Lattimore offers a unique opportunity to observe the processes by which a fragment of an ex-Communist witness's story has been expounded and tested—unique because of the almost "controlled" conditions of the "experiment." For what we have here is the development on two separate occasions, before two different Congressional committees, of testimony bearing on the same set of facts and tending to confirm or deny the same basic assertion: that Owen Lattimore was a member of the Communist conspiracy, acting under Communist directives to influence the course of American policy toward the Far East in conformity with the interests of Soviet Russia. And we have the "triers-of-fact," the two Congressional committees, arriving at diametrically opposed conclusions about the truth of that assertion.

We shall not be concerned here with who was right. Rather, we shall examine in detail the characteristic operations by which conclusions on this important issue of public policy have been reached and attempt to draw from our observations some tentative conclusions about the efficacy of the fact-finding processes used. We shall see what Budenz said and what he did not say, what questions he was asked and what questions he was not asked, what corroborative evidence was adduced and what was not adduced. We shall examine the political setting for its relationship to what was done and what was not done. And we shall ask whether enough evidence has been incorporated into the public record to enable an impartial observer to reach any conclusions.

The first of the two hearings in which Budenz developed his case against Lattimore was the State Department Employee Loyalty Investigation of March–June, 1950, which was conducted by a subcommittee of the Senate Foreign Relations Committee chaired by Senator Tydings of Maryland. The purpose of this hearing, which resulted in a printed record of 2,509 pages, was to investigate the charge made by Senator McCarthy of Wisconsin that a number of Communists—variously listed as 205, 81, and 57—were on the payroll of the State Department. How all this came to center on the figure of Owen Lattimore, a man who never worked for the State Department, is a matter we shall examine in a moment.

The second hearing was the investigation of the Institute of Pacific Relations undertaken by the Internal Security Subcommittee of the Senate Judiciary Committee, chaired by Senator McCarran of Nevada. This investigation, which examined allegations that the Institute was Communist-run and had improperly influenced the formation of foreign policy toward the Far East in the 1930's and 1940's, ran from July 1951 until June 1952 and resulted in a record of 5,712 pages of testimony and exhibits.

Both hearings ranged far afield from the question of whether Lattimore and certain others had participated knowingly in a Communist effort to influence American Far Eastern policy. Both hearings served as a means of massive inquiry into the failure of America's postwar Far Eastern policy, and especially into the reasons for the loss of China to communism. In the circumstances, the hearings inevitably gave rise to attacks and defense counterattacks over a broad range of American statecraft in which political passions took precedence over a full and fair exposition of facts. Nothing illustrates more vividly the influence of politics on the development of testimony than the manner in which Budenz came to be pitted on the witness stand against Lattimore.

III

On February 9, 1950, Senator McCarthy made his famous speech at Wheeling, West Virginia, in which for the first time he accused the Secretary of State of keeping a number of Communists on the payroll of the Department despite his knowledge that they were Communists. The number he mentioned then was 205. On other occasions it was 57. On February 20, when the Senator made his maiden appearance in the Senate as a spy-catcher, it was 81. The reaction in the Senate was immediate. On February 22, a resolution was adopted directing the Senate Foreign Relations Committe to conduct a "full and complete study and investigation as to whether persons who are disloyal to the United States are, or have been, employed by the Department of State." A subcommittee was constituted to undertake the investigation and Senator Tydings was appointed its chairman. On March 8, 1950, the Tydings Committee, as it came to be known, opened its hearings with testimony from Senator McCarthy. On March 13, the Senator identified Lattimore before the Committee as "one of the principal architects of our far eastern policy" and a man with a "record as a pro-Communist"—not one of Senator McCarthy's more vigorous denunciations. But before long the charge was greatly augmented.

Senator McCarthy informed the press that he had the name of the "top Russian espionage agent." In off-the-record conversations with reporters, he intimated that Lattimore was the man. On March 21, he testified before the Tydings Committee in executive session that he was willing to stake everything on the Lattimore case, and that if he was wrong, the subcommittee would be justified in not pursuing his charges further. He went so far as to assert that Lattimore was "the top of the whole ring of which Hiss was a part." By March 30, when Senator McCarthy delivered an omnibus speech in the Senate on Communist infiltration of the State Department, he was no longer quite so emphatic about Lattimore's role, referring to him as "one of the top Communist agents" and a "bad policy risk," and conceding that "in the case of Lattimore, I may have perhaps placed too much stress on the question of whether or not he has been an espionage agent." Nonetheless, the Lattimore case remained where the Senator had left it, the main prop for his charge about disloyalty in the State Department.

On April 6, Lattimore appeared before the Tydings Committee and categorically denied Senator McCarthy's charges. He asserted that he had never had anything to do with the formation of American foreign policy (it developed that he had never been officially connected with the State Department), denied Communist Party membership or Communist sympathies, and affirmed his loyalty to this country. After some questioning by members of the Committee, Senator Tydings made the following statement:

SENATOR TYDINGS   Dr. Lattimore, your case has been designated as the No. 1 case, finally, in the charges made by Senator McCarthy. You have been called, substantially, I think, if not accurately quoting, the top Red spy agent in America. We have been told that if we had access to certain files that this would be shown.

I think as chairman of this committee that I owe it to you and to the country to tell you that four of the five members of this committee, in the presence of Mr. J. Edgar Hoover, the head of the FBI, had a complete summary of your file made available to them. Mr. Hoover himself prepared those data. It was quite lengthy. And at the conclusion of the reading of that summary in great detail, it was the universal opinion of all of the members of the committee present, and all others in the room, of which there were two more, that there was nothing in that file to show that you were a Communist or had ever been a Communist, or that you were in any way connected with any espionage information or charges, so that the FBI file puts you completely, up to this moment, at least, in the clear.

It is interesting to note that this precedent-shattering revelation of FBI files was directed by the President at Senator Tydings' request after Senator McCarthy's repeated assertions that the files, if only they could be inspected, would offer substantiation for all his charges. Ironically enough, this McCarthy-instigated move appeared for the moment to have given the quietus to the Senator's charges against Lattimore.

However, the case was not over. There had been intimations earlier that a witness would be produced who would testify that Lattimore had been a Communist, and there was speculation that the witness might be Louis Budenz. The manner in which his name came to the committee's attention has never been made clear, but Budenz was subpoenaed to appear on April 20, 1950, two weeks after Lattimore's day of vindication. He appeared, according to his own statement, "as a reluctant if not unwilling witness." He had not been unwilling, however, to discuss Lattimore with friends of Senator McCarthy, and it seems fairly inferable that Budenz's appearance before the committee, regardless of his own personal feelings about testifying, represented an effort on the part of persons sympathetic to Senator McCarthy to pull the Senator's chestnuts out of the fire for him.

Budenz's testimony began with an identification of his own role in the Communist movement as managing editor of the *Daily Worker*. He explained that as a "leading member" of the Communist conspiracy he constantly received directives about the doings of a large number of people who were connected with the conspiracy.

. . . We had a liaison officer appointed who gave me instructions from day to day and in addition to that kept refreshing me on a list of about a thousand names which I was compelled to keep in my mind as to their various attitudes toward the Party, the various shifts and changes, whether a man had turned a traitor or whether he had not, and things of that sort. This list was not put down in writing because of the fact that it might be disclosed, consequently I was compelled to keep it in my mind, and this representative of the Political Bureau, the Politburo, kept refreshing my mind on this list of names. In that way I could examine a copy of the *Daily Worker* or any information or receive information intelligently.

He identified Jack Stachel as the man who served during a considerable part of his tenure on the *Daily Worker* as the liaison officer from the Politburo, the "dominant board in the Communist organization."

Budenz then described how the Communists infiltrated "various organizations and other key spots in this country." One such spot, he asserted, was the Institute of Pacific Relations, and he identified Frederick Vanderbilt Field as "one of the sources of the infiltration." Having established the existence of a Communist cell in the IPR, Budenz asserted that Lattimore was a member. He proceeded to enumerate five specific instances to support his assertion.

1. *Lattimore's Responsibility in 1937 for Placing Communist Writers in the Publication "Pacific Affairs."*

[MR. BUDENZ] In a specific meeting to which I refer, Mr. Lattimore was commended by Frederick Vanderbilt Field and Earl Browder for the fact that he had been responsible for the placing of a number of Communist writers in the organs of the Institute of Pacific Affairs, of which he was then the editor.

. . .

Field was present at that meeting and made a report at which he commended Mr. Lattimore's zeal in seeing that Communists were placed as writers in *Pacific Affairs*, and that this had been particularly noted during this last year, 1936 and 1937. Mr. Browder also referred to that, and it was agreed that Mr. Lattimore should be given general direction of organizing the writers and influencing the writers in representing the Chinese Communists as agrarian reformers, or as North Dakota nonpartisan leaguers.

SENATOR TYDINGS   Was Mr. Lattimore present at the meeting where this occurred?

MR. BUDENZ   Oh, no, sir. He was not there.

SENATOR GREEN   Do you know Mr. Lattimore?

MR. BUDENZ   Do you mean personally?

SENATOR GREEN   Yes.

MR. BUDENZ   I do not.

SENATOR GREEN   Have you ever seen Mr. Lattimore?

MR. BUDENZ   No, sir; I have not. As a matter of fact, however, I did not see Mr. Alger Hiss, either, and I knew him to be a Communist and so testified before the House Committee on Un-American Activities.

SENATOR GREEN   But you are not reasoning that everyone you have never seen and never heard may be a Communist. Is that your argument?

MR. BUDENZ   No, sir; that is not.

2. *Lattimore and the 1943 Change in the Communist Line on Chiang Kai-shek.*

MR. BUDENZ   In regard to another event that I could testify to, in 1943, at a regular meeting of the Political Bureau, at which Mr. Browder was present and others whom I could name, it was again officially reported that Mr. Lattimore, through Mr. Field, had received word from the apparatus that there was to be a change of line on Chiang Kai-shek. . . .

As a matter of fact what happened, according to the information received by us, was that from that time on we go after Chiang Kai-shek in the idea of a coalition government. The coalition government was a device used by the Communists always to slaughter those whom they brought into the coalition, and Moscow had some difficulty in advising the Communists to oppose Chiang Kai-shek, but at the same time to advise the public that we were still for Chiang Kai-shek, because they had to plead the coalition government, and coalition means that you do not denounce publicly the person you are coalescing with.

3. *"Consider Owen Lattimore as a Communist."*

[MR. BUDENZ]   In addition to that, in 1944 I shall be able to state that Jack Stachel, at the time Mr. Lattimore went to China as an adviser to Vice-President Henry Wallace—and by the way, Mr. Wallace's trip was followed with very great care and detail by the Communist Party—that at that time Jack Stachel advised me to consider Owen Lattimore as a Communist, which to me meant, because that was our method of discussing these matters, to treat as authoritative anything that he would say or advise.

4. *Lattimore and the "Amerasia" Case.*

[MR. BUDENZ]   Again in 1945, Senator, there arose the Amerasia case, the stealing of documents from Washington by Mr. Jaffe. I can say that, because he pleaded guilty and was fined $2,500.

. . .

[MR. BUDENZ]   Continuing, Senator, it was there reported by Jack Stachel that Mr. Lattimore had been in touch with some of the defendants, or they had been in touch with him, and that he had been of service in the Amerasia case.

5. *Lattimore and the Onionskins.*

[MR. BUDENZ]   Now, in addition to that, however, I would like to say that up until 1940 or '41—of course when I say it is a summary of my evidence, it isn't the full body of it. In 1940 or '41, up until 1940 or '41, the Politburo of the Communist Party issued throughout the country on onionskin documents which were official documents sent to the National Committee members, and also I can't say to my knowledge, but to my best information, officially received, sent to Moscow. These Politburo meetings were full of the whole discussions which were conducted. They were on onionskin paper and were sent to a common center through a mail drop and distributed to the members of the National Committee. I recall that very specifically in Chicago, for example, where we received them through Morris Childs, representative of the Communist Party there.

These documents in the discussions on the Far East referred to various people in the Party by their initials, because otherwise they would be disclosed, and in those documents in the discussion of Mr. Lattimore his name appeared under the initial "L" or "XL." I was so advised by Jack Stachel in the office in New York and as a matter of fact, these onionskin papers were considered so confidential that we were forbidden to burn them. We had to tear them up in small pieces and destroy them through the toilet. Then later we were ordered to give them to a common center.

As a matter of fact, much of the Communist devices are carried on through these onionskin instructions, which constantly are carried forward. The reason burning is forbidden is that it would create attention and would leave embers.

However, I do wish to state that on these reports to the Politburo, some of which may be available, though I don't know where they would be—there is the initial "L" or "XL" on Far Eastern affairs, which refers to Mr. Lattimore. We were so advised and instructed for our information.

The examination of Budenz was about as pointed an examination as has ever befallen any ex-Communist witness in a Congressional hearing. It concentrated on four aspects of his story that seemed open to question: the hearsay nature of his accusations, his failure to make them at an earlier time, his unfamiliarity with Lattimore's writings, and the improbability of his account with respect to the onionskin documents. Four examples of these lines of inquiry are given below.

The hearsay nature of his accusations. This point was so obvious from the outset of Budenz's testimony that one wonders why he did not disarm criticism by bringing it forward himself. But he did not, and it was pried out of him with telling effect. For example, with reference to his description of the 1937 meeting in which Field and Browder lauded Lattimore's work for the Party, Budenz was pressed by the committee's chief counsel, Mr. Edward P. Morgan, to recall just what Field had said about Lattimore, but he was unable to elaborate. Mr. Morgan continued to press Budenz about his personal knowledge that Lattimore was subject to Communist Party discipline. Budenz referred to reports he had received from Stachel, to which he attempted to give stature by emphasizing Stachel's role as the Party's chief disciplinarian. His interrogators were not satisfied with this response and continued the questioning until Budenz finally conceded:

MR. BUDENZ Outside of what I was officially told by the Communist leaders, I do not know of Mr. Lattimore as a Communist.

An extended passage of questioning by Senator Lodge attempted to pin down the nature of Budenz's knowledge about the "instructions" from the Communist Party that Lattimore allegedly had received.

SENATOR LODGE I would like, if you could say when, where, and how Lattimore received these instructions, or this instruction.

MR. BUDENZ Well, now, Senator, here I am in executive session, I suppose, and in this respect I will have to mention the fact that necessarily I did not follow Mr. Lattimore around. I only know that in Political Bureau meetings, which I attended, I heard instructions made that these things were going forward in the tremendous campaign which took place in book after book on this subject.

Now, that Mr. Lattimore personally had a conference with this gentleman or that, I cannot tell you.

SENATOR TYDINGS How was that?

MR. BUDENZ That he had a conference with this writer or that one, I cannot tell you because I was not present.

SENATOR TYDINGS I did not catch that.

MR. BUDENZ But, I have heard reports that this campaign was proceeding, and that it bore full fruit about 1943.

SENATOR LODGE Do you know, did any Communist worker tell you that he told Lattimore to start this campaign?

MR. BUDENZ Oh, yes; that was the substance of this report. That was why I was advised, not only that they had started—

SENATOR LODGE Who told you that?

MR. BUDENZ That was the report made in regard to this session in 1937. This was Browder's report, and Field's report.

SENATOR LODGE He told you that Lattimore had received these instructions?

MR. BUDENZ Yes; that he had received them—that is to say, first, I was thinking of the meeting when they said they were going to give them to him. Later on there followed this report and others verifying them, specifically Browder and Stachel confirmed that the instructions were being carried out.

SENATOR LODGE Did they say there they had given them, somebody going to see him at his house, or were they given to him over the telephone?

MR. BUDENZ No, No.

SENATOR LODGE   You don't know the procedure?

MR. BUDENZ   As a matter of fact, Senator, the Communists' reports to the Politburo don't go into details of that character. They give the general report on the campaign that is taking place, what is happening, and a general résumé of the situation.

SENATOR LODGE   So, you could not pinpoint all those details?

MR. BUDENZ   No; I never so claimed.

Budenz stated that he knew the instructions were being carried out because of the books and magazines that were being produced in response to them. Thereupon he was questioned about his knowledge of the books and magazines.

SENATOR TYDINGS   You have read all these articles yourself?

MR. BUDENZ   Which articles?

SENATOR TYDINGS   The ones to which you are referring.

MR. BUDENZ   A long time ago I glanced through them.

SENATOR TYDINGS   I would not say when, but you have read them all?

MR. BUDENZ   A long time ago, yes. I wouldn't say all of them, Senator, but—

SENATOR TYDINGS   A great many?

MR. BUDENZ   That is taking in too much.

These examples are fairly illustrative of the tendentiousness of Budenz's examination on the sources of his knowledge. The purpose and effect of this questioning was to create the impression that Budenz's knowledge was entirely of a hearsay nature and, further, that it was so general as to be valueless. Budenz himself, with the occasional aid of Senator Hickenlooper, attempted to bolster the quality of his information by stressing the conspiratorial nature of Party activities and the great importance attached to placing accurate information in his hands. His position, he averred, made it a matter of "political life and death" for him to know what he was talking about. These rehabilitative efforts were manful, but the net impression left by the persistent and hostile questioning of committee members and their counsel was that Budenz's story was dubious and unsubstantiated.

Budenz's failure to accuse Lattimore earlier. This point provided perhaps the most substantial source of doubt as to the validity of Budenz's testimony, and it was exploited to the fullest by the committee in its questioning. This questioning pursued two general lines. The first was aimed at pointing up the fact that Budenz had had frequent opportunities to divulge his knowledge about Lattimore but had failed to do so. Budenz's own statement provided the springboard for this inquiry. In developing his own stature as an authority on Communist penetration he repeatedly referred to his collaboration with the FBI. These references naturally prompted inquiry into the extent of his collaboration and raised the question of why he had never mentioned Lattimore's name. The substance of his answer was that he had more important people to deal with, which, as his questioners were quick to note, seemed somewhat inconsistent with the view he was now taking about Lattimore's importance as an exponent of the Communist line in policy toward China.

More damaging than this general failure to bring up Lattimore's name was the fact that there had been at least two occasions on which Budenz was squarely presented with the opportunity to link Lattimore with the Communist Party. Budenz's failure to do so, if he then believed Lattimore to be a Communist, could be characterized as, at the very least, evasive. The occasions are worth describing in detail, both because of their intrinsic importance and because of the light they shed on the difficulties of conducting an adequate examination of issues as sprawling and untidy as the question of whether Owen Lattimore, or any other man, had been a consciously participating member of the Communist Party.

The first incident concerned a magazine article that Budenz wrote for Collier's in 1949 entitled "The Menace of Red China." The article was concerned, among other things, with Communist influences on the formation of American policy toward China. Lattimore's name was not mentioned in the article. However, it developed that his name had been mentioned in an earlier draft of the article and then omitted after a conference with Leonard Parris, an associate editor of the magazine. The draft was made available to the committee. The strongest statement in it about Lattimore was that he had been "frequently referred to in [Communist] reports by Mr. [Frederick Vanderbilt] Field, and always in the most complimentary manner." This statement was deleted from the article on the basis of a discussion between Budenz and Parris, a transcript of which was introduced into the record of the hearing. The transcript, as well as the draft of the article, was handed to the committee by Mr. Abe Fortas, counsel for Lattimore. It is noteworthy that the committee deviated from customary Congressional procedure enough to permit Mr. Fortas to submit questions (but

not to ask them himself) which the committee's counsel then put
to Budenz. This uneasy compromise between Congressional and
judicial procedure did not work any too well. Mr. Morgan found
himself in the awkward position of propounding a series of questions which had been handed to him only a moment earlier and
with which he had no opportunity to familiarize himself. The results, naturally enough, were something short of perfect, but some
interesting material did emerge.

The most relevant extracts from the transcript of the interview
between Budenz and Parris read as follows:

Q. [by Mr. Parris] You have done one thing here that I think is not good.
By inference you implied that Joe Barnes and Lattimore are not
Communists exactly but are fellow travelers. . . .

A. I think probably what we ought to do is to leave out those names
entirely. Perhaps we can rephrase it some way. I said it merely to
show that they would add meat to what I was saying.

. . .

Q. On page 7 you say "This idea of the 'upstanding Chinese Communists, the great agrarian reformers,' was peddled everywhere from
that time on." You haven't given a single instance that it was peddled or that the idea was planted by the Communists. Give at least
one instance, or more than one if possible.

A. Lattimore and Barnes became champions of some of these ideas as
time went on.

Q. You're not saying that they acted as Communist agents in any way?

A. No.

Q. That ought to be quite clear.

A. Oh, yes.

Budenz's reply adroitly made use of the theory that Communists
have a policy of destroying their opponents by bringing libel suits,
and in doing so, seemed to reflect somewhat on Parris:

MR. MORGAN   Question by counsel for Mr. Lattimore: It is my understanding that at the time of this conference you did not claim that
Mr. Lattimore acted as a Communist agent in any way, and that is
still your view?

MR. BUDENZ   No, sir. I was very well aware, especially with Mr. Parris' peculiar questions which indicated to me that he might have a
particular viewpoint, that I was to answer in such a way as to avoid
Communist attack through libel, such as I know was their policy.
Consequently, this was not a discussion under oath. This was a discussion of an article, and I think that I have indicated quite well
there that Mr. Lattimore and Mr. Barnes were involved in this campaign.

MR. MORGAN   Further question: As a matter of fact, Mr. Lattimore states that he never referred to Chinese Communists as agrarian reformers or in any terms that meant the same thing. Can you tell us any specific instance in which you claim Mr. Lattimore did refer to the Chinese Communists as agrarian reformers?

MR. BUDENZ   Well, I would have to have opportunity to check on that, Mr. Counsel, but my statement against Mr. Lattimore is not that he personally stated this. He was always considered to be in a special and delicate position. But that he was given the responsibility of organizing this campaign.

MR. MORGAN   Mr. Chairman—

MR. BUDENZ   I am—I would like to have the privilege of submitting to this committee an analysis of Mr. Lattimore's writings in time. I have not had the opportunity to do so.

MR. MORGAN   Mr. Chairman, this document is, of course—I was not familiar with it, . . .

The issue was not further pressed at that moment but was returned to at a later point in the interrogation of Budenz:

SENATOR GREEN   Now, this morning you stated something that attracted my attention. I think, for your sake, we ought to clear it up. That was in connection with your discussion with the editors of *Collier's* about the article, and in explanation of some apparent discrepancy, you stated, "Well, this was a conference. It wasn't under oath."

Do you make a distinction between answers that are made seriously and without oath, and those made under oath.

MR. BUDENZ   No, sir; but I do make this statement: Here was a conference on my article. I know very well, Senator, that the Communists have a plan to harass and destroy a man by libel actions. When I received such peculiar questions from Mr. Parris, I immediately intended to shut him off, and as a matter of fact I am compelled to do that repeatedly. People come to me with all sorts of questions. I can't get rid of them.

In this case, I also was dealing with an article not yet completed, and I do not distinguish between under oath and otherwise, except in the sense that I cannot commit myself or permit myself to be attacked by someone who tried to draw me out.

SENATOR GREEN   You mean, under those circumstances, you are willing to put them off by stating something that is not true?

MR. BUDENZ   Well, I would not say—"not true," but that doesn't make the matter—

SENATOR GREEN   What expression would you prefer, having the same meaning—"false"? How would you put it? Put it in your own words.

MR. BUDENZ   Well, I would say, Senator, this: That for me to say to Mr. Parris that Mr. Lattimore was a Communist agent, in the way

that Mr. Parris was pressing me, would have been of no advantage
to the article, and would have, at the same time, have been a matter
of attack upon me.

The matter was not further developed. The reader will have to
judge for himself whether Parris (who was not called to testify)
had been "pressing" Budenz with "peculiar" questions.

The second occasion involved a communication between Budenz and a State Department investigator in 1947. An extended
quotation from the record at this point is in order, both for its substantive content and for a revealing glimpse of Budenz's demeanor
as a witness.

SENATOR GREEN   Did you talk to a special agent of the State Department in September 1947, about communism?

MR. BUDENZ   I don't recall that.

SENATOR GREEN   In September 1947 did you talk to any special agent
—in 1947—of the State Department?

MR. BUDENZ   I don't recall that, Senator.

SENATOR TYDINGS   Did you say, in that interview with this State Department agent that you were not prepared to pass judgment upon
the degree of Mr. Lattimore's association with the Party, that you
thought he was a sympathizer but that you were unable to recall at
that time any incident which definitely indicated that he was a member of the Party?

MR. BUDENZ   Well, I do not recall that, but if I did, it was in a telephone
conversation, and I am very evasive on the telephone, and with very
good reason, as anyone who considers how the Communists act, can
understand. I have to be very careful.

· · ·

SENATOR TYDINGS   Would you therefore deny that you said in 1947, to
any representative of the State Department, that you could not be
called at that time, you could not recall any incident which definitely
would indicate that Lattimore was a member of the Communist
Party?

MR. BUDENZ   I won't deny it.

SENATOR TYDINGS   You won't?

MR. BUDENZ   I would not deny it or affirm it, because on the telephone—

SENATOR TYDINGS   I am not talking about on the telephone.

MR. BUDENZ   Well, I am sure that the only time I ever talked with a
representative of the State Department, except in one specific case,
was on the telephone, and I did not give information on the telephone.

SENATOR TYDINGS   But, why would you not have said, rather that "I do
not recall at this time any instance which definitely indicates that
Lattimore was a member of the Party," why would you not have

said, if you did not want to talk on the telephone, "I do not care to discuss the matter on the telephone," or something else, other than the affirmative statement that you didn't recall any instance which definitely indicated that Lattimore was a member of the party?

MR. BUDENZ   I just used that device, if that is the case.

SENATOR TYDINGS   Would that put you in a position of making a statement that might not be true, or does it not?

MR. BUDENZ   Not necessarily, sir. Maybe I had not had Lattimore on my mind. You must understand, Senator, in regard to cases of this character, I had been very careful. That is to say, I do not make assertions unless I check very carefully on the case, and in checking up, know exactly what the facts are.

SENATOR TYDINGS   But, in this case you had nothing to check up on other than your conversation with Mr. Stachel, because he was the man that had previously—

MR. BUDENZ   Oh, yes; I may have had—

SENATOR TYDINGS   Excuse me, because I am directing myself particularly to the testimony that Mr. Stachel and some other people, I think it was Stachel who said "You are to consider Lattimore as a member of the Party?"

MR. BUDENZ   That is correct.

SENATOR TYDINGS   And you were outlined about more activities there, and you were told that Lattimore was very helpful—

MR. BUDENZ   That is correct.

SENATOR TYDINGS   You were also told that the movement was progressing very favorably and you knew Lattimore was head of the magazine.

Well now, if you had all that information in your mind, why would you say, in September 1947, that you did not recall at that time any incident which definitely indicated that Lattimore was a member of the Party?

MR. BUDENZ   I don't recall that statement, but if I made it, under the circumstances, I made it on the telephone, and therefore was not prepared, unless by very careful examination, which I always give, to make statements that are definite.

SENATOR TYDINGS   But, there is no record necessary for you to fix your —no record you could look up by research, you might say, in the case I have in mind, if Stachel told you that orally—why would you not have said, knowing this, knowing about Lattimore and knowing about the writers and knowing that Stachel had told you to consider Lattimore as a Communist, why would not you have said "I would like to talk about it with you, but privately," or "I don't care to discuss it," other than to make the affirmative statement that "I recall of no instance now that would indicate that he, Lattimore, was a member of the Party"?

MR. BUDENZ   Well, in the first place, I have only given information

fully to the Federal Bureau of Investigation. That has been my rule.
Secondly, I do not know people who promiscuously call me on the telephone and I have to be very careful.

SENATOR TYDINGS I appreciate that, but what I am trying to get at, Mr. Budenz, and I don't want to prolong it—

MR. BUDENZ I understand.

SENATOR TYDINGS I do not blame you for saying over the telephone, "I don't care to discuss it," or I don't blame you for saying on the telephone that, "This is something I might want to talk to you privately about"; but, instead of picking one of the things that would have protected the position you rightly wanted to protect, did you not say at that time, "I am unable to recall at this time any incident which definitely would indicate that Lattimore was a member of the Party?" And to convey the impression to your own Government, after you left the Communist Party, that you had nothing in mind that would show Lattimore was a member of the Communist Party?

MR. BUDENZ I did not have the time or energy to check carefully on the facts I had before me. I always do that, and I have made that reply, incidentally, more than once, along similar lines.

The effect of the questioning on these two specific occasions, and of Budenz's failure to mention Lattimore as a Communist, either in public testimony or in giving information to the FBI, at any time between his break with the Party in 1945 and Senator McCarthy's accusations against Lattimore in 1950, was to suggest that his testimony about Lattimore might have been a recent fabrication.

Budenz's unfamiliarity with Lattimore's writings. Budenz was extensively questioned about Lattimore's expressed views which appeared inconsistent with his being a Communist. This line of questioning not only tended to cast doubt on the accuracy of the information about Lattimore that Budenz had claimed to receive from his Communist associates, but served the further purpose of demonstrating Budenz's lack of acquaintance with Lattimore's work. Once again, the questioning was cued by Lattimore's counsel and executed, not too successfully, by counsel for the committee.

MR. MORGAN Further question: As a matter of fact, Mr. Lattimore states that he never referred to Chinese Communists as agrarian reformers or in any terms that meant the same thing. Can you tell us any specific instance in which you claim Mr. Lattimore did refer to the Chinese Communists as agrarian reformers?

MR. BUDENZ Well, I would have to have opportunity to check on that, Mr. Counsel, but my statement against Mr. Lattimore is not that he personally stated this. He was always considered to be in a special and delicate position. But that he was given the responsibility of organizing this campaign.

MR. MORGAN   Mr. Chairman—

MR. BUDENZ   I am—I would like to have the privilege of submitting to this committee an analysis of Mr. Lattimore's writings in time. I have not had the opportunity to do so.

MR. MORGAN   Mr. Chairman, this document is, of course—I was not familiar with it. . . .

Budenz was further questioned about a review of Lattimore's book, *Situation in Asia,* which appeared in the *Daily Worker* in 1949. The review criticized Lattimore for going "completely off the beam" in suggesting that emerging nationalism in Asia sought to remain independent of both America and Russia, and proceeded to criticize his conclusions about the struggle for power between those two nations. Although Budenz began by expressing hesitation about testifying on things that happened after he left the Party, he readily allowed himself to be drawn into opining on the treatment of pro-Communists in the Communist press. In so doing, he put himself in an "either-or" position that invited speedy retaliation from the chairman of the committee.

MR. MORGAN   Now may I ask you, as having been editor of the *Daily Worker,* was it ordinary or customary in reviews of books in the *Daily Worker* to speak critically of one who is projecting, so it has been stated here, a policy for the Soviet Union?

MR. BUDENZ   Yes, sir, I can explain to you that we had the policy in protecting people who are out beyond the Party proper, to criticize them with faint praise—that is to say, that is, to damn them with faint praise—rather, to praise them with faint damns, is the way I want to put it.

Now I can give to this committee examples of that, but I just will have to have time. However, I would like to analyze this, not as a member of the Party but for just a moment out of my experience.

In the first place, you will note that the whole emphasis here is on the "*Situation in Asia* criticizes United States Government policy in the Far East." You will note Mr. Lattimore's premise of the immediate action is approved. That is the important thing for Stalin. Communists don't go around saying, "We are Communists." They are pushing a certain line; I mean the Communists beyond the Party. This approves Mr. Lattimore's main premise, and it also comes as a conclusion of that where it says that what he is advocating, if followed out, certain things will have to be done.

What does it speak to Mr. Lattimore under all this extensive verbiage? It speaks to two things: that he puts forward a third-course idea, and, secondly, that he is still advocating capitalism in a way. Now, the *Daily Worker* knows that Mr. Lattimore in his position can do nothing else but be with capitalism as such. They know that this third force exists because it was discussed while I was in the Party, that it is something which the Communists have proposed from time to time; they constantly develop third forces. At the present moment they understand that it is practically impossible—I am only saying that, not as a far eastern expert, Mr. Chairman, which I am not, but merely from the discussions within the Party before I left—that it is impossible to develop a third force in Asia at the present moment. That is to say, either you are going to be with Chiang Kai-shek or you are going to be with the Reds. That is to say, you can't take a neutral attitude.

SENATOR TYDINGS   I do not want to be with either one of them in the situation right now.

Budenz's readiness to interpret what the *Daily Worker* had to say about *Situation in Asia* was put in a rather unfavorable light by a line of questioning that demonstrated his unfamiliarity not only with the body of Lattimore's work, but also with that very book.

SENATOR GREEN   You claim that Mr. Lattimore's views on China have changed in accordance with the change in the Communist line, is that your point?

MR. BUDENZ   I would not wish to be able to pass upon that until I have examined all of Mr. Lattimore's writings, as I have said.

SENATOR GREEN   How many of his books have you read?

MR. BUDENZ   Very few, in a very fragmentary way. I am not in a position to pass upon Mr. Lattimore's writings, except in a general way, except on his last book *Situation in Asia*.

SENATOR GREEN   Then, he might not have followed the Communist line in his previous books, I believe he has published 11.

MR. BUDENZ   That we can see when we analyze them, as far as I am concerned.

SENATOR GREEN   If you think that one book shows he is a Communist, because he is following the line, and the other books did not, what would be the weight or balance of evidence?

MR. BUDENZ   It would have to depend, of course, that is why I must analyze the book, we cannot talk about this in such shorthand terms. It seems to me, Senator, I would have to analyze the book.

Now as a matter of fact I have come here before the committee to testify to certain facts of my own knowledge, to the extent that I have been informed of them; so far as these other matters are concerned, I have not had the opportunity to analyze them. I have offered to analyze them and shall do so if the committee so desires.

SENATOR GREEN   How much of his published writings, I won't limit it to books, have you read?

MR. BUDENZ   Very few indeed.

SENATOR GREEN   How many?

MR. BUDENZ   Well, that I cannot say, offhand.

SENATOR GREEN   Have you read one book?

MR. BUDENZ   I have read hurriedly *Situation in Asia*.

SENATOR GREEN   Just looked it through?

MR. BUDENZ   Yes, sir.

His questioners put Budenz in an unfavorable position by citing instances of Lattimore's conspicuous deviation from the Party line (no doubt suggested by Lattimore's counsel) and asking how he could reconcile them with his assertion that Lattimore was a Communist. For example, he was pressed about Lattimore's position on the Russo-Finnish War and his support of the Marshall Plan.

MR. MORGAN   Dr. Lattimore testified, Mr. Budenz, that he participated in an organization which raised funds for Finland during the Russo-Finnish war in 1940. Would that indicate to you that he was a Communist sympathizer?

MR. BUDENZ   That he was a Communist sympathizer? That doesn't indicate that he was a Communist sympathizer. You would not necessarily have a Communist sympathizer connected with that, but it would not indicate that he was not a Communist. I mean to say that presence on that Finnish Committee were not guarantees that men were not members of the Communist Party. I don't know that this is quite the thing to do, Senator, but there has been a very famous name in the headlines from time to time. I know of a specific exemption given to a specific gentleman in this respect and to others. I don't know about Mr. Lattimore's case.

MR. MORGAN   Now, as a general proposition, would you say that contributing to Finland during this period of the Russo-Finnish war was or was not indicative of Communist sympathies?

SENATOR TYDINGS   You mean the Finnish-Russian war?

MR. MORGAN   Finnish-Russian war; yes.

MR.BUDENZ   I would say in general it was not indicative of Communist sympathies, but I would say, to my knowledge—and, as I say, I know of at least one instance, maybe more, where exemptions were granted to people who were in delicate positions to aid the Finnish campaign. The proposition was put up: A few dollars to Finland, what does that harm in the situation compared to protecting these comrades?

MR. MORGAN   The fact that Mr. Lattimore may have aided the Finns would not alter your conclusion in any respect?

MR. BUDENZ   It would not. That is to say, I don't want to be so arbitrary as that. I would give it consideration, but it would not alter it, knowing what I know.

MR. MORGAN   Dr. Lattimore referred in his testimony, I believe, to the fact that he had and does support the Marshall Plan. What observation would you make with respect to that, Mr. Budenz, if any?

MR. BUDENZ   Well, of course, now here I am testifying to events after I left the Party, and I hesitate to do that, Senator, but if my general opinion out of my experience is desired, I shall give an answer. That would not affect my judgment at all, considering his book, *Situation in Asia*, which I have only read very hastily, but I agree thoroughly with the *World-Telegram*, that Uncle Joe couldn't state it any better than Mr. Lattimore has done in his *Situation in Asia* when he states that the Soviet Union is looked to—I don't want to give an exact quote—with awe and wonder by the Asiatic peoples, whereas the United States is only regarded as the occasion for cannon fodder for them. Now that thing is just merely a popularized expression of an attack on imperialism by the Communists. Knowing that, and knowing that the Communists do give exemptions to men who are concealed, I would say that Mr. Lattimore—of course, I can only give my opinion here—could have been excused on the Marshall Plan in order to continue activities in the area to which he is assigned. There have been cases likewise of that to which I can refer if I am given time.

MR. MORGAN   It is your testimony, therefore, that the fact that Dr. Lattimore may support the Marshall Plan has no necessary bearing on whether he may or may not have been carrying out a policy sympathetic to the Communists?

MR. BUDENZ   If in his main line of assignment he continues to support the Stalinite policy, many things are exempted. That, however, does not indicate that I have any knowledge today of Mr. Lattimore's position.

This kind of incident put Budenz in the position of saying, in effect: What Lattimore did is less important than what I said.

Again and again, when pressed on deviations from the Communist Party line in Lattimore's writings, Budenz pleaded unfamiliarity with Lattimore's work and stated his intention of making an analysis of that work and submitting it to the committee. The printed exhibits contain no indication that such an analysis was ever made and submitted. The effect of this silence reinforces the impression that Budenz's charges against Lattimore were based wholly on what he was told by others, which returns us to the double question of the accuracy of Budenz's sources and the accuracy of his own recollection of what he had been told.

The onionskin documents. Nothing gave Budenz's story a more conspiratorial flavor than his account of the references to Lattimore as "L" or "XL" in Communist Party documents that were "issued throughout the country" but were so confidential that they had to be flushed down the toilet rather than being burned, because burning "would create attention and would leave embers." The committee treated this aspect of his story with polite skepticism, concentrating attention on the source of his knowledge and the availability of corroboration.

MR. MORGAN   Are any of these documents, to your knowledge, in existence?

MR. BUDENZ   Well, I would not know. The point of the matter is we had strict instructions to destroy them all.

MR. MORGAN   How do you know, Mr. Budenz, that the character "L" or "XL" was the designation for Mr. Lattimore?

MR. BUDENZ   That was told me by Jack Stachel on one of my visits to New York and, as a matter of fact, on several occasions.

. . .

SENATOR TYDINGS   Now, you also said that Lattimore was designated as "XL," I think, or something pretty close to that?

MR. BUDENZ   That is right.

SENATOR TYDINGS   As a Communist designation?

MR. BUDENZ   That is right.

SENATOR TYDINGS   Does his signature appear opposite that designation?

MR. BUDENZ   Oh no. That is onionskin instructions coming from the Politburo.

SENATOR TYDINGS   So, there was nothing to identify Lattimore with the "XL" on the onionskin itself?

MR. BUDENZ   Only the instructions given us by the Politburo.

The questioners were, of course, in no position to check on Budenz's assertions. At least, they were in no position to do so as long as his assertions comprised the only testimony in the record on the point. However, before the hearings were completed, additional testimony was adduced from persons who were in the best possible position to know the truth. These hearings provided a unique occasion for the full testimony of certain of Budenz's former associates in the Communist Party, who appeared in response to subpoenas and delivered themselves of statements which, if believed, contradicted Budenz's account, not only as to Lattimore's Communist affiliation but also as to Budenz's position in the Communist hierarchy. To this testimony we now turn.

The first witness after Budenz was Dr. Bella V. Dodd, a long-time worker in the labor movement, who cooperated with the Communists for a number of years, joined the Party in 1943, was elected a member of the National Committee in 1944 apparently in recognition of her prominence in labor work, and was expelled from the Party in 1949. It came to the attention of counsel for Lattimore that Dr. Dodd had questioned the accuracy of Budenz's testimony and, at counsel's suggestion, she was subpoenaed to testify.

She took sharp issue with Budenz on a number of points. First, she contradicted his version of the importance of his Party position, thereby inferentially weakening his assertion that he was in a strategic spot to pick up data about clandestine activity. She claimed, for example, that Budenz had been a member of the National Committee for a much shorter period of time than he had asserted and also that he did not begin to serve as managing editor of the *Daily Worker* until 1942 or 1943. On the basis of her acquaintance with him over a period of time going back to 1935 (it will be recalled that Budenz, too, had started out as a labor specialist), Dr. Dodd characterized him as "an ineffective man."

Further, she stated that she could not "bring into focus many of the things he says about the Communist Party." For example, she characterized his statements about Jack Stachel's role as "laughable," asserting that Stachel was "assigned to trade union matters at the time Budenz testified that Stachel was giving him names to be remembered and instructions regarding Professor Lattimore." Dr. Dodd went on to deride the idea that Stachel could possibly have given Budenz a list of 1,000 names to memorize, or, if he had, that Budenz could possibly have done so.

With respect to Lattimore, Dr. Dodd asserted that she had never heard his name mentioned as a Party member. She rejected with some scorn Budenz's account of seeing Lattimore's name referred to by code in Party documents:

Mr. Budenz says that Professor Lattimore was mentioned in secret Party memoranda as L or XL. This is playing cops and robbers with a vengeance. In the first place, I never saw an onionskin document such as Mr. Budenz says he was told to flush down the toilet. In the second place, if Professor Lattimore had been as close to the Party as Budenz claims, he would have been asked to come to Party headquarters for his instructions. Third, whatever errors we made in the Communist Party we did not fall into the habit of taking our methods from dime detective stories.

Oddly enough, the questioning of Dr. Dodd by the committee hardly brought out that she could have had very little direct knowledge of Budenz's sources of information about Lattimore, since she did not join the Party until 1943 and was not elected to the National Committee until 1944, whereas much of Budenz's testimony related to earlier events, such as the alleged meeting in 1937 at which Browder and Field were supposed to have referred to Lattimore's work for the Party. Although the point was obliquely raised, it was not pursued in detail, and little attempt was made to evaluate just how good a position Dr. Dodd was in to corroborate or deny Budenz's story.

The questioning by the minority members of the subcommittee, who should perhaps have been counted on to supply the necessary counterpoise, was highly ineffective. Senator Hickenlooper spent most of his questioning time in examining Dr. Dodd's views on questions that were, to put it mildly, rather wide of the mark. For example, it is difficult to see what relevance the following exchange had to the question at hand.

SENATOR HICKENLOOPER   Dr. Dodd, do you believe in the capitalistic form of government?

DR. DODD   I will tell you that the capitalistic system has done a great deal for our civilization. As an economist, I will tell you that the capitalistic system has certain weaknesses which are inherent in it, which will force a modification of our economic system of government. It cannot help it. We are a very different Government today, with the kind of unemployment insurance and pensions for trade unions, than we were 20 years ago.

SENATOR HICKENLOOPER   May I renew my question? Dr. Dodd, do you believe in the present system of capitalistic government that we have in the United States today, as it presently exists?

DR. DODD   I believe in the Government of the United States under its Constitution. I believe, as far as the economy of the Government is concerned, it is constantly evolving and shifting and changing as the needs of the people shift and change.

.   .   .

SENATOR HICKENLOOPER   You then are a Socialist today, in your own definition, right?

DR. DODD   I believe in the public ownership of the means of the production. I believe the time will have to come when the Govern-

ment will have to take more and more part in the productive processes.

SENATOR HICKENLOOPER You believe in Government ownership of
natural resources?

DR. DODD I certainly do.

SENATOR HICKENLOOPER And in transportation?

DR. DODD I certainly do.

SENATOR HICKENLOOPER And in communications?

DR. DODD I think it would help.

One can only conclude that a valuable opportunity to work out a
real issue of fact between witnesses, or alternatively, to demonstrate that Witness B was in no position to come to grips with assertions made by Witness A, was lost. The point is worth noting
because it is one that recurs with dispiriting frequency in Congressional hearings. The free-ranging nature of the inquiry, unbounded
by any formal requirements of proof and unchecked by the effective assertion of anyone's sense of relevance, tends to be at war
with the attempt to develop facts in an orderly way. While it is
questionable just how much light Dr. Dodd had to shed on the
Budenz charges, one is forced to the conclusion that whatever she
had was not properly developed by the examination process.

The witness that followed Dr. Dodd supported Budenz's position. His testimony is one of the strangest episodes in the annals
of the Tydings Committee. The witness was Larry E. Kerley, a
former FBI agent, and, at the time of his testimony, an editorial
staff writer for the *New York Journal-American*. He testified that
during his tenure with the FBI he employed as a confidential in-
formant a man named John Huber who served as an undercover
agent within the Communist Party from 1939 until 1946 or 1947.
The examination then proceeded as follows:

MR. MORGAN Now, knowing the nature of this inquiry, Mr. Kerley, do
you have any information of pertinence that you would like to lay
before this committee now?

MR. KERLEY Well, Mr. Huber, whom I have known these 2 or 3 years,
and came to my office about a week after the charges had originally
been brought against Professor Lattimore that he was a Communist
agent in this country, and Mr. Huber advised me that he had seen
Mr. Lattimore and had been in his company at a party in the early
part of 1946, in the home of Frederick Vanderbilt Field, who was
one of the directors of the Committee for a Democratic Far Eastern
Policy.

Now this is one of the front organizations of the Communist Party that has been named as subversive by the Attorney General. I asked Mr. Huber if known Communists had attended the party and he said that as far as—

MR. MORGAN   What I had in mind—I do not want to curtail your testimony, but I think that aspect of it must best come from Mr. Huber.

What I wanted, since you are here today, was whether or not you had any other information of pertinence to this committee in connection with this inquiry apart from Mr. Huber's testimony.

MR. KERLEY   Well, I do not know whether or not Mr. Huber is present, and that is why I was going to relate to you some of the conversations.

SENATOR TYDINGS   Would you mind if I ascertained whether he was, since it might have something to do with the length of your examination?

Is Mr. Huber present?

Is Mr. John Huber present?

(There was no response.)

SENATOR TYDINGS   He does not seem to be here, Mr. Morgan.

It developed that Huber, who had been subpoenaed to appear at the same time as Kerley and had come down to Washington from New York with him, had simply disappeared. He later turned up in New York, where he told reporters that he had "blacked out." His appearance had apparently been initiated by Senator McCarthy, on information from Robert Morris, the minority counsel to the Tydings Committee. His appearance was never compelled, although he was obviously in contempt of the Senate's subpoena. And the record was left in the strange position of having Huber's testimony given through the mouth of Kerley. Indeed, the committee did not abandon the point after it became obvious that Huber was not going to appear, but instead proceeded to question Kerley at length about Huber's story. This slipshod procedure was hardly calculated to frame an issue in terms responsive to further investigation. The result is described in a passage from the Tydings Committee's deliberations in executive session at the conclusions of the hearings. It is worth reproducing in its entirety for two reasons: It illustrates far more vividly than can mere assertion the shortcomings of the committee process as a means of eliciting and evaluating information, and it speaks eloquently, because unwittingly, of the political crosscurrents which so curtailed the effectiveness of the investigation.

SENATOR TYDINGS   We didn't get that other fellow that Senator Mc-Carthy had summoned and brought down here on a plane. He was down here in Washington and went home. We never even got him down here. He was sick, too.

SENATOR MC MAHON   I forgot about that "bird." Where is that "bird"?

MR. MORRIS   I hear he wants to come down.

SENATOR TYDINGS   Where did you hear it?

MR. MORRIS   From him.

SENATOR TYDINGS   Where is he?

MR. MORRIS   He is home in Mount Vernon. I spoke to him on the phone.

SENATOR MC MAHON   When?

MR. MORRIS   I guess it was about 10 days ago.

SENATOR MC MAHON   What did you talk to him about?

MR. MORRIS   He came and consulted me in connection with his appearance down here. He asked me if, in my opinion, he was in contempt, and I said, "Technically you are." He submitted a doctor's certificate. So he said, "What are you going to do?" I said, "Certainly, if I were you, I would write to Senator Tydings and tell him you are willing to come down here and testify in executive session."

SENATOR MC MAHON   Did you make any report as assistant counsel to this committee on this conversation?

MR. MORRIS   To Mr. Morgan? No; I didn't.

SENATOR MC MAHON   To any member of the committee?

MR. MORRIS   I don't know whether I mentioned it to Senator Hickenlooper. No; I don't think I did.

SENATOR MC MAHON   Did you mention it to Senator McCarthy?

MR. MORRIS   No.

SENATOR MC MAHON   Did you mention it to anybody in his office?

MR. MORRIS   In Senator McCarthy's office? No.

SENATOR MC MAHON   I am rather surprised, because I should think that information concerning a collapsible and disappearing witness—if you thought it was important enough to talk to him and give him advice—would be of some importance. I regret very much that you didn't notify the chairman of the committee.

MR. MORRIS   May I explain a little further?

SENATOR MC MAHON   Sure.

MR. MORRIS   I haven't been near my law office, I don't know, for a long period of time, and I got phone messages. I noticed he had been trying to reach me. He was trying to consult me sort of independent with respect to my position on the committee. He wanted, as he called it, some friendly advice as to where he stood and everything else. So, the advice I gave him was that he should write to Senator Tydings and say that he is perfectly willing to come down and testify. Now, what caused him to be so upset was the fact he had to testify in open session. Apparently, when he was first served, he was told by Mr. Tyler that he was going to be heard in executive session. When he got down here and saw all the klieg lights, he was very much disturbed, and he said he had an emotional upset; and I believe him, because the guy is very excitable.

MR. MORGAN   For the record, Mr. Tyler told him he didn't know whether he would appear in executive or open session, but that is neither here nor there.

MR. MORRIS   I am reporting on Mr. Huber's conversation.

MR. MORGAN   Just for the record, I want that to be clear.

MR. MORRIS   I said now that he is well again that he should come and send a letter to Senator Tydings.

SENATOR TYDINGS   If he came down here does anybody know what he would testify to? What is the point of bringing him unless he is going to contribute something to the sum total of knowledge essential to form an opinion on the matter before us? We had Mr. Van Buren down here who was widely heralded as a man who could tell everything in God's world, and if he had stayed in New York—he is a hell of a nice fellow—we would have known just as much as we know now. I don't want to take the time to have witnesses come down here unless we know they have got some pertinent information. There is no point in getting him down here, then finding he has nothing to contribute.

MR. MORRIS   Senator, don't misconstrue what I said now. I am answering Senator McMahon's inquiry about Huber. Here is the first time it came up, and I spoke of it as soon as I heard about it. I gave him advice. I didn't think it was in the capacity of assistant counsel. I think he came to me as somebody he could go to for assistance, and I gave him the best advice I could.

SENATOR MC MAHON   How many times have you conferred with him?

MR. MORRIS   Huber? Altogether, I must have seen Huber eight times. You see, he was one of the witnesses before the Westchester grand jury.

SENATOR MC MAHON   And you were connected with that case?

MR. MORRIS   Yes.

SENATOR MC MAHON   Is that where you first met him?

MR. MORRIS   That is where I first met him—possibly before that, even.

SENATOR MC MAHON   Were most of the meetings in connection with this?

MR. MORRIS   Yes.

SENATOR MC MAHON   How many times did you confer with him in relation to our matters?

MR. MORRIS   I would say two.

SENATOR MC MAHON   Would you fix the dates?

MR. MORRIS   It would be very difficult, Senator.

SENATOR MC MAHON   I don't mean the exact dates. I mean in relation to what was going on in the investigation. In other words, was it before he was supposed to appear before our committee?

MR. MORRIS   No. I met him once before he was supposed to appear, but I had no part of it or anything else. I just heard that he was going to be one of the witnesses.

SENATOR TYDINGS   Were you alone when you met him?

MR. MORRIS   No.

SENATOR TYDINGS   Who was with you?

MR. MORRIS   I think Mr. Sokolsky was present and Mr. Kerley. Mr. Sokolsky had nothing to do with it. It happened to be a social gathering at which these people happened to be present.

SENATOR TYDINGS   Anybody else?

SENATOR MC MAHON   Who is Kerley?

MR. MORRIS   He testified at the same time. It was a social gathering, Senator. I am trying to think of who else was present.

MR. MORGAN   Is our question whether or not we are going to call Huber?

SENATOR TYDINGS   Let us let the thing go.

MR. MORRIS   I am answering Senator McMahon's question. I am trying to recall who was present. The two that stand out are Kerley and Sokolsky. I don't think he even paid any attention to it.

SENATOR MC MAHON   Where was the meeting?

MR. MORRIS   It wasn't a meeting. It was at the home of J. B. Matthews, 410 West Twenty-fourth Street. He is a man who had—I know he always used to help me when I was in the Navy.

SENATOR MC MAHON   I know something about Dr. Matthews' background. That was before Kerley was supposed to appear with this man Huber?

MR. MORRIS   That is right, Senator.

SENATOR MC MAHON   Just a few days before?

MR. MORRIS   No. I think this was probably at least a week before, maybe 2 weeks.

SENATOR MC MAHON   Was that before you became associated with this committee?

MR. MORRIS   I don't think so; no.

SENATOR MC MAHON   That was when you were associated with this committee?

MR. MORRIS   I think so.

SENATOR MC MAHON   Did you make that known to the committee, the fact that you had had this meeting in regard to this witness?

MR. MORRIS   I don't think so, Senator. You see, it was a social gathering. Now, I was not there in my capacity as a counsel of the committee.

SENATOR MC MAHON   But Huber's appearance was discussed; wasn't it?

MR. MORRIS   Naturally, the Lattimore subject was in all the papers and everyone was talking about it.

SENATOR MC MAHON   Lattimore had already appeared.

MR. MORRIS   No. I don't know whether he had appeared, but Lattimore's name had been injected into the picture, and people were generally talking about Lattimore and evidence against Lattimore. I saw Huber there and I was rather surprised. I mean I hadn't seen Huber, I suppose, a month or 2 months, 6 weeks, whatever it was. So, I listened to what was going on. I just listened to what it was; I heard that Senator McCarthy had suggested he be called, I was rather surprised. They hadn't consulted me on it.

Extended comment seems superfluous. On the one hand, the majority members of the committee deliberately curtailed the investigative process at a point far short of what was necessary and feasible. On the other hand, the committee's minority counsel displayed what at the very least would seem to be a disingenuous attitude toward the work of the committee. The episode is all too typical of the way political considerations influence the development of the facts in a way that results in something less than a full and fair exposition.

The next witness before the subcommittee was Earl Browder, former Secretary of the Communist Party in the United States, who had been implicated by Budenz's testimony in the alleged infiltration of the Institute of Pacific Relations and, specifically, in the plans to use Lattimore to organize writers to follow the Communist line on Far Eastern policy. After sketching his career in the Communist Party, including his ouster as Secretary in 1945 and his expulsion from the Party in 1946, Browder was asked about the use of the IPR for Communist propaganda purposes.

MR. MORGAN   Was any effort made by the Communist Party to employ the Institute of Pacific Relations, and any publications of that organization, that that organization might have, to advance the policy that you say was the policy of the Communist Party with respect to China?

MR. BROWDER   We never considered such a thing as practical, for any serious consideration at all.

MR. MORGAN   Would you say that you did not employ the Institute of Pacific Relations for that?

MR. BROWDER   I would say very definitely that we did not.

MR. MORGAN   Did the Communist Party, to your knowledge, have individuals in the Institute of Pacific Relations or associated with the Institute of Pacific Relations, upon which you relied or depended or employed for the purpose of advancing this policy?

MR. BROWDER   No; it did not.

In answer to questions about Lattimore, Browder denied know-

ing Lattimore or ever having met him. This, of course, was not
inconsistent with the testimony given by Budenz. But Browder
went on to deny that he had ever heard Lattimore's name mentioned in Party circles and that he had ever discussed Lattimore
with anyone in the Communist Party. With specific reference to
the alleged 1937 meeting, Browder denied that any such meeting
had taken place. He also denied ever seeing Lattimore's name or
initials mentioned in any onionskin reports, such as those Budenz
had described, and went on to treat the question of the onionskin
reports in the following categorical terms:

MR. MORGAN   You mean, no such reports were received?
MR. BROWDER   I never heard of such reports, never saw such reports,
   and I doubt the existence of such reports.
MR. MORGAN   Was it customary, Mr. Browder, to have reports made
   in that manner on onionskin paper?
MR. BROWDER   On onionskin paper? Well, I certainly don't deny the
   existence of onionskin paper, in my office and every other office I
   ever had any connection with, usually used for manifold copies of
   letters, and so on, and for elimination of bulk in the storage of
   archives.
MR. MORGAN   What I have in mind, Mr. Browder, is not just the matter of onionskin reports on onionskin paper. I mean, was it customary in the Communist Party to receive reports in which individuals
   were designated by symbols, rather than by name?
MR. BROWDER   No; neither on onionskin nor bond.

Finally, Browder testified that he was familiar with Lattimore's
name, that Lattimore was such a prominent person that if he had
been a Communist, the fact could not have escaped his, Browder's,
attention, but that, on the contrary, Lattimore was known to him
"as a person of anti-Communist views, of a very decided and pro-
found character."

Browder then proceeded to attack Budenz's stature as a Communist. He described Budenz as a mere technician who had nothing to do with policy matters.

MR. BROWDER   Budenz was never anything but a technical man in the
   staff of the *Daily*. He was not a political man.
SENATOR MC MAHON   Didn't he have the title of managing editor?
MR. BROWDER   Yes.
SENATOR MC MAHON   Didn't that title carry with it the usual purposes
   of such a title on the newspaper?

MR. BROWDER   I don't know what the usual purposes of such a title are, but in our paper it means the technical editor.

SENATOR MC MAHON   What do you mean?

MR. BROWDER   The only field in which he was qualified was the technique of newspaper production. He was in charge of copy and so on. I suppose that, in a large modern newspaper, he would be what you would call the copy editor.

SENATOR MC MAHON   He had nothing to do with policy?

MR. BROWDER   No.

SENATOR MC MAHON   You regarded him as a loyal Party member?

MR. BROWDER   We had no reason at that time to question his loyalty, but we did discuss—question his capacity for anything beyond the technical newspaper production.

SENATOR MC MAHON   Was it customary for the contributors to your paper to call at the offices of the *Daily Worker* and leave their material, or was it sent in from time to time?

MR. BROWDER   Both—both.

SENATOR MC MAHON   You said that you had him in a conference for some work to be done on the Roman Catholic policy. What was the nature of that work, if you care to say?

MR. BROWDER   Well, he prided himself very much on his ability to spread communism among the Catholics, and we naturally humored that in hopes that it might develop something through it, and the conferences—

SENATOR MC MAHON   Louder.

MR. BROWDER   Conferences were held at his insistence, to discuss that problem.

SENATOR MC MAHON   He initiated that himself?

MR. BROWDER   Yes. He was the man who was also pressing it, and the necessity and the possibilities of spreading communism among the church members.

Browder's account is obviously at variance with Budenz's in many vital respects. Unlike the testimony of Bella Dodd, his testimony cannot be discounted on the ground of lack of firsthand knowledge. Plainly, either Browder or Budenz was lying.

Browder conceded that he knew Frederick Vanderbilt Field as a Communist, but denied ever having given Field any special missions of the sort described by Budenz, or having participated with Field in conferences relating to infiltration of the IPR and the use of Lattimore as an organizer of pro-Communist writers on Far Eastern policy.

Field followed Browder as a witness. In his prepared statement he denied ever having been associated with Lattimore in any connection except their work in the IPR, with which Field was connected from 1928 to 1940. He denied having had any association with Lattimore as a Communist. With respect to his own affiliation, he informed the committee that he was invoking the privilege against self-incrimination.

In the questioning that followed, Field refused to answer questions about membership in the Communist Party or about his acquaintance with any person but Owen Lattimore. So rigidly did he adhere to this policy that he invoked the privilege against self-incrimination in refusing to say whether or not he knew Dr. Philip Jessup. The committee accused him of acting contemptuously, and an examination of his testimony suggests that it is a fairly clear example of improper invocation of the Fifth Amendment. Curiously enough, he answered all questions about Lattimore with perfect freedom, while declining to answer questions about other persons who, if he was telling the truth about Lattimore, were known to him in the same innocent connection. One is forced to conclude either that Field was committing perjury in his testimony about Lattimore or that he was fashioning his own rules of pertinence with respect to the scope of the committee's inquiry.

His testimony about Lattimore is pretty well summed up in the following passages:

SENATOR TYDINGS   I might ask you again, for emphasis, if you have already answered it—Do you, or do you not of your own knowledge, know whether or not he is a member of the Communist Party?

MR. FIELD   To the very best of my knowledge, Mr. Chairman, Mr. Lattimore is not a member of the Communist Party.

SENATOR TYDINGS   Might I ask you if any time in any of your associations with Mr. Lattimore, in the conduct of the Institute of Pacific Relations, or in the publication of the magazine *Amerasia,* you saw or detected anything that aroused your suspicions that he was writing, not objectively, but—but rather objectively to accomplish a purpose that was not to the best interest of the United States?

MR. FIELD   No, I never did. On the contrary, I spent many years working for this research organization, in association with scholars; and it is quite evident that Professor Lattimore has the reputation of being one of the most outstanding scholars on the Far East in this country. He has a world-wide reputation in this sense.

SENATOR TYDINGS   Now, at any time during your association with this Institute of Pacific Affairs, and your position as chairman, I believe it was, of the editorial board, or on the editorial board of the magazine *Amerasia,* did you or do you know of anyone else who sug-

> gested, connived, or aided in putting Communist articles in that magazine through the medium of Mr. Lattimore?

MR. FIELD   No, I do not, Mr. Chairman.

SENATOR TYDINGS   Do you or do you not know of any time that Mr. Lattimore knowingly aided in the publication of an article that was written, so far as you know, by a Communist?

MR. FIELD   No, I do not, Mr. Chairman.

Field's testimony is inferentially contradictory to Budenz's, but not quite so directly as Browder's, because of his invocation of the Fifth Amendment on questions relating to his own activities, including possible attendance at the famous 1937 meeting. Curiously enough, even though Browder had testified that he knew Field, Field declined to say whether he knew Browder. Field's testimony also contradicts the hearsay account given by Kerley of Huber's attendance at a meeting at Field's house in 1946 at which Lattimore was present. Huber's story is also contradicted, it should be noted, by a telegram from Field's ex-wife stating that she was not and had never been a Communist and that Lattimore had not attended any meeting or party at the Field home in 1946.

The Lattimore phase of the Tydings Committee inquiry was concluded by the reappearance on the witness stand of Lattimore himself. He stated forcefully that the testimony against him came down to no more than the assertions of Budenz, and attacked those assertions in general and in specifics. It will serve no useful purpose to examine Lattimore's testimony in detail. It presented to one favorably disposed toward his cause a highly convincing defense of the integrity of his professional life. It was obviously so greeted by those who heard it. But to an entirely detached observer, there are disturbing overtones here and there that suggest somthing less than complete candor about his awareness of the Communist tendencies of some of those with whom he necessarily worked on Far Eastern problems. Like Budenz, Lattimore appeared to suffer from a complete inability to admit that he had ever been wrong, mistaken, uninformed, or naive. In the context of the Tydings Committee hearings, that jarring note is struck only occasionally. But it was to become a dominant theme in the IPR hearings two years later.

One final word about the Tydings Committee hearings. It became fashionable in some quarters in the years immediately following these hearings to refer to them as a "whitewash." An examination of the whole record does not seem to me to support that assertion if by it is meant a willful blindness toward available evidence that would tend to support the conclusion that Lattimore was a Communist agent. There was certainly enough opportunity to develop whatever evidence on that score was available. It does not appear from the record that there was any suppression of evidence, and one may be quite confident that the vigorous partisanship of the minority members of the committee would have resulted in exposure of any efforts to camouflage or conceal unpalatable truths.

That does not mean that the conduct of the hearings was immune to criticism. It was not. The questioning of witnesses showed lack of preparation. The manner in which the testimony was brought forth was chaotic. That is one of the great weaknesses of the Congressional inquiry as a fact-finding process, particularly when it is operating under as much pressure as this one was. The spring of 1950, immediately preceding the outbreak of the Korean War, was hardly a time when members of the Senate Foreign Relations Committe had nothing else on their minds but an investigation of Senator McCarthy's allegations about the State Department. But the fact that the diffusion of effort is readily explicable does not detract from its unfortunate effect. These hearings sprawled over a period of four months. There were long adjournments. There was little continuity. During the hearings, no one concerned appeared to have mastered the record in a way that would permit the effective examination of witnesses.

Two aspects of the committee's conduct deserve special criticism. The first is the failure to recall Budenz to the stand after the testimony of Dodd, Field, and Browder. Both in fairness to him and in the interest of sharpening the issues, he should have been interrogated on the many points of conflict between his testimony and theirs. The second is the committee's refusal to allow counsel for the minority to participate in the questioning of witnesses. No individual senator had the time adequately to prepare a line of questioning, and the questions directed by the various members of the committee demonstrated this weakness. The committee's chief counsel, Mr. Morgan, functioned with a conspicuous degree of fairness, considering the political pressure he was undoubtedly under. But the minority had no effective voice. One may surmise that the majority's decision not to permit questions by minority counsel was due in large part to the feeling that the gentleman who occupied that post, Mr. Robert Morris, was a close associate of Senator McCarthy's, and that the disruption that giving him his head would have entailed was not something they were willing to undergo. Whatever the tactical motivations for this decision, it made the conduct of the hearings appear something less than impartial, and as we have noted before, in matters of this sort the appearance of fairness may be as important as the reality.

IV

The second group of hearings in which the case of Budenz versus Lattimore was tried out in the public record began in July 1951, only a year after the conclusion of the Tydings Committee hearings. It was a year of many memorable events, including the beginning of the Korean struggle, and on the domestic scene it was a year in which the issue of communism in American life continued to make both news and votes. Senator Tydings, who headed the inquiry that had exonerated Lattimore, fell at the polls in November 1950 before the charge that he was "soft on Communism." His defeat was a sign of the mood of the times.

The IPR hearings grew out of the seizure by the Senate Internal Security Subcommittee of the files of the Institute of Pacific Relations, which turned out, on examination, to contain much data suggesting substantial influence by Communists on the work of the Institute. The inquiry was a far more wide-ranging one than that undertaken by the Tydings Committee, which was not itself (as has been earlier suggested) a model of concentration. Once again, however, the opposing figures of Louis Budenz and Owen Lattimore occupied the center of the stage.

This time, Budenz had his innings first. He testified before the committee on August 22 and October 1, 1951. There was little new in his testimony. What was new was the manner of his questioning by this committee, which was in complete contrast to the tone of his interrogation by the Tydings Committee. Clearly, the attempt was to build his stature as a witness and thus to characterize his information as being highly reliable. This time, the objections to his testimony as hearsay were met head-on at the beginning of the questioning, and this seeming disadvantage was turned to advantage.

MR. MORRIS   At the outset, Mr. Budenz, were you in a position in the Communist Party where you would have access to more secrets, to the identity of more people, than the ordinary Communist?

MR. BUDENZ   Most decidedly. Indeed, more than the normal member of the National Committee.

MR. MORRIS   Why is that, Mr. Budenz?

MR. BUDENZ   As managing editor of the *Daily Worker,* it was essential that I know the various delicate turns and twists of the line; not only of the line but of the emphasis of the line in the particular period of time.

THE CHAIRMAN   When you say "line" in that respect, what do you mean, Mr. Budenz?

MR. BUDENZ   I mean the Communist viewpoint at that particular moment, the Communist objective. This has nothing to do fundamentally with the Communist philosophy, except that it is an expression of it in action during a period of time. And that had to be emphasized in the *Daily Worker,* not merely as to what the line was but as to its various delicate nuances, if I may use that term. The *Daily Worker* is not a daily paper in the normal sense of the word. It is the telegraph agency of the conspiracy giving directives to the conspirators.

MR. MORRIS   On individuals?

MR. BUDENZ   On individuals likewise. It was a matter of political life and death to have a correct viewpoint of the various individuals who were dealt with by the *Daily Worker.*

．　．　．

SENATOR FERGUSON   And it had to be accurate for you to carry on; is that correct?

MR. BUDENZ   Communist information among themselves is absolutely accurate. It must be. It is the foundation of their work.

SENATOR FERGUSON   You see, we hear a lot said about so much evidence in this conspiracy being hearsay. And I am trying to get at the point as to what weight this committee can give to hearsay of this nature. Are you able to tell the committee now that in your opinion this is, let us say, a hearsay that deserves consideration by a committee?

MR. BUDENZ   This is an official communication between leaders of the conspiracy.

SENATOR FERGUSON   Among themselves?

MR. BUDENZ   That is right.

Although this interrogation of Budenz covered the same accusations against Lattimore that had been covered in his interrogation by the Tydings Committee, the presentation resembled more closely the development of a prosecutor's case than an attempt to evaluate the accuracy of a story. These hearings, unlike the Tydings Committee hearings, provided no counterbalance at all to the dominant tone of complete confidence in Budenz's veracity. For example, the evidence on the onionskin documents was given without the slightest indication that it had been seriously questioned by witnesses heard by the Tydings Committee. The only questions asked related to whether Lattimore's designation in these documents was an indication of his importance in the Communist movement.

Although the testimony adverse to Budenz in the Tydings Committee hearings was not specifically referred to, Budenz's testimony before the McCarran Committee suggested at several points an effort to repair the damage that had been done by what was said earlier. For example, Budenz stated that the use of onionskin documents terminated in 1940 or 1941. He had not so stated before the Tydings Committee. Whether this was a fresh piece of recollection we cannot, of course, judge. It served, among other purposes, the useful office of undercutting the testimony of Dr. Bella Dodd that she had never seen such documents, since she did not, by her own account, join the Communist Party until 1943. Rather, it would have served that function if any reference had been made to Dr. Dodd's impeaching testimony. There was none, nor was there any reference to the even more damaging testimony of Earl Browder.

In the friendly and deferential atmosphere of the IPR hearings, Budenz became considerably more expansive and less guarded in his statements. For example, he had told the Tydings Committee that Communists had infiltrated the IPR to a considerable extent. Under the friendly questioning of Mr. Robert Morris, counsel for the subcommittee, Budenz took a more categorical position:

MR. MORRIS   Now, Mr. Budenz, from the eyes of the then editor of the *Daily Worker* and a member of the National Committee of the Communist Party, what was your opinion of the Institute of Pacific Relations? What did you know of the Institute of Pacific Relations?

MR. BUDENZ   What I know is perhaps the better way to put it, because I was at Politburo meetings and in consultation with members of the Politburo constantly. As a matter of fact, day by day I was in consultation. And frequently I was at Politburo meetings because of my position. The Politburo in these discussions declared the Institute of Pacific Relations repeatedly to be a captive organization, completely under control of the Communist Party.

MR. MORRIS   You say the Institute of Pacific Relations was a captive organization?

MR. BUDENZ   That is correct.

MR. MORRIS   Completely under the control of the Communist Party?

MR. BUDENZ   That is correct.

He related a colorful anecdote to emphasize the closeness of the relationship between the Communist Party and the IPR:

MR. MORRIS   Mr. Budenz, would you say there was a cell, a Communist cell, operating within the Institute of Pacific Relations?

MR. BUDENZ   Yes, sir. As a matter of fact, Alexander Trachtenberg, in these Political Bureau discussions, emphasizing the importance of the work of this cell, described the Institute of Pacific Relations as "The little red schoolhouse for teaching certain people in Washington how to think with the Soviet Union in the Far East."

MR. MORRIS   I wonder if you would tell us who Alexander Trachtenberg is, Mr. Budenz?

MR. BUDENZ   Alexander Trachtenberg is one of the most important members of the Communist conspiracy in this country. He is the cultural commissar of the Communists in this country. He has published all the authorized works of Marx, Engels, Lenin, and Stalin, and all other works authorized by the Marx-Engels-Lenin Institute in Moscow. Through his hands these works have to go. He is technically the head of International Publishers, but he is vested with much more authority, with reference to the *Daily Worker*. He is in charge of the whole cultural work of the Party, or at least he was when I was in the Party.

MR. MORRIS   And is it your testimony that the Communists use the Institute of Pacific Relations to influence foreign policy?

MR. BUDENZ   That is right.

SENATOR FERGUSON   Is there any doubt in your mind, Mr. Budenz, that when a man like Trachtenberg is speaking about this being an educational process, this IPR, here in Washington—and I take it that is what is meant by the "little red schoolhouse"—that this was an actual fact, that he knew what he was talking about, because of his tie-in in the whole Communist activity?

MR. BUDENZ   Yes, sir; and because he knew it through the reports which were received from the Communists within the Institute of Pacific Relations, largely through Frederick Vanderbilt Field.

Note that Budenz gave stature to the "little red schoolhouse" characterization by emphasizing the importance of Trachtenberg. Throughout the record of these hearings there is ample indication of Trachtenberg's key role in the formulation and dissemination of Party ideology. It is surprising that Budenz did not emphasize Trachtenberg's role—indeed, he hardly mentioned it—in his testimony before the Tydings Committee. One wonders why the "little red schoolhouse" anecdote lay dormant in his mind for so long.

In Budenz's testimony on the relationship between Party membership and the activities of so-called Communist-front organizations, an exchange occurred which is illustrative of the tenor of the questioning in this hearing:

MR. BUDENZ   As I have said, to my knowledge 95 percent of the members of the Communist-front organizations are actually Communists, and the other 10 percent are thrown in there to give that appearance or that uncertainty of connection with the Communist movement.

MR. SOURWINE   Pardon me, Mr. Budenz. You have 105 percent. Will you settle for 90 and 10?

MR. BUDENZ   I would say it was 5 and 95 percent.

Mr. Sourwine was counsel to the parent Senate Judiciary Committee and shared with Mr. Morris, special counsel to the subcommittee, the conduct of the IPR hearings. His tone throughout, like Mr. Morris's, was one of violent hostility to witnesses accused of Communist affiliation, and of almost obsequious deference to their accusers. His action on the occasion quoted above is characteristic. He contented himself with tidying up Budenz's arithmetic and did not ask (nor did anyone else) for the basis of Budenz's rather surprising statement. As we shall see, Mr. Sourwine was not so complaisant in questioning witnesses whom he regarded as hostile.

The most important new development in Budenz's testimony was the elaboration on a subject that had received only passing mention during the Tydings Committee hearings. This was Vice-President Henry Wallace's mission to China in 1944, on which he was accompanied by Owen Lattimore and John Carter Vincent. Ironically enough, this new aspect of Budenz's testimony occasioned a far sharper challenge to his credibility than anything that occurred in the more skeptical atmosphere of the Tydings Committee hearings. Although its factual setting is complex, the controversy is worth examining.

It started, quietly enough, with a repetition of the charge that in 1944 Stachel had told Budenz to consider Lattimore a Communist. This time, however, the occasion for that remark was more fully described.

MR. BUDENZ   1944, the trip of Vice-President Henry Wallace. I don't know whether I can emphasize the importance of this trip to the Communists as much as it should be. It received a very great attention from the Politburo and it was constantly brought to my attention by Jack Stachel as the representative of the Politburo as a very important mission, which would redound to the benefit of the Communist cause in the Far East.

In that respect a great deal of dependence was placed on Owen Lattimore, whom I was told by Mr. Stachel at that time to consider a Communist—

MR. MORRIS   What do you mean, "consider a Communist"? Is that a technical word you are using?

MR. BUDENZ   That was a technical term we used which meant he was an authority from the Communist viewpoint. He was a Marxist authority.

MR. MORRIS   Was that warning given to you by anyone else at that time?

MR. BUDENZ   Well, there were many other references of similar character. I remember specifically Stachel's because my relations with him were very close and he was constantly giving me these instructions.

I do know that similar statements were made within the Politburo itself by other members in connection with Wallace's trip.

. . .

MR. BUDENZ   . . . Now, in order to be advised of such things as that, we were to rely on anything Lattimore might say or do that we would be aware of.

. . .

MR. SOURWINE   You mean that in connection with the Wallace mission the word was passed by the use of the phrase "consider him as a Communist," that with respect to that mission Mr. Lattimore might not be setting the line; he was giving the line, and he was interpreting that mission in Communist terms?

MR. BUDENZ   That's correct. He was a representative of the Party in the Wallace mission.

SENATOR SMITH   He was sort of a VIP in the movement?

MR. BUDENZ   That's right.

The emphasis was still, however, on the significance of what Stachel said about Lattimore rather than the significance of the work in which Lattimore was engaged. Later on the same day, Budenz charged for the first time that the Wallace mission was guided by the Communist viewpoint, naming Lattimore and John Carter Vincent, a State Department specialist in Far Eastern affairs, as the Communist agents who directed the Wallace mission toward Communist objectives. It should be noted that Budenz was asked about Vincent during an executive session of the Tydings Committee and at that time stated that he was not prepared to identify Vincent as a Communist.

After this testimony by Budenz, the newspaper columnist Joseph Alsop charged that the attack on the Wallace mission was, to his personal knowledge, unfounded. At the time of the mission, Alsop was aide to General Clair Chennault, Commander of the U.S. Fourteenth Air Force in China. He was in daily contact with Wallace and his aides while Wallace was in Kunming. Alsop wrote that the principal result of the Wallace mission was a cabled recommendation to President Roosevelt that the American commander in China, General Stilwell, be replaced. Stilwell was violently hostile to Chiang Kai-shek and the Nationalist Government and favorably disposed toward the Chinese Communists, whom he regarded as the only effective force that could be deployed against the Japanese, at this time everywhere triumphant on the Chinese mainland. This recommendation, which was followed by the replacement of Stilwell with Wedemeyer, was regarded by Alsop as a "profoundly anti-Communist act" which clearly demonstrated that the Wallace mission was not Communist-directed and that John Carter Vincent, who concurred in the recommendation, was not a Communist.

After the publication of the Alsop column, the committee recalled Budenz to the witness stand for the specific purpose of reviewing his testimony about the Wallace mission. He was shown the text of the Kunming cables and asked to comment on them in his role as an expert on the Communist Party line. First, he reviewed those portions of the cables that reported on Wallace's conversations with Chiang and on the general situation in China at the time. The following passage shows the tenor of his examination:

MR. MORRIS   Would you read each paragraph that you address yourself to, Mr. Budenz?

MR. BUDENZ   Yes. The first paragraph is in message I: "The discussion between the representatives of the Chinese Communists and those of the Chinese Government are taking place in Chungking, but the attitude of Chiang Kai-shek toward the problem is so imbued with prejudice that I can see little prospect for satisfactory long-term settlement."

MR. MORRIS   Is that an anti-Communist expression, Mr. Budenz?

MR. BUDENZ   Most decidedly not. It helps the Communists. If some person visiting the United States, of a diplomatic character, were to be represented to the American authorities today as prejudiced against the Communists, that would be of a kind, except that in this case Chiang Kai-shek has had civil war on his hands for a number of years, and Chiang Kai-shek's experience shows that he could not trust the Communists, and events proved he was correct.

MR. MORRIS   Will you address yourself to the second point in that cable, Mr. Budenz?

MR. BUDENZ   The second point is the sentence: "I emphasized to him the importance of reaching an understanding with Russia." This was the first point in the Communist drive at that time, in their literature and in the discussions with the Politburo. The necessity for what they called Russian-Chinese friendship.

And that was an authority purchasable, when you come realistically to consider it, only by the Chinese Communists coming to the front in China. That is what they understood.

Incidentally, this isn't exactly what the Communists were stressing at that time.

SENATOR FERGUSON   You feel no nation that is anti-Communist could have friendly relations with Russia?

MR. BUDENZ   I think history has proved it is impossible.

SENATOR FERGUSON   So a friendly relationship between China and Russia, real friendly relations, would have to be on the basis of both being Communists?

MR. BUDENZ   That is correct.

The implication of this testimony was that Wallace was led by his pro-Communist advisers, Vincent and Lattimore, to take a pro-Communist position in reporting to the President. Without anticipating later testimony that raised some doubt about the accuracy of Budenz's conclusion, it may be pointed out that in mid-1944 the proposition that a Sino-Russian understanding was vital to the successful prosecution of the war against Japan was hardly the exclusive property of the Communists.

After reviewing the reportorial portions of the Kunming cables, Budenz turned his attention to the recommendation that Stilwell be replaced by Wedemeyer. He did not discuss Stilwell's well-known anti-Chiang and pro-Chinese Communist proclivities, but instead attempted to reconcile the facts with his position by asserting that the American Communist line regarded the replacement as a "good compromise."

MR. BUDENZ   There is also a reference here to General Wedemeyer.

MR. MORRIS   Yes. Will you address yourself to that, Mr. Budenz?

MR. BUDENZ   Yes, sir.

General Wedemeyer, when he first came into public attention, was not opposed by the Communists. Indeed, the Communists felt that the compromise made with Wedemeyer was a good compromise. They were not opposed to Wedemeyer. They thought he was nonpolitical.

. . .

MR. BUDENZ   The Communists were very much opposed to General Chennault and didn't want him in the picture at all.

. . .

MR. BUDENZ   . . . What I wish to say is that General Wedemeyer in 1944 was not unacceptable to the Communists. Indeed, to a certain degree, they thought he was a good compromise, since it excluded General Chennault.

Budenz's testimony on the Communist view of the Wallace mission was summarized in this exchange with Senator Ferguson near the conclusion of his testimony:

SENATOR FERGUSON   I would just go back now to the first part that I asked about.

Again, you have testified before this committee and gave your reasons this morning for your belief that your testimony was true and accurate, the whole truth and nothing but the truth.

Do you now again say that it was?

MR. BUDENZ   I say it with more assurance than ever, because these documents I presented, as I have said, are only part of what could have been presented to this committee, and they confirm my contention, which was that the Communist Party Politburo, from its vantage point, thought that the Wallace Mission to Soviet Asia and China was being properly guided and would end in the way they wished it would end.

We have to appreciate what that objective of theirs was, knowing their objective during that particular period of time.

SENATOR FERGUSON   Do you feel their objective was carried out?

MR. BUDENZ   Absolutely, it was carried out.

On the basis of this conclusory statement, Alsop wrote to the committee asserting that Budenz's testimony was untruthful and requesting an opportunity to be heard. On October 18, 1951, he appeared before the committee. The substance of his testimony will be considered shortly. First, however, a word must be said about the difficulties of extracting that substance. Rarely in the

annals of Congressional inquiry has a witness been subjected to
so much badgering. Indeed, the most striking parallel is probably
the treatment of Lattimore himself by the same committee. Every
possible effort was made, both by counsel and by the members of
the committee, to blunt the edge of Alsop's testimony and to minimize the conflict between his firsthand account of what occurred
at Kunming and Budenz's testimony as to why the Wallace mission
was pro-Communist. Among many examples that might be cited,
the following exchange between Alsop and Mr. Sourwine illustrates the tendentious nature of the questioning and the enormous
effort made to prevent the creation of a clear-cut issue of credibility
between Budenz and Alsop:

MR. SOURWINE   If you are challenging Mr. Budenz' statement that the
Politburo was satisfied with the guidance given Mr. Wallace, is it
not necessary, in order for you to successfully challenge that, to
show that there was nothing accomplished by Mr. Lattimore and/or
Mr. Vincent which was in favor of the Communists.
    Do you feel you can successfully challenge Mr. Budenz' state-
ment by showing that Mr. Wallace did something that was not in
complete accord with the Communist line?
MR. ALSOP   I think I can successfully challenge Mr. Budenz' statement
by showing that the chief result—
MR. SOURWINE   No, answer my question.
MR. ALSOP   I am trying to answer your question.
MR. SOURWINE   You are not trying to answer it; you are trying to
evade it.
MR. ALSOP   I am not trying to evade it. If you will allow me to complete my sentence, I believe you will find I am trying to answer it.
SENATOR SMITH   Will the reporter read the question back?
    (The question was read back by the reporter.)
MR. ALSOP   I submit to you, Mr. Chairman, that if you can show the
main result of the Wallace mission was a profoundly anti-Communist
act, you successfully challenge Mr. Budenz' evidence.
MR. SOURWINE   Not unless you show that everything Mr. Wallace did
was the result of the influence of Mr. Vincent or Mr. Lattimore. If
Mr. Wallace did anything independently on his own, if he was not
a complete stooge of the Communists or a Communist agent—and
no one is alleging that and no one has alleged it—then what you
have just said is not the logical fact.
MR. ALSOP   Mr. Vincent participated and joined in this recommendation for the dismissal of General Stilwell. This was the extent of
guidance that Mr. Vincent gave Mr. Wallace.
MR. SOURWINE   That is different testimony. If that was the complete
extent of the guidance Mr. Vincent gave Mr. Wallace, then you are
coming around to the theory which was advanced, to wit, that there

was nothing accomplished which would have been pleasing to the Communists.

MR. ALSOP   If you will excuse me, Mr. Sourwine, I am saying what was accomplished with Mr. Vincent's participation and concurrence was profoundly displeasing to the Communists.

MR. SOURWINE   Put it this way: If Mr. Vincent through his influence on Mr. Wallace accomplished anything which was pleasing to the Communists, then Mr. Budenz' statement cannot be said to be perjury. Is that not accurate?

MR. ALSOP   Could you repeat that? You are getting so complicated, Mr. Sourwine, I did not understand your question.

SENATOR SMITH   I am certain I do not understand either one of you. Do you want the question read back, Mr. Sourwine?

MR. SOURWINE   I do not desire it.

SENATOR SMITH   Will the reporter read it back?

(The question was read by the reporter.)

MR. ALSOP   I would not say that that was accurate because it is a substantial disproof of Mr. Budenz' statement that Mr. Vincent guided Mr. Wallace toward the Communist objective. The principal guidance that Mr. Vincent gave Mr. Wallace was toward a profoundly anti-Communist objective.

MR. SOURWINE   There was no named objective, was there, Mr. Alsop?

MR. ALSOP   Well, Mr. Sourwine, what I am trying to show is that the main result of Mr. Wallace's mission was profoundly anti-Communist.

I think if you will permit me to proceed with the presentation of the very large quantity of documentation that I have, you will be convinced.

MR. SOURWINE   *Do you contend that Mr. Wallace's mission and its results were controlled entirely and shaped entirely by Mr. Vincent?*

MR. ALSOP   I do not so contend. I think Mr. Budenz grossly exaggerated in that report.

MR. SOURWINE   *If Mr. Vincent did not control what Mr. Wallace did, then nothing that Mr. Wallace did can be attributed to Mr. Vincent's influence, can it?*

MR. ALSOP   That is a question to me, Mr. Sourwine?

MR. SOURWINE   Yes, sir.

MR. ALSOP   I cannot possibly agree with that because Mr. Vincent did in fact join in guiding Mr. Wallace or influencing Mr. Wallace toward a profoundly anti-Communist act. This is the essence of the whole situation.*

This exchange, culminating in what we might call the "Sourwine fork," may be a prime example of debater's technique, but is surely not what ought to be expected in an impartial fact-finding inquiry.

---

* Italics mine.

Whether Mr. Sourwine's efforts were successful can be determined only after an examination of the substance of Alsop's testimony, to which we now turn.

We can briefly dispose of the issue of the reportorial portions of the Kunming cable, which Budenz characterized as being pro-Communist. Budenz implied that this material was inserted in the cables because of the pro-Communist influence of Vincent and Lattimore. Alsop testified that Lattimore had nothing to do with the cables and that, far from being pro-Communist, the cables simply contained an accurate description of the situation in China at the time and contained no statement which indicated a pro-Communist bias. So far, there might be thought to be nothing to choose between these opposing contentions, both being based on the opinions of their respective proponents. But Alsop went further and asserted that he himself was the author of the passages that Budenz characterized as pro-Communist.

The more important issue relates to the recommendation that General Stilwell be replaced by General Wedemeyer. It will be recalled that Budenz testified that this was viewed by the Communists as a "good compromise," since their objective was to prevent the appointment of General Chennault in General Stilwell's place. With respect to this assertion, as demonstrative of the malignly pro-Communist nature of the advice that John Carter Vincent allegedly gave to Wallace, Alsop's testimony can only be characterized as devastating. After testifying that Vincent strongly concurred in the view that Wallace should recommend Stilwell's dismissal, Alsop testified as follows:

MR. ALSOP   I also have a rather vivid recollection as to how General Wedemeyer came to be suggested for Stilwell's replacement. In brief, Mr. Wallace's first idea was to recommend General Chennault, of whom the Generalissimo had spoken to him highly and by whom he had been much impressed.

I looked to Mr. Vincent, hoping that he might interpose some objection to this suggestion of my own boss, but he went along with Mr. Wallace. That is why I remember Mr. Vincent's view on this thing.

So, it was left to me, who had served General Chennault since before Pearl Harbor, to oppose General Chennault's nomination as commander in chief in China. I had two reasons for doing so.

First, only General Chennault knew how to run an air force on a shoestring. Our shoestring was getting very thin. In those days the Fourteenth Air Force was the sole force in being to prevent thorough military disintegration in China. As Mr. Wallace later put it in this cable, General Chennault was needed on the job he was doing.

Second, and more important, General Stilwell had gone to very great lengths to blacken General Chennault's name at the Pentagon. Even if President Roosevelt decided to act on Wallace's recommendation, there was no hope at all that the President could ever persuade the Army and Air Staff to put General Chennault in Stilwell's place.

General Wedemeyer, who had great influence at the Pentagon, later I believe recommended General Chennault's promotion to lieutenant general, and it was refused.

The recommendation to recall Stillwell was certain to make enough row all by itself. If this recommendation was coupled with a nomination of General Chennault, the roof was quite sure to blow off. Hence, Mr. Wallace's idea was self-defeating.

Mr. Wallace and Mr. Vincent accepted these practical arguments of mine as being compelling, and thus it was I who "excluded General Chennault," to quote Mr. Budenz, and meanwhile the alleged Communist, Mr. Vincent, in fact approved the suggestion of this man whom "the Communists were very much opposed to and did not want at all," to quote Mr. Budenz again.

With General Chennault out of the picture, General Wedemeyer, whom I had seen in action when he visited Chungking in his then capacity as Lord Louis Mountbatten's deputy, was at length decided on. Thus Mr. Wallace's Kunming cable was at last roughed out in this discussion with Wallace, Vincent, and me. We drafted it together. I had a typewriter in the house and did the typing.

After Mr. Wallace signed it, the cable was sent through the consulate in Kunming, if I remember correctly. Mr. Wallace does not know how it was sent, as far as I recall. I took the signed draft off.

This was the way the accused man, Mr. Vincent, "guided" Mr. Wallace "along the paths" of the Party line.

Again I ask the committee to weigh Mr. Budenz' wholly unsupported testimony as to Mr. Vincent against these facts which I have presented.

Again I say it is not I who convicts Mr. Budenz of untruth; it is the facts that convict him.

The committee was not impressed with Alsop's assertion that the events he narrated demonstrated that Budenz had falsely accused John Carter Vincent of being a Communist. The ensuing questioning brought out the obvious point that Alsop had no personal knowledge whether Vincent was a Communist or not. Senator Smith of North Carolina then commented as follows:

SENATOR SMITH   I think you have answered it, and I think it is all right if that is what you said. Mr. Budenz made a statement. As I understood it, you challenged it, but now you say you did not have any personal knowledge of it, so that leaves it just where it was.

The implication is clear: There is no way to refute the testimony of Budenz when he says that X is a Communist. Budenz's testimony is inherently superior because he was once a Communist himself. The point is clearly made in another exchange between Alsop and Senator Smith.

SENATOR SMITH   You are correct that you could not prove that he was not a Communist, but Mr. Budenz, assuming he was truthful when he testified that Mr. Vincent was a Communist, could come nearer knowing if he himself was a member and they worked together than you could come near not knowing.

MR. ALSOP   Mr. Chairman, you are a former president, I believe, of the American Bar Association. What would be your judgment? Unsupported allegation for which not one shred of documentary evidence has been introduced stands on one side, and on the other side there is a mass of documentary evidence that the man behaved in the most contrary manner possible to that indicated by the unsupported allegation.

SENATOR SMITH   That is a matter of judgment, but if Mr. Budenz knew for a fact that he and Mr. Vincent were Communists, that they belonged to the same group, they swapped information, they consulted about Communist matters, whatever they did—I am not saying what is or is not because I do not know—but if Mr. Budenz said he was, people may not believe Mr. Budenz, you may not believe him and others may not believe him, but that is some evidence, at least, that Mr. Vincent was, according to what he said.

MR. ALSOP   I say the overwhelming weight of the evidence is against Mr. Budenz.

SENATOR SMITH   That is your judgment. It may be mine.

Despite the deference and solicitude with which Budenz was treated in the IPR hearings, the conflict between his testimony and that of Alsop (a presumably disinterested witness) produces a feeling of doubt. That doubt may not extend to his sincerity, although some may think that too is questionable, but it does encompass the important issue of his knowledgeability. The residual impression is that on this occasion Budenz may have been too eager to opine on a matter about which his information was incomplete and inaccurate. Since no one has come forward to challenge Alsop's account of what took place at Kunming, and since his testimony has been in substance corroborated by that of the other two principals, Henry Wallace and John Carter Vincent, it seems safe to conclude that it is an accurate description of what happened. If that is the case, it seems at the very least that the Communist hierarchy in New York in mid-1944, observing from afar the events in China, was mistaken about who its friends were. Whether it demonstrates any more than that about the accuracy or sincerity of Budenz's recollection will probably remain a matter of surmise.

It would take us far afield from this examination of the testimony of Budenz to consider in detail the interrogation of Lattimore by the Internal Security Subcommittee. That interrogation did not have much to do with Budenz's charges, but instead ranged over Lattimore's entire carer in Far Eastern affairs. Nonetheless, a few general comments about Lattimore's examination may be in order.

The dominant impression is of the complete breakdown of any orderly procedure of interrogation. The atmosphere of mutual hostility was so strong that the simplest of matters took page after page of question and answer to develop. There seems little question that the subcommittee and its counsel did everything in their power to harass and browbeat Lattimore and that he, in his turn, did everything in his power to express contempt and distrust for the operations of the subcommittee. It was not an edifying spectacle.

Matters got off to a bad start when Lattimore released the text of his prepared statement to the press before he began to testify. The statement contained a number of assertions that could easily be taken as questioning the subcommittee's good faith. Lattimore's appearance before the subcommitte opened with Senator McCarran's denunciation of the prepared statement. Lattimore was then permitted to read the statement into the record. "Permitted" may not be quite the right word, however. So frequent were the interruptions that often several pages of the printed record are filled with exchanges that separated the reading of one sentence in the prepared statement from another. The statement could probably have been read in its entirety in about two hours. Three full days, 223 pages of the printed record of the hearings, were consumed in the process.

In all, Lattimore was on the witness stand for 13 days and the record of his interrogation occupies 782 pages of the printed hearings. Three impressions emerge from a perusal of this material and hundreds of pages of other testimony bearing on matters covered in the interrogation of Lattimore. The first is of the enormous complexity of the subject. A definitive evaluation would require an encylopedic knowledge of Far Eastern affairs during the period from 1930 to 1950, plus a careful examination of everything said and written on the subject not only by Lattimore but also by every other contributor to the IPR publication *Pacific Affairs* and by every other scholar, journalist, and commentator who wrote on the subject. The job, if it had to be done, was one for a team of social scientists, not for a Congressional committee or, indeed, for any other trier of fact.

The second impression is of the extreme selectivity, bordering on unfairness, of the subcommittee in adducing evidence to document its case that Lattimore was a sympathizer with and promoter of Communist interests. For there can be no doubt that the committee had a case. This was not an attempt to inquire into the facts and reach a conclusion but rather an attempt to marshal facts so as to fit a predetermined conclusion. In this respect, the IPR inquiry appears, on balance, to have erred far more grievously than the Tydings Committee, although, as we have seen, that inquiry is open to criticism on the same score.

The third impression is concerned with Lattimore's conduct. Although the circumstances were trying in the extreme, there seems little doubt that Lattimore brought a great deal of trouble on himself by trying to launch a counterattack in the form of an assault on the committee's integrity. Leaving aside any question of principle involved in this kind of maneuver, it was certainly poor tactics. Furthermore, this belligerence was accompanied by some evasiveness and lack of candor under pressure of questioning. The combination is not a very attractive one.

A fair reading of all this material does not, in my judgment, come even close to substantiating the McCarthy-Budenz charges against Lattimore. What it does reveal is the picture of a self-assured amateur politico and inveterate busybody whose views extended over a wider area than his knowledge and who, while transparently not of the temperament to accept a "line" from the

Communists or anyone else, was more often than not to be found advocating positions on Far Eastern policy with which the Communists were in accord.

This judgment is in marked contrast to the conclusions of both the Tydings Committee and the IPR Committee, although it more nearly approaches the former than the latter. Pertinent extracts from both are given below. Their significance, for our purposes, is less a matter of which one was "right" than it is to demonstrate how easy it is for much the same evidence to be varyingly interpreted, in ways that depend on the bias of the observer.

The Tydings Committee concluded:

We find no evidence to support the charge that Owen Lattimore is the "top Russian spy" or, for that matter, any other sort of spy. Even the testimony of Louis F. Budenz, if given the fullest weight and import, could establish no more than the Communists used Lattimore to project a propaganda line anent China.
. . . We do not find that Mr. Lattimore's writings follow the Communist or any other line, save as his very consistent position on the Far East may be called the Lattimore line.
. . . Perhaps in many of his contacts, Mr. Lattimore has not exercised the discretion which our knowledge of Communism in 1950 indicates would have been wise, but we are impelled to comment that in no instance has Mr. Lattimore on the evidence before us been shown to have knowingly associated with Communists.

. . .

We would be remiss in not commenting on the manner in which the charges against Owen Lattimore have been presented. As in the case of other phases of our inquiry, we have seen a distortion of the facts of such a magnitude as to be truly alarming. Unfortunately, until now, it has been largely these distortions that have been before the American people.

The IPR Committee concluded:

Owen Lattimore was, from some time beginning in the 1930's, a conscious articulate instrument of the Soviet conspiracy.

As might be expected, the two committees also differed sharply in their evaluation of Budenz's testimony. The Tydings Committee set forth a careful summary of the Budenz charges and of the contradictory evidence adduced by Browder, Dodd, and others. Their general conclusions were summed up in the following paragraph in the report:

The subcommittee notes that the testimony of Mr. Budenz is in the nature of hearsay in that his evidence against Lattimore is founded on what he states he was told by or learned from others, identified as Communists. The subcommittee also notes that only since this investigation and the publicity concerning Lattimore in connection therewith has Budenz given information to the FBI concerning Lattimore, even though Budenz has been reporting for several years to the FBI on various Communist activities and personalities. We feel that there is significance in the fact that Budenz, at the time of preparing his *Collier's* article, to which reference has been made, did not present Lattimore in the same light that he did at the time he testified before us. Similarly in the case of Haldore Hanson, Budenz admitted that Hanson was named by him as a Communist for the first time during the course of our proceedings. Both Lattimore and Hanson would seem to have been such logical subjects for a report by Budenz to some Government agency that his failure to make such a report is necessarily puzzling, particularly in view of the fact that he reported them after the extensive publicity given the matter in the course of the McCarthy charges. While we understand that Mr. Budenz may have been unable to furnish detailed background material, it is regretted that he did not at least submit the names of these individuals to an agency of the Government before our proceedings. We recognize that Budenz has been used as a witness by the Government in other cases where his testimony was not hearsay and was corroborated. Here, of course, his testimony is hearsay and corroboration is, to a very great extent, lacking. This observation is necessarily not a reflection upon Mr. Budenz' veracity inasmuch as his testimony related to what he was told by Communists about whose veracity there is some doubt.

The IPR Committee, on the other hand, did not undertake an evaluation of Budenz's testimony. Indeed, the references to his testimony in the 226-page report are surprisingly sparse. When he is referred to, there is merely a statement of what he said with no attempt to provide an appraisal. Surprisingly enough, there is no extended treatment of the hotly contested issue of the Wallace mission, which has been described above. While the incident is referred to in a brief passage, there is no suggestion that Budenz's testimony was in any way challenged, and Alsop's name is not even mentioned. From this omission, and from the report's failure to deal at all with the problems created by the Budenz testimony, it seems clear that Budenz's testimony, even when challenged, was taken by the committee as expressing immutable truth.

Perhaps the major problem raised by the testimony of Louis Budenz is what he means when he calls a person a Communist. Once it is recognized that the source of his information is almost always hearsay rather than direct knowledge, it becomes apparent that much turns on where he gained his information. An air of formality and precision is lent to his identification of Communist affiliation by the frequently repeated assertion that his knowledge was derived from "official reports." This conjures up a picture of documentation, or at the very least, of some formality about the occasion on which the information was acquired. But on closer inspection it becomes apparent that an "official report" may be anything that one Communist says to another, or, at least, anything that one of Budenz's superiors in the Communist movement said to him. When Budenz testifies that he knows that a certain individual is a Communist from "official reports," it may mean nothing more than that Jack Stachel or someone of that sort mentioned the name, however casually, in a friendly way.

This possibility is considerably buttressed by the rather loose way in which Budenz uses the term "Communist." He plainly does not use it in a way that would coincide, for example, with legal membership in the Communist Party. One test he suggests is whether an individual or organization follows Soviet policy without deviation. (On that test, incidentally, Lattimore would not seem to qualify, in view of his opposition to the Soviet attack on Finland and his support for the Marshall Plan.) An even broader test is whether the individual's activity "lends itself to aiding the enemy of the United States, which is Soviet Russia." This test, if it can be called that, clearly depends on what views the individual applying it has about desirable policy for the United States. It is a short step from this test to the position that what is important is not whether a man is an actual Party member but rather whether one agrees with what he has said or done.

These two factors—a readiness to elevate hearsay to the status of authoritative fact and an expansive disregard for the niceties of actual Party affiliation—tend to interact in Budenz's testimony. Perhaps the most clear-cut example of this is his remarkable appearance before the House Committee on Tax-Exempt Foundations (the Cox Committee), in the course of which he rattled off the names of a number of eminent scholars and accused them of being Communists on the basis of "official reports." As one of those so accused remarked, "This is not evidence; it is mere denunciation." The rebuttal testimony of those named reveals a consistent pattern. All of them have maintained an active interest in political affairs.

All of them have been involved in activities in which Communists have also been involved. All of them have expressed the view that it is better to work toward desirable goals with persons who may be suspect than it is not to work at all.

This suggests what may be a plausible explanation for the conflict between the testimony of Budenz and that of so many whom he has accused of Communist affiliation. It may be that Budenz himself, as well as those who informed him, acting on the theory that those who cooperated with them in any respect were their friends in all respects, acquired a stock of names that jumbled inextricably all shades of conscious and unconscious collaboration. Add to this the uncertainties that the passage of a dozen or so years are bound to produce and the unconscious temptation to shore up unclear recollection with clear assertion, and it becomes quite plausible that many persons who were never actually conscious collaborators in achieving Communist objectives were so labeled by Budenz. It is not necessary, in short, that either Budenz or his victims be found to be engaging in conscious untruth. In many cases, including that of Owen Lattimore, it is more likely that the truth lay between them on ground that neither occupied.

The Tydings Committee hearings and the IPR hearings illustrate strikingly how easy it is for determined proponents of one or another fixed point of view to find in the inherent ambiguities of this kind of testimony support for the position they wish to espouse. And a major weakness of the Congressional investigation is its vulnerability to just such illegitimate use. That, rather than any question of who was telling the truth, is the important issue of public policy illumined by the case of Budenz v. Lattimore.

5 · LAUTNER

John Lautner's route to the witness stand was very different from that of the other three witnesses we have considered. Chambers, Bentley, and Budenz all defected after a prolonged period of disillusionment with Communism. For all of them, the break seems to have been a soul-searing experience, just as their involvement with Communism was a deeply felt emotional attachment. Lautner did not leave the Party; he was expelled. And what he lost appears to have been for him a job, not a mission. The difference between his case and the others is the difference between the amateur and the professional. Of the defectors, Lautner alone was a professional to whom Communism was a career, an organization man who advanced step by step in a bureaucracy only to lose his tenure when he became unacceptable to the concern's new management. His story gives a glimpse into the workaday side of the Communist movement, where a talent for the organizational chart and the tidy filing system is of more account than a passion for dialectics or an urge to be as one with the forces of history.

Lautner was born in Hungary on January 1, 1902. At the age of sixteen months he was brought to the United States but returned to his native land at the age of four. During the Communist Bela Kun uprising in Hungary following World War I, Lautner was drafted into the home guard, which was subsequently integrated into the Red Army. In the confused period that followed, Lautner was arrested as a Czech spy by the Rumanian Army, and after two months in a prisoners' compound, he was sent to Czechoslovakia. He never returned to Hungary. Lautner has testified that he was not a Communist during these years, and since he was only seventeen when he was expelled from Hungary, there seems no reason to doubt his claim.

In July 1920, he re-entered the United States and for several years lived an uneventful life as a laborer, first in the steel mills of Youngstown, Ohio, and then as a bricklayer apprenticed to his father until he obtained his own union card. In 1926 he became a citizen.

His growing interest in political action took him to New York in the spring of 1927 and he became involved in the International Workers Relief Organization, a working-class though non-Communist group. Like any young man, he began to make social contacts, and these contacts formed and furthered his career. Anomalously enough, it was through a Hungarian dramatic club that he met the people who sponsored his membership in the Communist Party. He joined the Party in 1929 and was assigned to the Yorkville unit in New York City. He was pointed in the direction his career was to take.

In 1930 Lautner was sent to the Hungarian National Training School, one of the nationality group institutions maintained by the Party. After this period of training, he was transferred to Detroit, where he began what became the predominant phase of his career in the Party, working with nationality groups. His first assignment was with the Hungarian Bureau, which had the mission of encouraging Hungarian-Americans to join the Auto Workers Industrial Union, at that time a prime target for Communist infiltration.

And so began the round of assignments that might as well have characterized the advance of a promising young junior executive in a business enterprise. Each assignment a job conscientiously done, a step up the ladder. The young man favorably impresses his superiors. He gets better assignments. He is on the way. And so it went for Lautner. A few years in the provinces—Detroit, Canada, Cleveland. Then back to the home office in New York with more responsibilities and greater recognition. What he did day in and day out, what the pattern of his life was, we do not know. His career as a Communist is known, but one wonders how his daily life differed from that of more mundanely situated people.

In 1936 Lautner was assigned to West Virginia and the difficult job of recruiting for the Party in the coal and chemical industries. By then he was important enough to be called back to New York at regular intervals to consult with the National Committee of the Party. Among the many influential friends he made was Elizabeth Gurley Flynn, whose durability as a Party tycoon is virtually unmatched. Some fifteen years later, Lautner's testimony helped bring about the only significant interruption in her career, her conviction in a Smith Act prosecution.

Lautner's advancement was marked by the honor of membership on the presiding committee of the National Convention held in 1940. The following year he was sent to the National Training School in New York, a very selective "command" school for seasoned Party leaders. This mark of recognition came his way through Roy Hudson, who, with Bob Minor, was running the Party's affairs during the absence of Earl Browder, then confined in the federal penitentiary in Atlanta. Between his stint at the National Training School and his induction into the Army in 1942, Lautner served in the Party's Language Department, which was headed by Avro Landy, and then as Secretary of the Hungarian Bureau and as Secretary of the Hungarian Section of the Party-affiliated International Workers Order.

Lautner's career in the Army, beginning in November 1942, seems to have been similar to his career in the Party, the talents previously recognized in the one now apparently recognized by the other. After basic training he was sent to the Military Intelligence School at Camp Ritchie, Maryland. He was assigned to duty with a Psychological Warfare Unit, first in Algeria and then in Bari, Italy. Here he came into contact with some Hungarians in a British unit, with ultimately disastrous consequences for his career. Although Lautner claimed to have been completely uninvolved in Party activities during his Army career, one of the Hungarians whom he met at that time later denounced him as a Titoist when, in 1949, the Communist regime in Hungary tried and executed Laszlo Rajk, one of their erstwhile leaders, on charges of spying for Tito. Although the Rajk trial received a good deal of publicity in this country, there was no public mention of Lautner's involvement and he was apparently unaware that his name had been brought into the trial. However, some Communist leaders in this country received private information about his alleged complicity and, as we shall see, became suspicious about his fidelity. Ironically enough, the Hungarian Communists later admitted that Rajk had been innocent of the charges brought against him and he was posthumously "rehabilitated." That came too late, however, to help Lautner, who by then had been expelled from the American Communist Party.

Throughout his military career Lautner was, he later insisted, and there is no evidence to gainsay it, technically severed from the Party and did nothing to forward the ends of the Communist movement. He did, however, stay in touch with Party affairs through correspondence with his old friend Elizabeth Gurley Flynn.

During these years the Party had been transformed under Earl Browder's direction into the Communist Political Association and had temporarily abandoned its militant role in favor of cooperation with the war effort. At the time of Lautner's discharge from the service in the summer of 1945, the Party was preparing to reconstitute itself and Lautner attended the New York State Convention and the National Convention, which accomplished this return to proletarian militancy. Since he was then unattached to a district of the Party and therefore could not attend as a regular or alternate delegate, he was invited to attend as a "fraternal" delegate.

Early in 1946, Hal Simon, a member of the New York State Secretariat, gave Lautner the task of helping to organize the building trades section of the Party in accordance with the new "concentration" policy. On one occasion, Lautner described that policy: "The Communist Party concentrates upon the main decisive industries and in this industry on the main decisive factories, and in these main decisive factories on the main departments, and in these main departments on the key people."

After "concentration" on the building trades, Lautner moved to the Chelsea region and "concentration" among longshoremen and transportation workers. In May 1947, Bob Thompson, a member of the National Committee and state chairman of the New York Party, recognized Lautner by appointing him to the State Review Commission. This commission, Lautner later testified, was entrusted with preserving and guarding the Marxist-Leninist line against deviationists. It selected promising Party members for special education and promotion, reviewed the disciplinary proceedings of subordinate committees, and guarded against spies and "stool pigeons." This assignment, combining as it did high administrative duties, a kind of judicial function, and security police work, represented the apogee, as well as the beginning of the end, of Lautner's career in the Party.

In 1948, after the indictment under the Smith Act of the national leaders of the Party, including Dennis, the Party's secretary, Lautner's "police" talents came into their own. He was given charge of security arrangements at the 1948 National Convention and, during the trial, was entrusted by Dennis with hiring bodyguards for the defendants and with locating safe meeting places for the National Board. At the same time he was, he claimed (although the claim was disputed by Elizabeth Gurley Flynn), appointed to membership on the National Review Commission.

After the Dennis indictment, with its promise of hard times for American Communists, Lautner's main work was preparing the New York Party to go underground. These were nerve-wracking days, and suspicion and distrust apparently burst out among the comrades. Lautner soon suffered a fate not unknown among counterespionage agents. In carrying out his task of guarding against spies and traitors to the Party, he aroused suspicions about his own reliability, partly because of security failures for which he was held responsible, and partly because of his involvement in the Rajk affair. Rightly or wrongly, and this later became a matter of some controversy (with the truth, as it was so often in those trying days for the Communists, hidden in the clatter of charge and countercharge) he was suspected of being an FBI informer. According to Lautner, it was only *after* the inquisition and expulsion that he contacted the FBI. At any rate, he was relieved of his delicate assignment and sent to do less sensitive work in Cleveland.

There, in January 1950, in a setting that he later described in dramatic detail and with telling effect on the witness stand, Lautner was lured to a dingy cellar by Party hatchet men, stripped naked, and subjected to an inquisition. Only the sheer accident of having left a comrade's name at his hotel, he hinted, saved him from worse than inquisition. Trained as he was in the folkways of the Party, Lautner was not surprised to read in the *Daily Worker* a few days later that he had been expelled from Party membership.

His next move reveals the Party bureaucrat at his most typical. He appealed to the National Review Commission of the Party for a hearing and reinstatement. The Communist Party had been his life; there was no other, no higher authority to which he could appeal. Not surprisingly, he received no reply to his appeal. He then collected his unemployment compensation and went fishing. For the next several months, he subsequently declared, he read and meditated—possibly reflecting wryly on the course of events that had led to his predicament. Finally he got in touch with the FBI, offering his services to the Department of Justice in its prosecution of Communist leaders and organizations. Here was a prize catch, as the Justice Department was quick to realize. Lautner became a "consultant" to the Department and embarked on a new career as the Government's chief witness in a series of Smith Act trials and Subversive Activities Control Board hearings.

II

From 1952 to 1956, Lautner appeared as a principal witness in no less than 25 proceedings relating to the issue of Communist penetration. Over and over again he told his story. Nine of these appearances were before the Subversive Activities Control Board in proceedings to compel the registration of Communist-action or Communist-front organizations. Of these, by far the most important was what is often referred to as the "parent" proceeding, brought to compel the registration of the Communist Party itself. Fifteen other proceedings were Smith Act prosecutions against "second-string" leaders of the Communist Party ranging from New York to Hawaii. Lautner's remaining appearance was in a proceeding relating to Communist infiltration of public education conducted by the New York State Board of Regents.

These were years of intensive official concern with the problems of Communist penetration, of fact-finding for informational purposes, and of fact-finding as a basis for invoking official sanctions against Communists and their allies. It was this second type of fact-finding in which Lautner's testimony played a predominant role. The distinction between the two, which was referred to in Chapter 1, is necessary for an understanding of the significance of Lautner's testimony and the processes by which it was elicited. Lautner was not engaged in supplying public information. He was testifying in proceedings designed to put some people in jail and to impose other unpleasant consequences on other people and organizations. When that much is at stake, testimony is very carefully elicited by its proponents, here attorneys for the Government, and equally carefully tested by its opponents, here attorneys for the Communist defendants. This is the kind of process to which Chambers was subjected twice, in the two Hiss trials, Bentley only once, in the first Remington trial, and Budenz far fewer times than Lautner. Moreover, Chambers, Bentley, and Budenz testified mainly before Congressional committees. Not so Lautner. These sharply drawn adversary proceedings were the main arena of his testimony. For a witness, such proceedings are truly ordeal by combat. And they are much less satisfactory than Congressional committee investigations for developing a story in the large, for providing nice nuances and psychological insights. Lautner's testimony has none of the drama that marked the Congressional appearances of the other three. This was plain hard work.

Twenty-five proceedings in four years is a lot. But their significance is not merely quantitative. In each of them Lautner was taken over the same general areas of testimony. These testimonial occasions, therefore, afford an unmatched opportunity to observe the process by which a witness's testimony is built up, shaped, and refined. We can see at work the process by which the weaknesses discovered in an earlier appearance are glossed over and rectified in a later one. The testimony takes on a life of its own, growing not only from the matrix of the witness's recollection of the primary events about which he is testifying but also from the directing force of the testimonial occasions themselves. And we can see the cross-examiners at work, probing, testing, impairing, and when they can, destroying, not just in the context of a single testimonial occasion but using the results of previous cross-examinations and grasping whatever advantage they can from the fact that no one can possibly tell the same complicated story in precisely the same way 25 different times. How does the testimony stand up? Where does the balance of credibility lie? What testimony is strengthened, what weakened? And, perhaps most important, what segments of testimony by their very nature are unaffected by this kind of sustained examination and re-examination? These are questions for which we hope to obtain answers in this examination of Lautner's testimony.

We shall begin by narrating the substance of Lautner's testimony, keeping in mind that what we have is an extraordinarily concentrated distillation of thousands of pages of testimony. There follow some general observations on the cross-examination to which the testimony was subjected on various occasions. We shall then consider the corroborative and contradictory testimony elicited from other witnesses, as well as additional factors bearing on the reliability of Lautner's testimony. Next we shall consider some of the variations in substance and style produced by the diversity of occasions on which Lautner testified. Finally, we shall present a few tentative conclusions about this testimony and its significance for our basic inquiry about the efficacy of fact-finding processes.

Before we embark on these lines of inquiry, however, something should be said about Lautner's testimonial style, which is directly related to his role as a Communist functionary. Lautner's testimony reveals an almost complete absence of the passion and personal involvement that so strongly characterized the testimony of Chambers, Bentley, and Budenz. Lautner rarely revealed the fervent commitment to Communism, or the equally fervent rejection of it, that was so often evident in the testimony of the others. Having apparently accepted Communism according to Lenin's dictum that it was "not a dogma but a program for action," Lautner went about the performance of his Party functions in a matter-of-fact way. This workmanlike approach is equally characteristic of his testimonial performance for the Government. Once, when pressed by defense counsel on the question of pecuniary profit from his role as an ex-Communist witness, he disdainfully replied that he neither lectured nor wrote books—an obvious aspersion on the activities of other ex-Communists.

It may be that the relative absence of a sermonizing tendency in Lautner's evidence suggests a greater degree of objectivity on his part than is inferable from the testimony of, say, Louis Budenz. On the other hand, his relative lack of personal involvement may suggest to some, as it often did to defense counsel, a possible susceptibility to suggestions from government investigators and lawyers. Whatever the conclusion, and both may have some truth in them, a study of Lautner's testimony sheds little light on what it was about the Communist movement that bound its adherents so firmly to it.

III

Lautner's experience with the Communist Party spanned two decades in which he observed and worked within the Party structure as a student, an instructor, and an active, high-level functionary. As a student he became versed in at least the rudiments of the Marxist-Leninist doctrine. As an instructor of Party organization he became thoroughly familiar with the Party structure and the personnel who occupied positions of prominence within that structure. As a section organizer, district representative, and functionary in the post-1945 reorganization of the Party, he added practical experience to his knowledge of Communist theory.

Perhaps his main value to the Government was his familiarity with the post-1945 purposes and activities of the Party. Lautner is the only defector who enjoyed close personal relations with the top functionaries during this period and consequently observed the course of Party developments after the repudiation of Browder's policies.

The synopses of his testimony given below all relate to areas of his experience that especially illuminate the theory and structure of American Communism.

In the spring of 1930 Lautner was assigned to a three-months training program at the 1930 Hungarian Training School in New York. His courses included "Marxism-Leninism," "Political Economy," "History of the Russian Revolution," "Dialectical Materialism," "The Program of the Sixth World Congress," "The Communist Manifesto," and "The Program of the Communist International." His instructors included the notorious J. Peters, described by Lautner as an organizational specialist on cadre work for the National Committee, and author of *The Communist Party: A Manual on Organization*; Louis Bebrits, member of the editorial board of the Hungarian-American Communist Party paper known as *Uj Elore* and later Minister of Transportation in the Hungarian Communist Government; Gus Majer, Secretary of the National Hungarian Bureau in 1930–31; John Gyetvai, a member of the editorial board of *Uj Elore*, who was removed in 1931 following a factional struggle and who, after World War II, was Minister to Turkey for the Hungarian Government; John Santa (Santo), an editor of *Uj Elore* and section organizer in the Bronx; Louis Weinstock, later a member of the National Review Commission, who was elected to the National Committee in 1945; and several lesser lights.

In *U.S.* v. *Silverman*, Lautner testified that Gyetvai "stated that the purpose of the school was to develop a core of party functionaries through the Marxist-Leninist education . . . given in this school." The school was held in district headquarters of the Communist Party and about twenty "promising young" Party members from all over the country attended. In the Board of Regents hearing, Lautner testified that the class was addressed by J. Peters, who told them "that the party is investing a lot of money, time and talent in developing us as professional revolutionaries, and he hopes and the party as such hopes that we will live up to the estimate of the party . . . that we will become professional revolutionaries."

This testimony served to emphasize the foreign domination of the American Party as well as its adherence to a program of action leading to violent overthrow of the Government.

In recognition of his work in West Virginia, Lautner was selected to attend the 1941 National Training School, a three-month, full-time school in New York City. According to Lautner, the school never convened in the same place for more than one day, but was held in homes in various parts of the city. This bit of local color no doubt contributed to the Government's attempt to portray the Party as a clandestine, conspiratorial organization. Despite the school's floating nature, Lautner claimed, the students had at their disposal "all the writing, collected works of Lenin, [and] all the works of Stalin." The student body was a select group of seven leaders of state party organizations.

The classical Communist literature and leading contemporary Communist writings were studied. A course on Marxism-Leninism was given by George Siskind, described by Lautner as one of the leading functionaries of the Party, who was director of Agitation-Propaganda in the New York State Party in 1933 and was director of national cadres for the Party after 1945. Lautner relied upon Siskind's instruction when testifying about Communist objectives. "The History of the Communist Party of the Soviet Union" was taught by Sam Carr, who in 1931 was Executive Secretary of the Canadian Communist Party and who in 1949 was detained on Ellis Island in connection with the Gouzenko spy case. Other courses given in the school were "Political Economy," taught by Jacob

"Pop" Mindel, head of the National School Commission and director of the National Training School; "Party Organization," taught by John Williamson, a member of the National Committee, Labor Secretary of the Communist Party, and Organizational Secretary; "Party Problems," by Roy Hudson, a member of the National Committee until 1945; "Communist Party and the Trade Unions," by Jack Johnstone, a National Committeeman in the 30's; "Problems in China," by Rudy Baker, a district organizer in Detroit and reputedly a long-time Comintern representative; "Imperialism," by Avro Landy, head of the Nationality Groups Commission; "Negro Problems," by James Ford, National Committeeman until Browder's expulsion; and a "Marxist version" of American history, by Francis Franklin, onetime national leader of the Young Communist League, who was later expelled from the Party because of difference of opinion with the leaders.

As in the case of testimony on the 1930 Hungarian Training School, this testimony showed the Party's objectives and served as a basis for the assertion that the 1945 reconstitution picked up a consistent thread of seditious activity.

When Lautner returned from the Army in June 1945, he had conversations with Williamson and Elizabeth Gurley Flynn, members of the National Committee. Flynn told Lautner about William Z. Foster's criticism of Browder and about the reversal of attitude by leading functionaries toward Browder's "Popular Front" policies. Williamson informed Lautner of the imminent special convention and instructed him to prepare himself by reading the Draft Resolution of the National Board, the Duclos letter, and pre-convention articles in the *Daily Worker*. The letter by Jacques Duclos, a leader of the French Communist Party, had excited considerable ferment within the Party and is described by Lautner as a factor in the decision to hold the 1945 convention. The letter was extremely critical of Browder's policies, declaring that they were deviations from Marxism-Leninism. The Draft Resolution accepted the Duclos letter and called for a reconstitution of the Party.

At Williamson's invitation, Lautner attended the New York State Convention, which preceded the National Convention by a week. Lautner testified that at the State Convention Foster gave a report in which he endorsed the Duclos letter, criticized Browder's errors, and urged a return to Marxist-Leninist principles. About 500 people attended the convention. They selected a delegation to the National Convention, and by a unanimous vote passed a resolution urging a reconstitution of the Party.

The National Convention was held in the Fraternal Clubhouse in the Times Square area on the last three days of July 1945. About 100 people attended as delegates, alternate delegates, and fraternal delegates. It was closed to anyone who was not a delegate. Lautner attended as a fraternal or guest delegate at Williamson's invitation, and was assigned to the Veterans' Committee. He was also given the task of supervising a stairway that led to a room where stenographers were making copies of the proceedings. Lautner claimed that he was present at all the general sessions.

The main report was given by Foster. Lautner related a summary of this report.

Foster in his report to the convention analyzed the revisionist errors that Earl Browder committed under his leadership.

In his report he accused him that he deviated from the Marxist concept of economy . . . he accused Browder of giving up the vanguard role, the leading role of the Communist Party . . . of denying the imperialist monopoly nature of capitalism . . . And then in his report Foster dealt with the effect of this revisionist leadership on the Communist movement . . . in the United States and its effect elsewhere, and called upon the Party membership to restudy the basic principles of Marxism-Leninism, vigorous efforts to eradicate all vestiges of opportunism and revisionism from the ranks of the Party, and to rebuild, to go back and rebuild the Communist Party of the United States.

Lautner testified that Williamson, Secretary of the Political Association, made two addresses—one on the reconstitution of the Party, and another in which he read the Party constitution to the Assembly. Because of its verbal inconsistency with the idea of forcible overthrow, the 1945 constitution has been a hurdle to the basic theory of the Smith Act prosecutions. On numerous occasions Lautner testified that in fact there was a contradiction in the constitution, insofar as it purported in its preamble to support both the United States Constitution and the "principles of Marxism-Leninism." When describing Williamson's address on the constitution, Lautner usually related an incident that took place while the sections were being read. A delegate called from the floor:

"Where is the dictatorship of the proletariat in this preamble?" According to Lautner, Eugene Dennis stepped in at this point and answered, "It's there, even the blind can see it." The implication apparently was that orthodox Communist objectives were to be understood even though not explicitly stated.

The convention also heard a general disavowal of Browder's policies by the Party's leading functionaries. Jacob "Pop" Mindel, among others, gave a self-critical speech, pointing out "how even he, a Marxist-Leninist scholar and theoretician, could be duped by Browder's revisionist policies."

The convention concluded with a unanimous decision to adopt the constitution, and that was the end of Browder and the beginning of the end of the American Communist Party as a force in American life.

Lautner claimed that when he returned from the Army he found that the Party structure had undergone extensive change— "there were large community clubs in various parts of the city . . . there were no shop units to speak of, or industrial units or sections at that time." This, he implied, indicated the temporary "open" character of the Communist Political Association, in contrast to the disciplined militancy that had preceded it and was to follow. With the formal reconstitution of the Party at the 1945 convention, the Party began a three-pronged program: to reorganize, to re-educate, and to carry out a concentration policy in the "decisive industries," according to the policy set out by Foster at the 1945 convention.

Large clubs were broken up into smaller groups. New sections were established and other clubs were streamlined. A survey was made of industrial workers, and industrial sections were established "in furniture, needle trades, [and] on the waterfront." Other sections were created among the longshoremen, cement workers, teamsters, and electrical workers. Professional sections were also established.

The concentration program consisted of recruiting members in the "decisive" sectors of the industry. Lautner testified that New York County was divided into six concentration regions. He served with the reorganization committee and then was assigned work with the No. 1 region—Chelsea—where the "main concentration problem" existed among the transport workers.

As part of the re-education program Lautner taught classes of 20 to 25 students who were Party functionaries among the bakers, furriers, and members of the building trades. From 1946 to 1949 he instructed them on the history of the American Communist Party, the organization of the Party, political economy, and Marxism-Leninism. In these classes, held in the Jefferson School, the Roosevelt Building, and Party headquarters, Lautner used all the classic books in the Little Lenin Library, and Foster's Report to the 1945 convention and the Program of the Communist International, among other documents. If not introduced before, these documents usually were brought in at this point in Lautner's testimony.

Lautner bolstered this testimony by referring to a preliminary conversation with Alberto Moreau, the head of the School Commission in New York, who assigned Lautner to teach. According to Lautner he was instructed on pedagogy and on the content of his courses. An outline of the courses listing the material covered was another aid to Lautner's testimony. Lautner's claim of adherence to the true Communist line was further strengthened by his assertion that his classes were attended by other leading functionaries whose purpose was to supervise his teaching. While the main point of this testimony was to explain what was taught, it served the equally important function of demonstrating the monolithic adherence to the Party line that characterized the training activities. Since Lautner's testimony revealed that indoctrination, rather than discussion, characterized the Party's pedagogical activities, the characterization of the Party as a militant action group was presented to the jury.

After the Dennis indictment Lautner's main responsibility was to prepare an underground organization for the New York Party. A number of meetings were held with the State Secretariat—Bob Thompson, Hal Simon, and Bob Norman. Thompson told Lautner that according to Foster's report on the experience in Europe, only 10 per cent of the Party would remain intact should the Party be declared illegal. Consequently, plans were made to integrate 10 per cent of the members into an "organized force that was supposed to fight in an organized fashion, to fight back into legality."

Lautner described the underground plan as having two aspects, "vertical and horizontal." Vertically, the underground was to have seven levels—state, area, county, region, section, subsection, and unit. Each level would be organized in groups of three, with initiative moving from the top to the bottom level. The state leadership formed the apex of the triangle. Each of the three members of the state leadership—the political head, the organizational head, and the trade union mass organization head—was to appoint three members at the area level. Each of these three in turn made three appointments at the next lower level, and so on down to the unit level. Hence, with the exception of those in the top and bottom strata, each person would know only six others—the two others of his group of three, the one who made his appointment, and the three that he appointed. Lautner testified that when he left the Party the underground had been established and was functioning at all seven levels in New York and that the same organizational plan was being used elsewhere.

Lautner used the term "horizontal" to describe the reserve leadership and communications and propaganda system to be available to the various levels. Although he did not himself use the analogy, the resemblance to line and staff functions in a military organization seems apparent. It was to this staff phase of the underground program that Lautner devoted most of his efforts. Lautner helped to obtain photo-offset equipment, short-wave radio sets, and mimeograph machines to equip the Party for its underground operations. A small flat-bed hand mimeograph machine was made for the lower levels of the organization. The machine could be disassembled so that it would not be difficult to conceal. Lautner instructed functionaries from other states in the use of the machines. He claimed that when he left the Party, over 600 such mimeograph machines had been manufactured, 300 were being manufactured, and the Party planned to order another 300. Besides working on underground communications equipment, Lautner worked at finding proper meeting and contact places and made plans for hiding Party leaders in the event that it became necessary.

This line of testimony, which was relatively untouched on cross-examination, must have done much to confirm the view that the Party was a close-knit conspiratorial organization.

Although Lautner described the circumstances surrounding his expulsion from the Party in many hearings, such testimony may at first glance seem irrelevant to any of the issues in a Smith Act prosecution, and its admissibility was usually challenged as irrelevant to any issue before the tribunal. Judge Harlan, upholding the conviction of the second-string Communists in *U.S.* v. *Flynn,* explained that this testimony was admissible on at least two grounds: "that the Party functioned not as an ordinary political party but in a covert, deceptive, violent, and highly disciplined manner such as might be expected of a revolutionary organization," and "that although provisions of the Party constitution seemed to belie a revolutionary purpose, the constitution was not in practice faithfully followed"—the Government's so-called "Aesopian" theory. The same explanations serve to demonstrate the relevance of much else in Lautner's testimony.

Late in 1949 the Party became suspicious that Lautner was in communication with the FBI. In February 1949, Lautner had received reports in his capacity as head of the New York State Review Commission about the suspicious activities of Angela Calomiris, who later appeared as a witness for the Government in the *Dennis* case. Apparently he had failed to give his superiors adequate warning about her probable defection. About the same time, according to Lautner, a Party member called him about a phone call received by the member's wife. The caller had given his number, which the Party member gave to Lautner. Lautner scribbled the number on his office pad. The number belonged to an FBI agent. Apparently someone in the Party's security apparatus found the number and traced it. This set of circumstances bred suspicion that Lautner was an FBI agent, or at least that he was sheltering informers within the Party. And, on the basis of the Rajk affair, some leaders of the Party also had become suspicious that Lautner had made friends among Titoists while he was overseas, or that he was an international spy. When questioned on cross-examination about these possibilities, Lautner categorically denied having been anything but a loyal Communist until his expulsion from the Party.

Suspicion that he was a traitor to the Party led, Lautner claimed, first to an unsuccessful attempt to have him liquidated behind the Iron Curtain, and then to an unceremonious inquisition in a Cleveland cellar, where his life was threatened and his membership in the Party terminated.

In November and December, 1949, Louis Weinstock, one of

the principal Party leaders in the labor movement, advised Lautner to go to Hungary to do Party work. Lautner testified that he
went to Thompson to discuss the matter and Thompson "willingly
approved." About this time Lautner was talking to Weinstock
about other matters when Howard Johnson, educational director
of the New York Party, inquired about Moses Simon's arrest in
Hungary as a British agent. "Weinstock curtly told him, 'You mind
your own business.'" This incident in the context of later events
caused Lautner to believe that the Party hoped to have him liquidated in Hungary. What apparently saved Lautner, who dutifully
applied for a passport, was that his application was denied because
of this country's strained relations with Hungary.

At this point Jack Kling urged Lautner to go to the Midwest
with him for further work on the underground project. The State
Secretariat approved Lautner's transfer and on January 14, 1950,
Lautner left for Cleveland to meet Jack Kling. He checked in at
a Cleveland hotel, had lunch, and went to a theater with Kling.
They walked around until late evening when a car picked them
up and took them to a house in the Kingsbury Run section of Cleveland. Kling told Lautner to go down to the cellar. He entered the
cellar and found two men playing cards who ordered him to un-
dress. The men had guns, knives, and rubber hoses. After his
clothes had been searched, Solly Wellman, a Party leader from
Detroit, and Joe Brandt, a Party leader from Ohio, entered the
cellar with Jack Kling and the driver of the car. They accused
Lautner of being a "traitor," "spy," and "stool pigeon." In the room
was a recording machine and another machine that they said was
a lie detector. Lautner was asked how long he had been a CIA
member and what his relationship with the Field brothers was.
When they asked whom he knew in Cleveland, Lautner mentioned
that he had left Kling's name at the hotel desk. Apparently this
frightened his interrogators, for after making him sign a confes-
sion, they released him and told him to meet them the next day
at a downtown restaurant. The next day Lautner went to the appointed place, but no one appeared, so he left Cleveland and returned to New York.

On January 17, Lautner read of his expulsion in the *Daily
Worker*. He sent a letter requesting reinstatement to Trachtenberg, chairman of the National Review Commission, but received

no answer. Lautner testified that although the constitution provided that no one could be expelled without a hearing and a review of the decision, the only "hearing" he received was the Cleveland cellar inquisition. This line of testimony, with its spy thriller overtones, was undoubtedly quite effective in depicting the ruthlessness of the Party's leaders and the divergence between their professions of peace and their militant practices.

Another major area of testimony, particularly important to the Government in the Subversive Activities Control Board proceedings, concerns the relations of the Communist Party of the United States with Russia, with the Communist International (Comintern), and with other Communist parties—the issue of foreign domination.

Prior to the enactment of the Foreign Agents Registration Act in 1940, the Party was openly affiliated with the Comintern. Many American Communists—Earl Browder, Bob Minor, Gil Green, and William Foster, among others—represented this international organization, according to Lautner. After passage of the Act, this open affiliation ceased and the relationship became covert. The main link between the U.S. Party and the Communist International then became Gerhardt Eisler, whom Lautner knew in the '30's under the name of Edwards. Eisler, of course, is known as an international agent of the Comintern. After his deportation from this country in 1949, he went to East Germany, where he became Propaganda Chief for the Communist-dominated regime. Lautner testified to having had several contacts with Eisler in the 1930's. According to Lautner, when Eisler spoke "we were very attentive to what he had to say, and what he did say, well, he should know, he is the representative, and what he says is the Party line. There was no questioning of [his] judgment."

After 1945 Lautner saw Eisler shortly after the latter's release from Ellis Island and again a few days later at Party headquarters. Lautner also saw him in 1949, when Eisler gave a speech at a New York restaurant to a gathering sponsored by the Civil Rights Congress in honor of the Communists released from Ellis Island. Lautner was asked: "Did Eisler to your knowledge ever undertake to influence the Party activities in this country, after 1945?" Lautner replied, "Yes."

Other evidence of foreign domination given by Lautner included testimony that the Communist International controlled the Profintern, and that the Trade Union Unity League, with which Lautner worked in Detroit, was affiliated with the Profintern. Lautner claimed that the policy of the Party in the early '30's was "to build a Red revolutionary trade union movement under the leadership of the Profintern." Lautner also recalled an oath of allegiance to the Soviet Union read by Carl Brodsky at a gathering in Madison Square Garden. Additional evidence of the foreign control of the American Party was provided by Lautner's description of a conversation with Jack Kling in January 1950. Lautner showed Kling a pamphlet, written by Browder after the 1945 convention, in which Browder stated that all major policies during his leadership "had the previous knowledge, consent and active support of the decisive International Communist Leadership." "Kling's only comment was a smile, and he [said], 'if this is not stool pigeon work on the part of Browder, then nothing is,'" a remark that was doubtless intended by the witness to be taken as an admission that what Browder had written was true.

Lautner also described the attitude of the propaganda organs of the American Communist Party toward the Soviet Union. He claimed he could not remember any instances when *Political Affairs*, the *Communist* (predecessor of *Political Affairs*), or the *Daily Worker* ever took issue with or criticized the Soviet Union "or any of [the] people's democracies."

Soviet Russia Today, the official organ of the Friends of the Soviet Union, was distributed "as widely as possible by the Communist Party." Lautner said that he saw Teddy Bayer, the business manager of this publication, going to the finance office at Party headquarters every two weeks.

Although the American Party did not affiliate with the Cominform when it was formed in 1947, Lautner testified that *For a Lasting Peace for a People's Democracy*, the official publication of the Communist Information Bureau in Moscow, was flown into the United States and supplied to functionaries by the Party.

In the 1941 National Training School Lautner claimed he made a study of the question of allegiance, and one of the conclusions he drew from *The History of the Communist Party of the Soviet Union*, and from other sources was that in the event of war with the Soviet Union, the primary allegiance of a Party member would be to the Soviet Union. Lautner also testified that in classes supervised by Ben Semonofsky, the New York County school director, he taught the difference between "just and unjust wars," and cited the defense of the Soviet Union as an example of a "just" war. He also taught that it would be the "task" of every Communist to support Russia against the United States in the event of war.

In short, Lautner testified that "essentially the Party follows the policies of the Soviet Government over here." Peaceful coexistence is merely "one of the tactics in the struggle against imperialism," and he had been taught that peaceful coexistence is really impossible.

Indicating the relationship of the American Party to Party organizations in other nations, Lautner testified that in the 1930's the Canadian Party drew upon American cadres for its development. The Cuban and Puerto Rican Parties were dependent upon the American organization for finances, and at least two people known to Lautner were sent to Cuba or to Puerto Rico to assist in Party organization.

The picture thus drawn of an interlocking group of national Parties, all owing ultimate allegiance to a common source, was of substantial importance in buttressing the Government's case that the American Communist Party was under Russian control. It was heavily relied upon by the Board in reaching its conclusion that the Party was subject to the registration provisions of the Internal Security Act.

Having been both an instructor and a student in the main Communist schools, and having had extensive experience as a Party functionary, Lautner was an ideal witness for explaining the meaning of Marxism-Leninism and its peculiar terminology. He could recall declarations of policy made by prominent Communist scholars and philosophers, declarations that were assertedly not fully understood by others.

Lautner testified that the true meaning of Marxism-Leninism was known only to "initiates" in the Party, those having a special indoctrination in Communist theory. Hence, the 1945 and 1948 constitutions, which apparently uphold the United States Constitution and prohibit force and violence, would not deceive the insider, who would know that Marxism-Leninism is incompatible with such attitudes.

According to Lautner, the objective of the Party is to establish the dictatorship of the proletariat by means of a proletarian revolution. As defined in Lautner's testimony, the "proletarian revolution" is the "violent shattering of the bourgeois state." The Party is to decide when the conditions are proper for a revolution. Lautner claimed he was instructed that "this whole epoch since the turn of the century is ripe—there is a revolutionary situation."

Lautner's testimony about the teaching of the theory of "Exceptionalism" at the 1941 National Training School brought up the question of alternatives to forcible overthrow. According to Lautner, he was taught that this theory, which holds that some countries could make a gradual transition from capitalism to socialism, was not applicable to the United States. The point of Lautner's testimony was that the Communist leaders here anticipated that change would have to come about by violent means. Of course this theory is the cornerstone of the case the Government was trying to build.

IV

In most proceedings, and especially in the earlier trials, Lautner was given a vigorous and extensive cross-examination that covered nearly every conceivable motive for falsifying, tested his recollection of detail, and used his testimony as a platform for developing the defense's thesis.

A standard method of impeachment employed in all proceedings was to dwell at length upon Lautner's remuneration from the Government with the object of making his status as a professional witness manifest, and therefore suspect, to the trier-of-fact. Another method was to question Lautner about his failure to tell the truth on various occasions while he was a member of the Party—the annulment proceedings in which he perjured himself by claiming that his wife refused to become a Catholic, his marriage to a Jewish woman in which he apparently held himself out as a convert to Judaism, and his passport and army questionnaires in which he signed statements that he was not a member of a subversive organization and that he supported the Constitution of the United States.

Although the cross-examinations in most proceedings covered the same ground, emphasis and technique varied among cross-examiners, with different stress and varying degrees of success. The various modes of attack are illustrated by the cross-examination in the Los Angeles Smith Act trial. By questioning Lautner about his experiences in Detroit and West Virginia, the examiner attempted to point up the depressed social conditions of the 1930's and inferentially to establish the legitimate, nonviolent purposes of the Communist Party. Lautner was questioned about hunger strikes, violence of employers and police against the working class, and evictions of the poor in Detroit. He was asked about captive mines, company towns, and low wages in the mining towns of West Virginia, where he was the district organizer. Lautner's experience in West Virginia was used to show that the Party attempted to use open political methods there until it was suppressed by the Dies Committee. His cross-examiner forced Lautner to admit that the Party was listed in the phone book and was not a covert organization.

Lautner's failure to recollect events or writings that had favorable implications for the defense was contrasted with his familiarity with exact page references in certain texts during direct examination by the Government. The examiner thus quite dramatically questioned the genuineness of Lautner's memory on direct examination, creating the suspicion that he had been told what to say and that his testimony was biased.

Finally, a major portion of the cross-examination was concerned with impeaching Lautner's familiarity with Marxism-Leninism. Lautner's testimony on direct about instructions he gave and received and about the 1945 convention was used as a vehicle for bringing before the jury other Communist writings that tended to contradict the theme of Lautner's direct testimony or at least to indicate that its accuracy was confined to an earlier period or special circumstances.

The cross-examination in the New York "second-string" prosecution (*U.S.* v. *Flynn*) included all of the above techniques and represented the most comprehensive effort to destroy Lautner's testimony. For a period of 16 days attorneys questioned Lautner about all phases of his Party experience. One examiner spent days reviewing Communist theory, testing Lautner's recollection and consistency and at the same time conveying to the jury through his questions (whether Lautner's answer was favorable or not) the impression that Communist theory was not incompatible with the peaceful establishment of socialism.

In the Hawaiian Smith Act prosecution (*U.S.* v. *Fujimoto*) the cross-examiner first concentrated upon discrediting Lautner by questioning him at length about the amount of pay and other benefits he received as a witness for the Government. The remainder of the examination was perhaps the most intensive and effective questioning Lautner ever underwent about his knowledge of Communist theory. Lautner was used as a sounding board for the defense's theory and at the same time made to appear as though he really had very little understanding of Communist principles.

Perhaps it was Lautner's fear that the cross-examiner was succeeding in discrediting his testimony that now and then led him to make embarrassing statements. At one point, having been led through a line of questioning designed to produce the response that Marxism-Leninism was not a dogmatic philosophy but rather a flexible science, Lautner was finally asked whether Marxism-Leninism could be understood by merely hearing someone read isolated excerpts from textbooks. Perhaps recalling the isolated passages favorable to the defense position with which his cross-examiners had taxed him, he unequivocally responded that this could not be done. Of course, counsel instantly reminded Lautner that the Government's case on direct had consisted mainly of having Lautner identify a text and then reading a selected passage from it to the jury.

The examination in the *Fujimoto* trial seriously impaired Lautner's testimony on direct concerning the revolutionary purpose and readiness of the Party. Lautner was forced to resort to *Foundations of Leninism,* a book written in 1920, to substantiate his allegation that revolutionary conditions existed in the post-1945 period. After attempting to digress and to evade the question by describing statements to the contrary as "tactical resolutions," Lautner was finally forced to admit that the "objective conditions" for revolution did not exist in the United States.

In the New York Board of Regents hearing, the primary weapon of the cross-examiner was the inconsistent statement. By 1953, Lautner had given several thousand pages of testimony. The cross-examiner apparently selected the questionable areas and led Lautner into statements that conflicted with earlier responses. This hearing also illustrates another method of impeachment used more in later proceedings; Lautner's failure to mention certain subjects in earlier proceedings, particularly his failure to mention force and violence in the first Subversive Activities Control Board hearing, was pointed out to the trier-of-fact.

In the Philadelphia Smith Act trial (*U.S.* v. *Kuzma*), the cross-examination was directed mainly toward developing the peaceful tenor of Marxism-Leninism in the post-1945 period. Perhaps the most effective part of this examination was the demonstration, through Lautner's responses, that even if the Party advocated revolution, it had not been teaching revolutionary techniques and otherwise was not equipping its members for anything but an ideological struggle.

From *U.S.* v. *Kuzma* (1954) on, the examinations of Lautner fall into one or more of the above patterns. For the most part, the intensity of cross-examination seems to have abated measurably in later trials, perhaps because both direct testimony and cross-examination had by then been polished smooth by repetition, until little opportunity remained for surprise on either side.

V

We shall now examine the processes by which proponents of Lautner's testimony sought to strengthen it and those by which his opponents sought to impeach it. We shall pay particular attention to areas of conflict that gave rise to situations reflecting favorably or unfavorably on the reliability and relevance of some of Lautner's statements.

At the outset of this examination, a cautionary word is in order. To avoid a distorting emphasis on the shortcomings of Lautner's testimony, it should be kept in mind that the material which is here compressed into a few pages is extracted from literally thousands of pages of testimony. Anyone familiar with the trial process knows that even the most honest, forthright, and accurate witness is likely to fall into occasional lapses and inconsistencies. If the human memory were a perfect recording instrument, the elaborate processes of examination and cross-examination would be to a large extent unnecessary. Taken literally, the maxim *falsus in uno, falsus in omnibus* is an impossible counsel of perfection. The important question here is whether the limits of tolerable error have been exceeded. That judgment cannot be made on a mere quantitative count of errors.

There are not many areas in which the testimony of other witnesses covers the same events as Lautner's testimony. That is particularly true of testimony about the post-1945 situation, the area of Lautner's greatest utility to the Government. On the other hand, there is a great deal of overlap in testimony about Communist ideology. Here, perhaps the most important corroboration comes from the testimony of an objective expert. In the SACB proceeding against the Communist Party, the Government called Dr. Philip Mosely, Director of the Russian Institute and Professor of International Relations at Columbia University, a leading expert on Soviet Russia and Communist doctrine. He confirmed Lautner's evaluation of American Communist doctrine at many points, including the theory of "just and unjust wars" and the influence of the Duclos letter on the reconstitution of the Party.

A number of ex-Communist witnesses corroborated aspects of Lautner's testimony. The comparatively unimportant nature of this corroboration precludes the need for any detailed narration of its content. A few examples will suffice.

Paul Crouch testified that he knew Lautner and worked closely with him in the late 1930's: "We were both southern district organizers of the Party."

Joseph Kornfeder claimed that he conferred with Gerhardt Eisler, whom he knew as a Communist International representative, in Cleveland in 1933, thereby corroborating Lautner's testimony about Eisler. William Odell Nowell (who attended the Lenin School, was a delegate to the Seventh World Congress, and was an Educational Director of the Party until he left it in 1936) also testified that he knew Eisler as a Communist International representative under the name of Edwards in the 1930's. Nowell testified that the Auto Workers Union was affiliated with the Trade Union Unity League, which, in turn, was affiliated with the Profintern. He confirmed Lautner's testimony that Peters's Manual was in use in the Party up to 1935.

Manning Johnson (Party member from 1930 to 1939, member of the Central Committee from 1936 to 1938) testified that he was taught that in the event of war with Russia it would be the duty of a Communist to "bring about the defeat of the government of the U.S.and to secure a victory of the Red Army." He also identified Eisler as a Communist International representative having "Edwards" as an alias. Johnson described instructions he received in the 1930's about how the Party would function if it decided to go underground. The instructions he related parallel the instructions Lautner received when he began to work on the New York Party underground with respect to the organization of the membership and the use of printing presses and mimeograph machines. Johnson also agreed with Lautner about Williamson's positions in the early 1930's, Gil Green's position as head of the Young Communist League, and the positions of other prominent figures in the Communist organization.

Frank S. Meyer (British Communist who transferred to the American Party in 1934 and left it in 1946), an instructor at the Jefferson School of Social Science and a close friend of Budenz, also identified Eisler as Edwards. He also testified that Gil Green was head of the Young Communist League in 1934 and district organizer in the New York district in 1943.

It is obvious that very little of this testimony was significant. The identification of leaders of the open Communist Party could have been established by reference to published documents. That is true of much testimony given by former Communists, including Lautner himself. To make this point is not, of course, to attack the veracity of the witnesses.

Their veracity did not, however, go unchallenged. The testimony of two of these witnesses, Johnson and Crouch, as well as that of a third, Matusow, was stricken from the record of the SACB proceeding against the Communist Party at the direction of the Supreme Court after the Party made substantially uncontested allegations that these three had committed perjury in other proceedings relating to the issue of communism. It should be noted that the wholesale lying of which they were accused was of an entirely different order of magnitude from the occasional inconsistencies that are bound to enter the testimony of even the most scrupulously honest witness.

Another category of corroborative witness was the secret FBI agent. These people joined the Party at the instance of the FBI and, in some cases, managed to attain positions of some prominence. Their success may be a commentary on the almost pathetic eagerness of the Party to attract recruits.

Perhaps the most important of these witnesses was Mary Stalcup Markward, who served as an FBI agent within the Party from 1943 to 1950 and who was a member of the district board for Maryland. Her veracity was attacked in the SACB Communist Party proceeding. At the Supreme Court's direction, the Board re-examined her testimony at the same time as that of Crouch, Johnson, and Matusow, but found her to be a credible witness. Her testimony is not particularly startling. She agreed with Lautner about the Party's new orientation after the 1945 convention and agreed with his assessment of the importance of the Duclos letter in bringing it about. She also corroborated his testimony that propaganda material prepared by the Cominform was made available to Party functionaries, thereby lending further support to the Government's contention that the Party was under the domination of the International Communist movement directed from Soviet Russia.

In one instance, there is some corroboration for parts of Lautner's story from a defendant in a Smith Act prosecution. Elizabeth Gurley Flynn, who took the stand in her own behalf, agreed that Lautner had been a close friend of hers and testified that she had been a witness to his wedding. She also corroborated his identification of certain well-known leaders of the open Party. None of this agreement, however reassuring it might be to one concerned about Lautner's general familiarity with the Communist Party, was in the slightest degree significant. Indeed, it tended to emphasize the relatively innocuous character of much of Lautner's information.

As might be expected, Lautner's testimony contradicted that of defendants in Smith Act prosecutions on the very few occasions when they covered the same ground. Unfortunately for comparative study, very few Smith Act defendants testified in their own behalf, and of those who did, fewer still had anything to say responsive to Lautner's testimony. The principal exception was Elizabeth Gurley Flynn, who was perhaps the most forthright of the defendants in the various proceedings and who happened to be well acquainted with Lautner.

On several occasions, Flynn disagreed with Lautner about what the facts actually were and how they were to be interpreted. For example, she insisted that Lautner was never a member of the National Review Commission. On the contrary, she testified, Lautner as a close friend complained to her on several occasions between 1947 and 1949 about not being appointed to the National Commission, and asked her to intercede for him. On cross-examination, government counsel attempted to show that the chairmen of the state committees were invariably appointed to the corresponding committee at the national level. When asked about certain specific persons and their positions, Flynn began to balk about "naming names" and finally was held in contempt.

Flynn claimed that she did not know Gerhardt Eisler to be a Communist International representative (an almost incredible assertion) and did not know him under the name of Edwards. She denied that he ever attended National Committee meetings. She went further and averred that there had been no directive or instruction from the Soviet Party, to her knowledge, since 1938.

Lautner had testified that elaborate security precautions were taken at the 1949 convention to ensure that only delegates gained entrance to the convention floor, and that the press was confined to the foyer, where it was "fed press releases." Flynn, however, maintained that the convention was open to the public and the press. It would appear that on a matter of this sort the facts could easily have been ascertained, but so far as the record shows they were not.

Lautner had testified that Dennis initiated the proposal at the 1948 convention that the National Committee have only 13 members, the existing National Board with the addition of Miss Flynn. Flynn testified that the proposal was arrived at by the caucuses of the state delegations and announced by Dennis. The issue involved was, of course, whether the Party was authoritarian or democratic in practice.

Flynn claimed that Foster's book, *The Twilight of World Capitalism*, published in 1949, was printed in over 100,000 copies, given wide circulation, and used for instruction in Party classes. (The book's thesis was that a united front coalition government could obtain majority support in the United States.) Lautner had denied hearing of the book while in the Party. Here again, the record fails to resolve a question whose answer should have been ascertainable.

The most important source for the impeachment of Lautner was Lautner himself. While the main outline of his story remained relatively unchanged throughout the many proceedings in which he testified, there are a number of instances in which a careful comparative reading reveals inconsistencies and intrinsic contradictions. While these instances do not bulk large overall, they tend to raise some question about Lautner's accuracy and sincerity as a witness and, in particular, about his readiness to fit his evidence to the exigencies of the moment. A sampling of seven instances is given below.

(1) One rather questionable area of testimony is Lautner's account of the period from June to August, 1945, the period immediately following his discharge from the Army, which includes the important event of the 1945 Party convention. In particular, his testimony about the Duclos article or letter raises doubts about his veracity. The letter was highly critical of Browder's deviations during 1944–45 and was important to the Government in establishing the revolutionary aspect of the Party purpose after 1945. In 1952, before the SACB, Lautner mentioned the letter as a "factor" in calling the 1945 convention. When asked where he first read the article, he replied: "It was the *World Telegram* or the *New York Times*, or both. And then a day after, or so, in the *Daily Worker*." In the *Flynn* (1952) case and in subsequent proceedings, Lautner claimed that he read the article at the direction of Williamson, the National Secretary of the Political Association, in the *Daily Worker*. In *U.S.* v. *Forest* (1954), Lautner was asked whether the letter was printed in papers other than the *Daily Worker*. Lautner responded: "I recall that it was published in the *World Telegram* but I didn't read it in the *World Telegram*; I heard about it."

The "directions" from Williamson were not mentioned in early testimony. However, in later proceedings these alleged directions were used to identify other incriminating documents. In the *Forest* case, for example, Lautner remembered an incriminating letter written to the *Daily Worker* of July 9, 1945, by one of the defendants as an article he had read at Williamson's direction. In the 1952 SACB proceeding the opportunity and motive to mention Williamson's "directions" had been clearly present, but nothing was said on the subject. Lautner was asked what he did and where he went after his release from the Army. In response, he gave a meaningless account of meetings at Party headquarters with Dennis and Foster and then with Williamson and Stachel, in which the subject of his new assignment—whether or not he should be sent to Ohio as a functionary—was discussed. These meetings were alluded to in the *Flynn* case, but there Lautner placed them *after* the 1945 convention, which would have been too late for him to receive the directions which he claimed to have had. One suspects that the directions became a convenient device for introducing through Lautner contemporaneous documents that might not otherwise have been admissible.

Another conversation alleged to have taken place during this period takes on increasing significance as it is alluded to in subsequent hearings. Lautner described a meeting with Flynn about a week after his release from the service. Flynn allegedly discussed in detail the Party's attitude toward Browderism. The conversation was not mentioned in the SACB hearing. In 1952, in *U.S. v. Flynn*, Elizabeth Gurley Flynn denied having had such a conversation with Lautner. In the 1953 proceedings before the SACB against the Jefferson School of Social Science, Lautner added to his account of this meeting as given in the *Flynn* case, stating that Flynn also told him that the Party maintained a liaison between Browder and President Roosevelt.

Lautner also alleged that at the time of this meeting, about a week after his release from the Army, he had already been reassigned to work with the Hungarian National Bureau and the Nationality Groups Commission—another conflict with his testimony in *Flynn*, where he stated that the conversation with Party leaders about his assignment occurred after the 1945 convention.

(2) In most hearings, the subject of the 1943 *Schneiderman* decision was broadened upon cross-examination. In that case the Supreme Court reversed a decision that a Communist leader should be deported on the ground that it had not been shown that

the Communist Party was subversive. The authority of this decision was considerably weakened by subsequent cases. Nevertheless, the defense made much of its favorable implications and of Justice Murphy's comment that a tenable interpretation of Communist theory might be that force would be used only to counteract force. This was buttressed by reference to a declaration by William Z. Foster that Murphy's suggestion was an acceptable formulation of Communist theory.

In the California Smith Act trial (which, by an interesting coincidence, took its name from the same William Schneiderman who had been involved in the 1943 case), Lautner was questioned about his answer, "no," on an army questionnaire about participation in subversive activities. (The time in question was late 1942 or early 1943, prior to the favorable decision in the Supreme Court in *Schneiderman.*) Lautner stated: ". . . and at that time the Schneiderman case was pending in the U.S. Supreme Court, and the U.S. Supreme Court brought a decision on that case and, therefore, in all honesty and truthfulness I answered that question 'no.' "

But in other hearings, when the *Schneiderman* decision was brought up by defense counsel, Lautner seemed very reluctant to allow the defense to develop its favorable import. Although it had become a familiar line of cross-examination by 1955, when asked about it then, Lautner testified:

A. I have no recollection of it.

     .   .   .

Q. At any time?
A. Well, I was in the Army. Once I heard in 19— I was in Africa when on the radio I heard something about some kind of Schneiderman decision. That is the only reason I have at the moment and that was . . .
Q. You have heard about the decision; is that a fair statement to say?
A. Well, I don't know what decision you are referring to. There may be more than one decision. I heard about one decision in 1943. I was in Africa—I was on detail.
Q. You have no recollection of having heard of this decision that I am talking about?
A. Well, what is this decision that you are talking about, Mr. Seltzer? You are talking about this decision. I don't know what this decision is.

After being confronted with his testimony in the *Flynn* case, where he had admitted the importance of the decision to the Party, Lautner answered questions about it.

(3) In 1949 Foster wrote a book, *The Twilight of World Capitalism*, which has a number of passages that are consistent with the defense's interpretation of Communist theory. In the *Silverman* case (1955), Lautner testified that he received a copy of the book in his box at Party headquarters. Then, upon further questioning, he stated:

I may have read it . . . I think I did read it once. . . . *I did, and I took issue on certain things with Foster on that.* And in '50 he admitted he made mistakes.*

On redirect Lautner stated: *"All I recall, that I got the book and I drew certain conclusions myself from this book . . ."**

But, in the *Flynn* case in 1952, Lautner had testified: "I don't recall that book, no." And then: "I have no recollection of reading the book, but I know about the book."

Q. Mr. Witness, I am asking you, is that a fact, that you personally disagreed with the position stated in that excerpt which I read from Foster's book?
A. Foster disagreed with Foster.

. . .

A. I don't take any position on what Foster says. I don't take a personal position on it.

. . .

A. I didn't take any position on it.

(4) A recurring topic for cross-examination was Lautner's initial conference with the FBI. Before the SACB, Lautner testified that the first "conference" lasted 15 minutes. Lautner stated he was told he would be contacted and a few days later he was called by telephone and went to the New York office of the Bureau. He didn't recall whether the conference was long, and when asked what transpired, he replied:

To tell the truth, there was a period at that time where the Federal Bureau of Investigation was not so sure about me because they knew that I was not an agent, and they had ideas that I was trying to tell them a story over there, that I was trying to give a story to the FBI and get into the good graces of the FBI. That suspicion was there for quite some time. If that is what you want to have, I don't know.

---

* Italics mine.

In later proceedings Lautner did not mention his suspicion that the FBI did not trust him. In the *Flynn* and *Board of Regents* proceedings, Lautner stated that his first conference lasted four or five hours and continued the next day. When shown his testimony before the SACB, Lautner claimed that he considered the 15-minute session with the FBI to be a "meeting" and not a "conference." The cross-examiner then pointed out that the term "conference" was used in the question before the SACB.

(5) *The History of the Communist Party of the Soviet Union* was always one of the main Government exhibits, and Lautner usually testified to his familiarity with it, prior to the introduction of passages from the book. In most proceedings, he mentioned the use of it in his 1946–48 classes. But in both the *Flynn* case and the *Silverman* case, he also mentioned giving seminars on the book: "I had one—about three or four seminars on the *History of the CPSU* in West Virginia." In *U.S.* v. *Fujimoto,* when the defense was attempting to bring out statements in the book consistent with its theory of the case, the following testimony was taken:

A. I read the *History of the CPSU* but I have no recollection of that quotation.
Q. Did you ever teach—
A. *The History of the CPSU,* no.
Q. No?
A. No, not as a subject matter.
Q. Did you ever use it in any course that you taught?
A. Oh, yes. I used it but I used it in relation to the subject matter that I was teaching.

(6) In the *Frankfeld* case (1952), Lautner was asked about having prepared his testimony in advance in certain cases.

Q. Isn't it true, Mr. Lautner, that the questions and answers that you have given here on direct examination were written out beforehand and gone over by you?
A. That is not correct. The testimony that I have given here is my testimony.
Q. But were these questions and answers written out beforehand?
A. No. That is not true.

But in the *Flynn* case (1952), he testified as follows:

Q. In the Baltimore case (*Frankfeld*), in the Washington case, and in the California case, isn't it true that the questions put to you by the

attorney, and the answers you gave were written out beforehand?
That is the only question I am putting to you, Mr. Lautner.
A. Yes.
Q. That is true?
A. Yes, in consultation with the attorney based on my testimony.

(7) In his extensive testimony on theoretical questions, Lautner was at times inconsistent and even contradictory. For example, in *U.S.* v. *Kuzma* (1954), he testified as follows regarding
Communist theory:

Q. Has there been any occasion since June 1945, when the Communist
Party has said that there were objective conditions for a revolutionary situation?
A. Well, the Communist Party says, and I thought, and I was taught,
too, that this whole epoch since the turn of the century is ripe—
there is a revolutionary situation. Stalin in his *Foundations* defines
it. I can find it for you.

But in *U.S.* v. *Fujimoto* (1952), he had answered the same
question differently:

Q. Let me ask you this: Can you tell me at any time since June 1945,
when there have been objective conditions in the United States of
America which the Communist Party have said constitute the objec-
tive conditions for a revolutionary situation?
A. At this moment I cannot recall. No, I don't think objective condi-
tions prevailed since or did—
Q. Your answer is then, that no such objective conditions prevailed since
June 1935.
A. That is right.
Q. '45 rather.
A. Yes.
Q. Is that right?
A. Yes.

In *Kuzma* when this contradiction was pointed out, Lautner
explained, a little lamely, that his answer in *Fujimoto* was confined
to the United States, whereas in *Kuzma* it referred to the world
situation.
Again, in *U.S.* v. *Kuzma* (1954), he was asked:

Q. Now at the bakers and furriers school didn't you teach there that war
between the United States and the Soviet Union was not inevitable?
A. I didn't teach that.

But to the same question in the *Flynn* case in 1952, he had answered:

Q. All right, didn't you teach your classes that the Communist Party took the position that a war between the United States and the Soviet Union was not inevitable?

A. Yes.

Q. And didn't you teach your class that the Communist Party took the position that war between the United States and the Soviet Union could be avoided?

A. Yes, that is correct.

Lautner reconciled this testimony by stating that this line was "tactical" and the question was "tricky."

Before the Board of Regents of the State of New York, in 1953, the following exchange took place:

Q. As a matter of fact, were you not specifically taught during your membership in the Communist Party, not to memorize passages and propositions from Marxist-Leninist writings?

A. That is not true, also.

But, again in the *Flynn* case, in 1952, Lautner had answered:

Q. Let us confine our attention now to the writings of Lenin, the selected works, collected works, the Little Lenin Library. When you studied these writings of Lenin, you were taught not to learn by heart certain isolated passages and propositions from Marxism-Leninism, were you not?

A. That is correct.

Q. Were you not taught, Mr. Witness, that no passage from Marxist-Leninist writings can apply to any and all situations?

A. I was taught that there is a certain— There is a basic—

. . .

A. I can't answer that question yes or no. What I was taught—

Q. You were also taught not to apply certain passages to any and all situations, isn't that right?

A. That is correct.

Q. You were taught that no passage can apply to any and all situations, weren't you?

A. That is correct.

On another question, he answered the Board of Regents as follows:

Q. And were you not taught, Mr. Witness, that the authority of the Communist Party cannot be sustained by violence but only by the confidence of the working class?

A. Well, once a dictatorship of the proletariat is established and the Party is the ruling party—

Q. Please, Mr. Witness.

A. Not in those words.

Q. You weren't?

A. No. Not in those words.

In the *Fujimoto* case the previous year, he had not been reluctant in answering:

Q. And according *to what you were taught*, did he say in that book that the authority of the Party is sustained not by violence but by the confidence of the working class?

A. That is what Stalin said, yes.

Q. And did he say that the confidence of the working class in the Communist Party is not gained by violence, because violence would only kill it, did he say that?

A. Yes.

All of these instances of inconsistency have one thing in common. They show a progressive hardening, from early to later proceedings, in Lautner's attitude toward his former comrades. He became more and more reluctant to say anything that might conceivably be construed as helping them.

One result of repeating testimony on several occasions is that inconsistencies develop from one occasion to the next, increasing the area of exposure to effective cross-examination. We have noted some instances of this tendency in Lautner's testimony. But there is another result. As the witness gains some practical experience in what will be asked of him, his testimony about events and circumstances described in earlier hearings becomes refined and expanded. Points on which he has been subjected to challenge are modified to disarm attack; points that were not stated categorically tend to harden into fixed positions and to carry greater impact. Again, this is a natural tendency to which all witnesses are probably subject to some extent. The question is whether the variations remain within tolerable limits. Lautner testified with increasing self-assurance and positiveness as he retold his experiences. Testimony that at first seemed ambiguous or aimless later became sharp and forceful. In the 1952 SACB proceeding against the American Communist Party, for example, Lautner was ques-

tioned about the purpose of the Hungarian National Training
School. He responded: "The purpose was . . . to bring together
from the country as a whole promising young Party members and
put them through a Party education and to develop Party functionaries out of them." In 1955, Lautner's response to the same
question was: "This school had one purpose in mind, and it was
so stated: to develop out of the student body professional revolutionaries for the coming period."

Here are three more examples of the evolution of Lautner's
testimony.

(1) Before the SACB in 1952, Lautner testified that in his
classes the Program of the Communist International "was referred
to. It was not used. It was referred to as reference material." Three
years later, in *U.S.* v. *Forest,* Lautner volunteered: "I taught the
Program of the Communist International." In the same year when
asked about this document in *U.S.* v. *Silverman,* Lautner claimed
it was used "as the basic Stalinist program around which Stalin
consolidated his leadership and eliminated all the opportunists."

(2) The colorful term "Aesopian" had been used repeatedly
by Budenz in his testimony about the 1945 and 1948 constitutions.
Lautner had frequently interpreted the same documents as Budenz, but generally had referred to them as "self-serving." In 1955,
however, Lautner used Budenz's characterization in describing the
1948 constitution, and defined the historical meaning of the term
for the edification of the jury.

(3) The objectives and policy of the Party were important to
the Government's case before the SACB, and Lautner was provided with a number of opportunities to describe them. Defense
counsel in later proceedings made much of the fact that despite
his voluminous testimony, he never once used the expression "force
and violence." However, later testimony abounded with the expression. For example, in *U.S.* v. *Forest* (1954), Lautner described
the objectives of the Party as "the destruction by force and violence
of capitalism and its government as speedily as conditions will
permit in the name of the working class led by the Communist
Party in alliance with the sections of the Negro people and the
petty bourgeoisie."

What may be a negative aspect of Lautner's evolution as a
witness is his relative unresponsiveness, either through lack of

candor or through faulty recollection, to cross-examiners' questions, which, if answered directly, would favor the defense position or impair his usefulness to the Government. Again, this tendency is not an unnatural one; but in proceedings where so much was at stake it is somewhat disturbing to find evidence that a witness had made the cause in which he testified so strongly his own that he seemed, on occasion, to have abandoned the role of witness for that of advocate.

For example, although Lautner elsewhere claimed that his principal duty was to build the influence of the Communist Party with the United Mine Workers in West Virginia from 1936 to 1940, when asked on cross-examination in the Los Angeles case (1952) whether coal miners' wages were very low, Lautner responded: "I don't know. I did not work in the coal mines. I didn't get any paycheck and I don't know. How would I know what the wages were?"

Since the Government's theory was that the 1948 constitution's clause purporting to proscribe force and violence was nothing but window-dressing inserted in the constitution because of the *Dennis* indictments, the presence of the same provision in the 1938 constitution (as amended up to 1942) was a significant piece of evidence for the defense. Lautner, when questioned about this constitution, claimed to have no recollection of it, even though he was a delegate from West Virginia to the convention that adopted it.

While Chairman of the State Review Commission in New York, Lautner apparently wrote a report about informers in which he said: "Persons who were morally corrupt or suspected of moral corruption were likely candidates for FBI informers." This report was an understandably popular topic for cross-examiners, but Lautner would not recall it.

After having obtained the court's assistance in the attempt to get Lautner to answer, defense counsel asked Lautner: "Is it not true that you knew generally that trade unionists kept their membership secret in many instances because they were fearful they would be discharged if their membership in trade unions was known?" Despite his experience in West Virginia in the late 1930's and his work in Detroit in 1930 where he claimed he "recruited some (workers) who worked in the Ford Plant, who are working there right now," Lautner's answer to this question was: "I give you an answer, an answer with a little explanation because a 'yes' or 'no' doesn't answer this particular question that you raise because I am speaking now—you asked me to speak as to my knowledge, what do I know about persecution in the trade union movement and obviously—"

In addition to these illustrations of the evolution of Lautner's testimony, there are many instances of his having given a definite response in one proceeding but modifying, qualifying, or claiming not to remember the response in a later proceeding.

VI

It has become something of a commonplace to assert that informers' testimony is highly suspect in general and that this is especially true of the testimony of ex-Communists. Such generalizations about types of witnesses are not very useful. Ultimately, the testimony of a witness must stand or fall on its own merits. Nevertheless, there are problems that arise when the testimony of a particular witness who happens to be an "informer" is being evaluated. It may be a useful exercise to consider some of these problems as they apply to Lautner's testimony, if only to demonstrate the danger of unsupported generalizations on the subject.

First, there is the general issue of motive for falsification. It seems generally true that former Communists experience a strong reaction against their old allegiance and, in many cases, manifest an intense desire to do everything they can to abjure it. One also suspects that many former Communists abjure one set of absolutes in favor of another, that what formerly was the purest white becomes for them the deepest black, and that this tendency renders their account of the past suspect. In Lautner's case, notwithstanding the unpleasant nature of his expulsion from the Party, there is little to suggest any such motive for falsification. Neither the form nor the content of what he had to say exhibits the zeal of the reformed sinner.

It is true that Lautner profited financially from his testimony. Indeed, his career as a consultant to the Department of Justice appears to have been considerably more lucrative than his work as a Party functionary. It may be surmised that he was aware that this source of wealth might quickly dry up if his testimony was not helpful, and that this gave him a motive to see that it was.

This factor is an imponderable one and could be factually evaluated only if we had available transcriptions of Lautner's earliest interviews with the Justice Department.

He may have had other motives for giving false testimony. As a participant in what has now been branded as unlawful conspiracy, Lautner could himself have been subjected to criminal penalties, although the statute of limitations barred his prosecution by 1953, three years after his withdrawal from the conspiracy. And if, as seems possible, he falsified his naturalization papers in some material respect, he may still be liable to denaturalization and deportation.

Motive for falsification aside, there are other problems. One is that Lautner may not have been what he represented himself as having been, a bona fide Communist. In several of the earlier proceedings, defense counsel attempted to establish that Lautner might have been an FBI informer, or at any rate, that he might have lost faith some time before he left the Party. The evidence supporting this assertion is tenuous and need not be recounted at length. It comes down to what may be the rather suspicious circumstances under which Lautner retained certain bits of documentary evidence about his activities in the Party, coupled with extremely vague intimations that he may have been a "Titoist" or some other species of deviationist during a portion of his connection with the Party.

In many of the proceedings, counsel intimated that much of Lautner's knowledge may have come from sources other than his memory. Lautner denied having read the transcripts of this testimony. But as a consultant to the Department of Justice, he claimed to have done research in preparation for testifying. How far his subconscious may have merged later study with earlier memory is an interesting psychological question. Lautner admitted having one aid to his memory: in a number of the Smith Act trials— *Flynn, Frankfeld, Schneiderman,* and *Silverman*—and before the Subversive Activities Control Board and the Board of Regents— his questions and answers were written out beforehand by the attorney.

VII

A study of a witness's testimony that is focused primarily upon intrinsic consistency, as this one necessarily has been, seems foredoomed to be indecisive. Many events and conversations must be taken as uncontradicted, particularly in the Smith Act trials, since those who were in a position to affirm or deny did not (with the notable exception of Elizabeth Gurley Flynn) take the stand in their own behalf. Even where there is a conflict in testimony about the same event, one is left with the choice between one memory and another, between a biased professional witness and a biased Communist defendant.

Furthermore, the line of inquiry is limited by the nature of the fact-finding process and the particular exigencies of the problem under scrutiny. Areas of testimony that arouse suspicions in one proceeding may not be followed up in another. Extrinsic evidence is, for the most part, not available, and the rules of evidence further restrict one's perspective. Since the scope of direct examination controls what can be inquired into on cross-examination, instances which have embarrassed the witness in one proceeding may be avoided in another.

As we move from fact to theory, the problem is compounded. It is most difficult to evaluate Lautner's testimony about Communist theory, since the ultimate issue is itself cloudy. Were it clear, Lautner's testimony could easily be evaluated; but his testimony would then be unnecessary. Since the over-all issue in these proceedings was the "true" attitude of the Communist Party, Lautner's testimony must be accepted or rejected ultimately on the basis of one's own evaluation of the documentary evidence about Communist doctrine. It seems clear that "force and violence" is involved in Communist theory, but force and violence when? Only as a means of preventing an oppressive minority from perpetuating itself, as the Party contended, or as an inevitable step in the Communist accession to power, as the Government maintained?

The ultimate question is: What did the term "Marxism-Leninism" mean to those who were accused of having embraced the doctrine? The term comprehends the whole tangled skein of Communist theory, as expounded by Marx, Engels, Lenin, Stalin, and other party classicists. In defining the term, Lautner testified that Communist theory looks to the use of "force and violence" to "smash the bourgeois state" and to establish the "dictatorship of the proletariat." It was the use of the term "Marxism-Leninism" in the 1945 constitution that was the basis of Lautner's characterization of the constitution as misleading insofar as it appeared to eschew force and violence. But elaboration of the connotations of "Marxism-Leninism" leads into a quagmire of esoteric terminology.

Lautner relied heavily on his training and experience in giving answers that substantiated the Government's view of the nature of Communism. His knowledge of the literature from attendance at schools, presence at national conventions, teaching activities, and discussions with leading Party functionaries served as the basis for introducing into the record the real case against Communism—the horde of documentary exhibits, including classic texts, pamphlets, and newspaper articles published over many decades and emanating from diverse sources. Excerpts from these documents were read into evidence by government attorneys. Other excerpts were read by defense attorneys. The ultimate problem of judgment is not unlike that involved in determining whether a book is "obscene," and may be just as inherently difficult, if not impossible, to resolve. Judgment about fact becomes so intertwined with fact that it is impossible to say where one begins and the other leaves off.

If those who led the Communist Party believed in and advocated the overthrow of the Government by force and violence at the first opportunity of success, as the jury verdicts in the various Smith Act cases must have concluded they did, then the great bulk of Lautner's testimony is consistent with the truth and perhaps overly conservative at times. If, on the other hand, those same leaders advocated forcible overthrow if and only if the proponets of the existing order would themselves resort to force to prevent peaceful change, then Lautner at least exaggerated and perhaps told knowing falsehoods. And if neither of those two polar positions represents the "true" nature of American communism, Lautner is guilty of oversimplification, a vice which may well have been inherent in the nature of these proceedings.

Since much of Lautner's testimony concerned verifiable (although unverified) facts, it seems that the inconsistencies and other deficiencies in his testimony culled from the many thousands of pages in which that testimony has been reproduced may well be trivial and insignificant. In that sense, the conclusion must be reached on a fair appraisal that he is a "reliable" witness.

On balance, however, a favorable judgment as to Lautner's "reliability" must be put in proper perspective. Reliability does not automatically ensure significance. What the proceedings in which Lautner played so large a role sought to resolve were large and complicated questions about the nature of American communism. The forms in which these questions were cast for purposes of legal fact-finding were themselves somewhat oversimplified. The Smith Act asks for a determination whether certain individuals advocated the "duty, necessity, desirability, or propriety of overthrowing or destroying the government . . . by force or violence." The Internal Security Act requires a finder-of-fact to say whether an organization is "substantially directed, dominated, or controlled by the foreign government or foreign organization controlling the world Communist movement." These questions do not evoke the full complexity of motives and objectives animating the Communist movement over time. But, oversimplified as they are, these questions place a heavy burden on fact-finding processes, involving as they do an inquiry into beliefs and attitudes that do not necessarily manifest themselves in overt action and whose evolution can be understood only by recapitulating decades of history.

Legal fact-finding processes simply are not equal to the demands placed upon them by these proceedings. Edmund Burke's famous remark about the difficulty of indicting a whole nation suggests the corollary that legal processes are not intended for the job of trying a chapter of history. The judgmental processes involved in ascertaining the nature of the American Communist movement and in understanding those who were engaged in it pose, ultimately, a task for the historian rather than for the trier-of-fact.

6 · CONCLUSION

We are back at the starting-point of this inquiry. What can we say about the efficacy of official fact-finding processes in the light of these accounts of the testimony of four ex-Communist witnesses? Has the operation of the processes under scrutiny afforded a basis for even a fragmentary set of conclusions about the witnesses and their stories? I think that my conclusions on this score are due the reader, even though it is the process by which the testimony has been elicited rather than its credibility that is primarily at stake here. Therefore, I shall start this summing-up with some brief comments on the witnesses and their testimony.

No aspect of any of these witnesses' stories has been more fully explored or more searchingly tested than the testimony of Whittaker Chambers as it refers to Alger Hiss. Nor has there often been, by the standards of the litigation process, more sweeping vindication for a witness. The jury had to believe either Hiss or Chambers, not on marginal details but in the large. Further, in order to believe Chambers, it had to reject all reasonable doubts in favor of Hiss. This it did. Nothing in the transcript of the trials or in what took place after the trials leads me to think that the jury was unjustified in reaching the conclusion that it did. Absent further information of a kind we are not likely to get, it seems to me that the suspension of disbelief in which so many engaged for so long ought to be abandoned.

That said, the case remains enigmatic in its larger aspects. As I have pointed out, much testimony might be compelled that would bear materially on the question of the extent and degree of Hiss's Communist affiliations. And other aspects of Chambers's story that remain largely uncorroborated, notably his denunciation of Harry Dexter White, would likewise be clarified by further examination of other witnesses. Much material exists to support an analysis of the Harry Dexter White case. But I doubt that any very firm conclusions could be reached without the development of substantially more evidence than is now in the public record.

Finally, there is the question of Chambers's demeanor as a witness. His testimony strikes me as being on the surface far more candid, far less evasive and less defensive, than that of any of the other witnesses. This, perhaps, is not too surprising. Chambers was obviously a man of great intelligence and sensitivity, with a gift of self-expression. Whether that gift may not sometimes have been used to mask a less than candid response is a troubling question. What seems clear is that his forensic talents glittered in the dramatic atmosphere of the Hiss trials. Whether or not he was invariably a truthful witness—whether or not his dramatic capacity and his lively sense of self-protection may at times have got the better of accurate recollection—Chambers emerges, for me at least, as a largely convincing witness.

By contrast, no witness's story is better calculated to inspire mistrust or disbelief than Elizabeth Bentley's. The extravagance of her claims about her espionage contacts, the vagueness of her testimony about the content of the secret material that she allegedly received, the absence of corroboration for most of her story, and, above all, her evasiveness as a witness, all combine to raise serious doubts about her reliability. And yet, hers is clearly no story invented out of whole cloth.

Her relationship with Golos, who allegedly masterminded her espionage work, is amply corroborated, as is the fact of her relationship with Remington and several others of the supposed contacts. Moreover, most of her contacts had ideological affiliations that might well have predisposed them to cooperate with her. Finally, the refusal of many of those whom she accused to come forward with denials or explanations, though it is inconclusive, must weigh heavily in any judgment formed on the basis of a record as indeterminate as the present one.

If it were not for Miss Bentley's exploitation of her experience for profit, I would be a good deal less skeptical about much of her testimony. But the tendency in her book to embroider a narrative for dramatic effect quickens one's suspicions that the same tendency may exist in her sworn testimony. As I have pointed out, those suspicions are often confirmed. Far more than the testimony of Whittaker Chambers, Elizabeth Bentley's testimony seems to require that a good deal more evidence be adduced before firm conclusions can be formed: evidence from persons who have so far remained silent, evidence from the investigative files of the FBI.

If one accepts the main outlines of Miss Bentley's story, there remains the question of what the people with whom she was in contact thought they were doing. In the case of the Silvermasters and Ullmann, it is tolerably clear that if the facts were at all as Miss Bentley asserted they were, her contacts must have known that their activity was designed to transmit official secrets to a foreign power. But that is not necessarily true of the other participants in the alleged Silvermaster ring, most of whom did not, by Miss Bentley's own admission, know her. Nor is it necessarily true of some of her individual contacts, such as Redmont, Miller, and Lee. The range of possibilities is wide, and we shall probably never know just where along the spectrum from knowing acts of espionage to innocent indiscretion the truth lies.

The Remington case afforded the only opportunity for an exhaustive cross-examination of Miss Bentley. That opportunity was not fully utilized, both for reasons of trial tactics and because of the unavailability of potentially impeaching material. Her questioning before Congressional committees was hardly calculated to test her credibility.

In lawyers' terms, I would say that Miss Bentley has made out a prima facie case, that the burden of going forward is on those who would disprove her account, but that she is not entitled to a directed verdict in her favor.

As a commentator on Communist aims and objectives Budenz is impressive, although we may doubt that the Party was ever quite as monolithic as he portrayed it. That doubt, however, is created more by the views of historians who have studied the American Communist Party than it is by anything contained in the record of Budenz's numerous examinations and cross-examinations.

Indeed, it may be fairly observed that proceedings of the kind involved in this study are less well suited for providing any kind of basis for conclusions about general Communist aims and objectives, or about the philosophical underpinning of American Communism, than they are for demonstrating what did or did not happen on any given occasion.

When it comes to the delineation of facts, the testimony of Budenz is, in the main, of a hearsay nature. We cannot know how well he remembers what he was told or how accurate it was in the first place. The testimony of other ex-Party members suggests that he may have exaggerated his position in Party councils. It is accordingly difficult to evaluate his "official reports" with the slender information we have.

In his examination by the hostile Tydings Committee he was evasive when pressed. His testimony about Lattimore was particularly vulnerable. Why had he not accused Lattimore sooner, particularly when occasions on which he might appropriately have done so were not lacking? When pressed on that matter, he tended to filibuster rather than to answer directly. That is not in itself an indication of unreliability, but it suggests an unwillingness to admit the possibility of mistake, a trait that can quite unconsciously influence a witness's recollection.

More important than any of these considerations is the question suggested at the end of the chapter on Budenz's testimony: To what extent has he allowed his judgment of who is and who is not a Communist to be shaped by his own views of desirable public policy? One wonders how many of Budenz's fellow-travelers are people who simply found themselves in the same place at the same time on errands of their own. No doubts on this score seem to have plagued Budenz, or, for the most part, his interrogators.

John Lautner's workmanlike role in the Communist movement is echoed in his stolid, pedantic, and relatively unshakable testimony. To be sure, he has been tripped up on more than one occasion. He has also been evasive, militantly self-justifying, and all the other things one might expect of a man who, late in life, finds himself in the unenviable position of repudiating his life's work. Yet he gives the over-all impression of close familiarity with the Party's ideology and, more important, with the day-to-day details of its operation.

Strongly in Lautner's favor as a witness is the fact that unlike the other three, he has not carved out an extra-testimonial career as an ex-Communist. He has been paid, and paid well, for his testimony. But he has not had the additional impetus to fabricate that comes from the creation of a public image that must constantly be refurbished by yet another round of revelations.

The frequent repetition of Lautner's story gave rise, as we have seen, to a number of inconsistencies. It also resulted in opportunities for him to sharpen the lines of his testimony, to supply point where it had previously been lacking. But viewed in the total context of his testimony, the inconsistencies appear relatively minor, and the net impression is of a conscientious effort to recall the details of his past.

As I have suggested, the questionable areas in the testimony of the ex-Communist witnesses relate mainly to detailed assertions of fact that are difficult, if not impossible, to verify on the basis of the available evidence. There is enough corroborative testimony and enough extrinsic evidence to sustain acceptance of the main outlines of the story told by each of the witnesses. However, it seems obvious that firm conclusions about the reliability of the witnesses should not be ventured on the basis of the present public record without a systematic examination of the shortcomings of the processes used to elicit and test the evidence.

The residual doubts may not be very important in the total context of what these witnesses have said. Certainly there has been little in the way of established disproof. But a common thread of attitude and personality runs through all of the testimony examined, which restrains a cautious observer from giving it wholehearted credence. All four of these witnesses, to say nothing of the many other ex-Communists whose testimony has been peripherally examined, appear to have forsaken one set of absolutes for another. The urge for self-vindication appears to be so strong that anyone who is not with them must necessarily be against them. This tendency is most noticeable in Budenz's case, but it afflicts the others as well. Then there is the troublesome matter of pecuniary motive. All these witnesses have admittedly profited financially from their roles as denouncers of the hated Communist conspiracy. While they cannot be blamed for wanting to salvage what they could from the wreckage of their lives, their interest in being "useful" witnesses is obvious. And "useful" has meant, all too often, useful to the immediate political purposes of their interrogators. It would be surprising if this interest did not result in exaggerations and even in occasional distortions.

The almost feverish pursuit of publicity that surrounded the development of so much of this testimony has undoubtedly contributed to the unsatisfactory state of the record. We have observed in detail instances in which that was so. Moreover, the tendentious nature of all the proceedings, which we shall examine in a moment, imposed additional limitations on the development of the facts. Hence, to the extent that the testimony of these witnesses leaves doubts unresolved, the witnesses, those whom they accused, and their interrogators may all have been in varying degrees the victims of a set of processes that are generally unsatisfactory for dealing with an important social problem.

If the four preceding chapters have not lent some support to my unenthusiastic appraisal of these processes, further statements to the same effect at this point will surely be fruitless. Nonetheless, it may be useful to point out systematically the shortcomings reflected in the analysis of specific testimony.

A question that must first be answered is: "shortcomings" viewed from what perspective? Is a perjury trial an adequate vehicle for determining whether X lied or told the truth on a given occasion? I think it is, or at any rate I am not prepared to suggest a better one. Is a Congressional investigation an adequate vehicle for arousing public opinion? Quite obviously it is, especially with the help of modern mass communications, as is shown by the rise and fall of Senator McCarthy. Is that same Congressional investigation an adequate vehicle for discovering the facts about an alleged danger and placing them before the public? Here the answer, based on the results of this study, must be No. It is from the perspective of official fact-finding as a basis for public enlightenment —and hence, if democratic theory has any merit, as a basis for rational action—that the processes here examined fall short.

If we were looking at the situation as of 1945 or 1946, when it was becoming apparent that American Communism was shedding all pretense of being a native radical movement and that our Government and other public institutions had been infiltrated by Communists, what should we be interested in knowing? We should presumably be interested in getting as coherent an account as possible of the nature of the Communist movement and the extent of Communist infiltration—by whom it was carried on, what they did, what their objectives were. Our job, in short, would be what we have traditionally regarded as the historian's job: to find out, in Ranke's classic phrase, *wie es eigentlich gewesen*—how it really happened. But compiling this history properly and swiftly would require the use of tools not in the possession of any historian, or of any private person. If it were to be done, it would have to be done by public agencies, armed with the power to compel people to tell what they knew and equipped to test and evaluate what they were told; and it would have to be done in an objective spirit of inquiry, without rancor and without a thought to gaining present political advantage by capitalizing on past blunders.

It was not done. Competing pressures of policy and the lack of a properly equipped and sufficiently disinterested organ of inquiry combined to frustrate the goal. What institutional factors caused this failure? Can we do better in the future? These are the questions to which the rest of this chapter is devoted.

II

We have been dealing with testimony developed, in the main, in three types of proceedings: Congressional investigations, administrative hearings, and court trials. In the next few pages, I shall say something about the advantages and disadvantages of each of these vehicles for eliciting and testing the stories of ex-Communist witnesses.

Congressional investigation has two great advantages: it is open-ended and it is nonadversary. Its scope is limited only by its constitutive authorization, which usually amounts to no limitation at all. That scope is vastly useful in developing testimony as a coherent whole, untrammeled by considerations of relevancy or materiality to a predetermined subject matter. It is no accident that the main outlines of a witness's story are usually to be found in the transcripts of a Congressional investigation rather than in the records of an administrative or judicial hearing. Compare, for example, Elizabeth Bentley's testimony before the House Un-American Activities Committee in 1948 with her testimony in the Remington case. The Committee record, for all its meanderings, contains the essence of her entire story, or at least makes it available to the reader who is willing to perform a certain amount of carpentry on it. The record of the Remington trial, by contrast, is intelligible only to one who is already familiar with the contours of Miss Bentley's story.

The other great advantage of the Congressional inquiry is that it takes place, at least in theory, in a nonadversary setting. Since winning or losing "the case" is not immediately at stake, witnesses are likely to speak more freely. To be sure, a witness may become a trifle slipshod when there is no formal cross-examination, but an informal cross-examination may be just as serviceable, as it was, for example, in the questioning of Budenz by the Tydings Committee and its counsel. In the ideal Congressional inquiry, the witness will be pressed without being bullied or intimidated. He will be allowed to tell his story in his own way, without the interruptions and altercations that mark a hotly contested trial.

These advantages, while theoretically impressive, are in practice rarely exploited to their full extent, and are in any event more than offset by several crippling disadvantages. Chief among these are politics and publicity. We have traced examples of both, and of their interplay; the point is too obvious to require extended comment. As long as the Congressional inquiry serves as an instrument of politics, a means by which political points are won and lost, its utility as a fact-finding institution in a highly charged context is bound to be sharply limited.

Less obvious but equally disadvantageous is the flimsy structure of the typical investigation. The committee members are busy men. They are forever having to leave the hearing room to go to the floor of the House or the Senate, or to some other, equally pressing committee meeting. Members wander in and out. The presiding officer may change several times during a single session. Sometimes the new man does not quite catch the drift of what has gone before. The whole business is apt to be quite unsystematic. The cure for all this is supposed to be the committee staff, particularly the committee counsel. But, as we have seen, staff members are not always adequately prepared. And the caliber of personnel, while outstanding in some cases, often leaves something to be desired.

Deficiencies in the organization and quality of staff personnel are in theory remediable, although there are undoubtedly limits to what can practically be done in these respects. For one thing staff positions on Congressional committees are an important form of patronage, and it is Utopian to suppose that this advantage will ever be voluntarily foregone. But even if we assume that improvement is possible, the staff is still the servant of the committee members. However fair-minded and competent staff members may be, they are powerless to prevent their masters from using the investigative process as a political platform.

The same observation applies to the structure of committee hearings. There is a fuzziness and lack of focus in all but the most firmly guided Congressional hearings that is perhaps the inevitable concomitant of their free-ranging and flexible character. More careful preparation for the hearing may sometimes mitigate this difficulty, but rarely overcomes it; an able counsel may preserve his sense of order, but he must defer to the Committee's sense of the priorities of the moment. Particularly when an inquiry lasts several weeks or longer, the place of the individual pieces in the total composition is often obscure. Loose ends have a tendency not to get tied up. A witness says that he will supply certain information later. Later turns out to be never. Or a suggestion is made that certain rebuttal testimony be called. Everyone agrees that it should be called, and then nothing more is heard about it. Names are tossed out, never to reappear. Confusion becomes the governing principle. The investigative proceeding becomes merely a demonstrative proceeding, and not a very good one at that. Instead of serving as a means for digging out evidence, evaluating it and reaching reasoned conclusions, the Congressional investigation in this context has shown itself to be just a vehicle for placing "facts" in the record without any real effort to ascertain either their probative value or their significance.

Palliatives for all this have often been suggested, ranging from elaborate codes designed to regulate every aspect of committee behavior to general admonitions to be fair. None of them answers the basic objection that the Congressional investigation is potentially an instrument of political strategy, and that it takes only one determined man to convert the potentiality to fact. There is much force in Walter Lippmann's observation that the problem "is not one which is likely to be solved by an ingenious idea." Beyond that, it may be observed that increased competence on the interrogators' part is also necessary, and that more fairness does not automatically bring with it increased competence.

The principal virtue of the court trial, viewed from the standpoint of objective fact-finding, is the opportunity it affords to test the credibility of witnesses. At its best, in the hands of able and well-prepared counsel, cross-examination becomes the great engine for the discovery of truth that Wigmore termed it. But it is not often seen at its best in the trials we have reviewed. And its necessary concentration on one detail at a time leaves the impression of a pile of tiny colored stones that no one has bothered to fit into a mosaic.

Even when the issue is as comparatively narrow as the question of perjury in the Hiss and Remington cases, the ramifications of fact tend to sprawl untidily. In the Smith Act proceedings, where it sometimes seems that history itself is on trial, one is left with the overwhelming impression that the trial process is simply not equal to the demands being made of it.

Of course, the trial is not expected to produce neatly done up bundles of history. But our inquiry is limited to its efficacy as a device for establishing the facts about one or another aspect of the Communist conspiracy. There it plainly falls short. The adversary process simply is not well adapted to the intelligible sequential ordering of complex factual data. The criminal trial is not designed for that purpose and cannot be expected to achieve it. Viewed as an instrument of fact-finding, it always falls into one of two difficulties: either it leaves out too much to be informative or it includes too much to be orderly.

What then of the administrative inquiry, that great compromise between the trial and the legislative investigation? The answer must turn on what is being inquired into. There are undoubtedly many theoretical advantages to the use of the administrative process for the development of complex factual issues. These advantages are often realized in practice, as in rate or route proceedings in regulated industries, where the hybrid legislative-judicial hearing is plainly superior to either of its sources. But the efficacy of the administrative proceeding depends on the focus given it by its constitutive authorization.

The principal use to which the administrative proceeding has been put in the context of the Communist issue is the determination, under the Internal Security Act, of whether certain organizations are Communist-dominated. The hundreds of thousands of pages accumulated by the Subversive Activities Control Board have their uses, but they do not adequately serve the function of telling us "how it really happened."

The principal difficulty has been the tendentious nature of the proceedings. Their object is to compel the respondent organizations to register as Communist-dominated. Various disabilities follow upon such a designation. As a consequence, the hearings are devoted to the proof or disproof of an overly simplified question of fact—indeed, a question that may not admit of a rational answer. Consequently, the SACB proceedings lack the flexible and open-ended quality that is the Congressional investigation's chief merit.

These strictures apply, of course, to the particular administrative tribunal that Congress elected to create, not to any administrative tribunal that might have been created. Conceivably a standing administrative tribunal armed with a broader and more flexible charter than Congress gave the SACB would work. My ideas on this point are implicit in the subsequent discussion of alternative instruments of inquiry for the future.

From the point of view of public enlightenment, it appears that none of the three kinds of institutions made available for the interrogation of ex-Communists is satisfactory. Before we turn to a consideration of alternatives, however, it is necessary to comment on two deficiencies in the mechanism of proof that have contributed significantly to the inadequacy of the public record: the privilege against self-incrimination and the inaccessibility of the files of official investigative agencies, notably the Federal Bureau of Investigation.

III

The Immunity Act. The obvious solution to the difficulties of proof posed by the privilege against self-incrimination lies in the device of compelling testimony in exchange for immunity from prosecution. That device has been resorted to by Congress on many occasions. Most relevant to this discussion is the Immunity Act of 1954, whose provisions are described in Chapter 2. The Act may be used either by a Congressional committee or by a grand jury. Its use so far has been confined to the grand jury, perhaps because of doubts about the constitutionality of the provision relating to the role of the judiciary in compelling testimony sought by a committee of Congress. Some substantial objections to the Act are set forth in the opinion of the dissenting justices in *Ullmann v. United States,* the case that upheld its constitutionality. The dissenters argue that the principle of the privilege against self-incrimination does more than merely protect a witness against criminal prosecution; it is meant to guarantee to the individual the right of privacy from governmental invasion of his life—he has an indefeasible right to be let alone. Of course, if this absolutist position is accepted, discussion is at an end. But the position has not been accepted as a constitutional prohibition, and it seems of doubtful value also as an expression of legislative wisdom.

There are only two real questions, it seems to me. First, what purposes are sought by permitting the exchange of immunity for testimony? And second, what safeguards are available to ensure that the deleterious impact of compulsory testimony will be minimized? These questions can be answered only after an examination of the legal processes in which the immunity provisions are, or might be, given effect.

The grand jury, of course, has the advantage of secret proceedings. But for purposes of creating a public record, that becomes a disadvantage. The grand jury makes its proceedings known in two ways, by indictment or by presentment. The indictment is plainly inappropriate to our purposes; it is merely a conclusory allegation that certain named persons have committed a crime. The presentment, on the other hand, reflects the historic function of the grand jury as a kind of roving inquisition into the management of public affairs. That function has, however, fallen into disuse, particularly in the federal jurisdiction, with which we are concerned. Moreover, the cross section of the community that the grand jury is supposed to reflect, however well suited it may be to some inquisitorial functions, may not be the most appropriate agency for evaluating questions about Communist infiltration.

The other available institution is the Congressional committee. It is here that opponents of the Immunity Act find the most to feel uneasy about. The prospect of a free-wheeling legislative circus, using the Immunity Act at whim to force revelations for whatever motive, is one that may well give pause. All the defects of the legislative inquiry that we have examined might well be magnified by the use of this great power, so instinct with the possibility of oppression.

There is the further possibility, rarely adverted to but certainly present, that witnesses compelled to testify under the Immunity Act may simply commit perjury, particularly where verification of their testimony is not readily available. If perjury does indeed occur in these circumstances, one would expect its incidence to be roughly proportional to the influence of politics and publicity on the hearing in question. If a witness knows that his testimony will be exploited for political advantage, if he knows that his private life will immediately become public property, his motive for evasion or even downright lying is correspondingly strengthened. If that is so, the danger of widespread perjury would be at its greatest in a Congressional investigation. It seems only reasonable that an institution whose history has demonstrated neither fairness nor competence as a characteristic virtue should not exercise powers greater than those which have already led to what is at best a spotty performance.

The question of the Immunity Act, then, is inseparably entwined with the question of the appropriate agency to be entrusted with its power.

The Jencks Principle. The investigative files of the FBI and similar agencies are jealously guarded by their custodians. It is right that this should be so, since they presumably contain great masses of unevaluated information whose indiscriminate release would injure to no purpose not only some of the nation's citizens, but the nation itself. Still, the security of these files is not absolute. There are interests to be served by permitting disclosure under some circumstances.

That this is so is illustrated by the Supreme Court's decision in *Jencks* v. *U.S.*, holding that a defendant in a criminal prosecution is entitled to examine statements made to an investigative agency by a witness against him, so that the defendant may take advantage in cross-examination of any inconsistencies between the witness's testimony in court and his statement to the investigative agency. The *Jencks* decision was followed by an Act of Congress prescribing in great detail the circumstances under which a criminal defendant might be allowed access to such statements. This in turn has been followed by a considerable volume of case law, interpreting Congress's none-too-clear statute. We need not be concerned here with the technicalities and refinements of the *Jencks* rule. What is relevant to our purpose is an adequate elaboration of the *Jencks* principle and its application to the problem of discovering the facts about American Communism.

The principle, broadly stated, is that a defendant should be given access to all relevant evidence that might assist him in his defense. This in turn rests on a notion of fundamental fairness which insists that the Government may not bring its power to bear on the individual and at the same time conceal information in its possession, a notion that has been reflected in an established line of criminal cases.

It is not immediately apparent why this salutary principle should be confined, first, to criminal proceedings, and second, to protecting the individual's interest. Criminal proceedings are not alone in exposing an accused person to infamy and ruin. The Congressional investigation may be an equally potent instrument to this end. Simple justice suggests giving a person accused of misconduct before an investigating committee the opportunity to discover whether his accuser has made materially inconsistent statements in the past. But over and above this question of fairness to the accused, may there not also be good reason on the public's behalf to insist that accusations of Communist complicity be checked against the accuser's previous *in camera* statements? Without this aid, we are forced to gauge the iceberg's dimensions by what appears above water.

Two examples previously discussed should make the point clear. Would not an impartial fact-finder be better able to evaluate Budenz's charges against Lattimore if he had a complete record of what Budenz had said in private to the FBI? And would not the important question of the timing of Elizabeth Bentley's approach to the FBI be answered if that agency's files could be opened to the extent necessary to expose data relevant to that question? Many more examples could be cited, but I think the point is solidly established, at least with respect to the desirability of full disclosure. There are, however, other aspects of the problem that must be taken into account.

These lead us back to the question of who ought to be entrusted with the power to compel this kind of disclosure. It has become a cardinal principle of relations between the executive and legislative branches of the Federal Government that the confidentiality of investigative files must not be breached. The experience of the McCarthy era suggests the danger of permitting access to investigative files purely on the *ipse dixit* of a Congressional committee. One solution might be to vest discretion in some executive official to determine when files should be exposed, but experience shows that political influences are by no means confined to Capitol Hill. Attorney-General Brownell's attack on former President Truman, fortified by declassification of secret files on Harry Dexter White, is a clear example (whatever one's view may be of the substantive merits of the case) of the use of confidential information for political purposes. We cannot keep that kind of thing from happening occasionally, but we need not make it a regular principle of executive power. Another possibility, leaving it to the accused to decide whether the files should be exposed, ignores the public interest in disclosure, which might well conflict with the accused man's desire to be let alone.

I am compelled to conclude that the solution, if there is one, lies in the creation of a new instrument of government, one deliberately designed for the kind of inquiry we have been discussing. There is nothing original about this conclusion, but it may take on added force when made in the light of and as a consequence of the kind of investigation of existing processes that has been undertaken in these pages. We turn now to a discussion of possible instruments.

IV

What specifications ought to be required in a new instrument of government fit to be entrusted with the great powers that inhere in the Immunity Act and in the *Jencks* principle? There are three that strike me as being of paramount importance: its object must be to find facts rather than to apply sanctions; it must be free of political pressures; its results rather than its processes must be given publicity. It is evident that these specifications are not met in any existing instrument of the Federal Government in the United States, but possible models do exist elsewhere, both in this country and abroad.

Perhaps the closest case in point is a British institution, the Tribunal of Inquiry. Its purpose has been described by Professor Herman Finer in the leading study on the subject as "removing a quasi-political misdemeanor from the political arena because the proof should be quasi-judicial, but not taking the case to a law court because the problem is quasi-political." It would be hard to frame a more apt description of the kind of problem we have been discussing.

A Tribunal of Inquiry is constituted upon resolution by both Houses of Parliament, in the words of the enabling statute, "for inquiring into a definite matter described in the Resolution as of urgent public importance." It has the powers of a court of law to compel testimony, although it is accorded greater latitude in framing its procedures and in the evidence that it considers. It is typically chaired by a Justice of the High Court; there are usually two other members, who are likely to be senior members of the Bar. The members are appointed, in effect, by the Cabinet. The Tribunal's proceedings are usually public though it may choose in some instances to hear evidence in private. It conducts its inquiry in an orderly and expeditious fashion and renders a report that states its findings of fact. That is all. There is no prosecution and no persecution. If individual public servants are found to have betrayed their trust, they resign without waiting to be removed, so general is the acceptance of the Tribunal's fact-finding.

The procedure of convening a Tribunal of Inquiry is rarely resorted to, a fact that may help to explain its effectiveness. There have been only two instances in the last fifteen years. The first of these demonstrates the Tribunal's success in delving into a highly complex, not to say confused, mass of facts and extracting from them a coherent and orderly account of what happened. The Tribunal investigated an allegation that certain Ministers of the Crown and other public officials had accepted presents from private persons in return for favorable official action. Four interrelated incidents and a dozen different public officials were involved.

The Tribunal, chaired by Mr. Justice Lynskey and assisted in its work by the Attorney General (a member of the same political party as the accused officials!), sat for twenty-six days and heard fifty-eight witnesses, nineteen of them represented by counsel, all of whom were entitled to cross-examine witnesses and frequently availed themselves of the opportunity. The Tribunal's report examined the allegations relative to each transaction and each official whose name was brought into question. Two officials were found to have acted improperly. The meticulous nature of the Tribunal's work is exemplified by its report on the principal malefactor, the Parliamentary Secretary to the Board of Trade. He had been accused of improper dealings with four named private persons; he was declared to be blameless with regard to two of them, but to have betrayed his trust with the other two. He and the other official found to have behaved badly immediately resigned. Just as important, the Tribunal made detailed findings exonerating the other officials whose activities had been questioned.

A noteworthy aspect of the Tribunal's work was the speed with which it acted. The Tribunal was appointed on October 29, 1948; it heard evidence from November 15 to December 21. Its report was rendered in January 1949. The contrast with the typical Congressional investigation is striking. The members of the Tribunal, of course, had no competing demands on their time.

The other Tribunal of Inquiry in recent times had to consider a matter of equal gravity—an allegation that there had been an improper disclosure of an impending rise in the Bank of England's interest rate, to the advantage of certain financial concerns. The affair took place in September 1957. A Tribunal consisting once again of a Justice of the High Court and two senior barristers was appointed in November. The Tribunal sat for twelve days during December, heard 132 witnesses under oath, many of them represented by counsel, took written statements from 236 other persons, and issued a report in January 1958, concluding that the allegations were unfounded. In dealing with some of the more abstruse questions of high finance, the Tribunal had the aid of officials of the Treasury, who conducted the investigatory phase of the inquiry at the Tribunal's direction.

Another British institution provides other aspects of a model relevant to our problem. That is the Royal Commission of Inquiry and its slightly less prestigious counterpart, the Departmental Committee. Unlike the Tribunal of Inquiry, the Royal Commission is established not to find particular facts but to investigate a general situation and supply a basis for making legislative or other official policy. To put it another way, the Tribunal's fact-finding is adjudicative; the Royal Commission's fact-finding is legislative. The Commission's work may not eventuate in legislation, but it is performed with the possibility of legislation in mind and in aid of that possibility. This difference in function is reflected in the comparative looseness of procedure in setting up a Royal Commission and in carrying on its work. There does not appear to be any general legislative authorization for Royal Commissions comparable to the Tribunals of Inquiry (Evidence) Act. A Royal Commission is constituted by a command of the Crown directing the prospective members to investigate a given subject, which is defined in the Terms of Reference. In practice, the Crown requests a Commission at the instance of the Cabinet or of a particular minister within whose sphere of interest the subject matter falls. Parliament may in theory impede the establishment or functioning of a Royal Commission by withholding funds, but I know of no instance in which this has been done. A Departmental Committee is indistinguishable from a Royal Commission except that it is constituted by direction of a minister, e.g., the Home Secretary, rather than of the Crown.

The members of a Royal Commission or Departmental Committee are almost always drawn from private life. Depending on how technical the subject of inquiry happens to be, the members may be either experts in the specialty involved or simply prominent members of the community who can be expected to bring common sense and good judgment to bear on any problem confronting them. Ordinarily the Commission has a secretary, who is a civil servant, assigned to help it. His function is to generate the production of evidence, to assist the Commission in keeping track of the evidence received, and to aid in formulating the report that constitutes the normal end product of the Commission's work.

The procedure of a Royal Commission is not fixed by law. Ordinarily, the Commission takes evidence, in either oral or written form, from anyone who desires to be heard. The Commission has no subpoena power; all its witnesses appear voluntarily. The questioning of witnesses is done informally, without any regard for the rules of evidence or other niceties of the adversary process. This is natural enough, since there is nothing adversary about the process either in form or in substance. The Commissioners have no ax to grind; nothing is at stake for them; their responsibility is to do a good job of considering the facts and arriving at a proposed solution.

Royal Commissions are as frequent as Tribunals of Inquiry are rare. There are usually several in being at any given time. Depending on the complexity of the problem confronting it, a Royal Commission may be in existence for a few months or for several years. Once a final report is rendered, the Commission, having fulfilled its only function, goes out of existence. If legislation results, as it often does, that is the work of other hands. The Commission's job is simply to get the facts in an orderly way and to propose a solution if one seems called for. Its work product usually consists of two items: a report, which narrates the procedure it employed, lists in detail the facts it has found, and makes recommendations; and the Minutes of Evidence, a transcript of the testimony it has heard and the written submissions it has received. If the subject of inquiry is of general public interest, the Commission's report is given wide publicity and is, in itself, a powerful stimulus to legislative action.

The best-known result of the Commission device in recent years is undoubtedly the Report of the Committee on Homosexual Offences and Prostitution, popularly known as the Wolfenden Report. It is a particularly striking instance of the utility of such a report as a basis for drawing public attention to a difficult social problem and stimulating intelligent public discussion of that problem. The Committee* was appointed by the Home Secretary in August 1954 to consider whether changes in the criminal law relating to homosexual offenses and to prostitution ought to be made. The Committee, chaired by Sir John Wolfenden, consisted of fifteen members, among whom were two doctors, two clergymen, one senior barrister, and one judge. Owing to the delicate nature of the subject, the hearings were conducted entirely in private, a rather unusual procedure, and no Minutes of Evidence were published. The Committee sat for sixty-two days over a period of three years, and

---

* A Departmental Committee rather than a Royal Commission.

heard evidence from a large number of interested persons. The Report was rendered in September 1957 and occasioned an intense and protracted public debate, both within and without Parliament, centering on its most controversial recommendation—that homosexual conduct engaged in privately by consenting adults should no longer be treated as a criminal offense. That recommendation has so far failed to be enacted into law, although other, less controversial changes in the law recommended by the Committee did gain enactment.

While there was obviously a wide divergence of opinion about the wisdom of the Committee's recommendations, there is no doubt that its careful and dispassionate analysis of the facts about law enforcement in the field of sexual conduct made a valuable contribution to public enlightenment on both sides of the Atlantic. It does not seem farfetched to suggest that there are many problems of social importance in this country that would similarly benefit from the careful and disinterested scrutiny of a fact-finding body clothed with official powers but free from political pressures.

In fact, *ad hoc* fact-finding boards or commissions are not unknown in the United States. On the federal level there is nothing like the Tribunal of Inquiry, but there have been commissions set up exclusively for fact-finding purposes and manned predominantly, although not exclusively, by persons of stature drawn from private life. The twelve-man Hoover Commission of 1947–49, for example, was constituted by joint action of the President and Congress to investigate ways of tightening the organization and increasing the efficiency of the executive branch of government. And there have been many fact-finding boards set up by the President without statutory authorization, notably in the field of labor relations. On the state level, there is New York's Moreland Act, the closest American analogue to the British Tribunals of Inquiry (Evidence) Act. Under this statute, passed in 1907 during the governorship of Charles Evans Hughes, the governor is authorized to appoint one or more commissioners "to examine and investigate the management and affairs of any department, board, bureau, or commission of the State." A Moreland Commissioner has the power to issue subpoenas and to take testimony under oath, and he may employ counsel and other staff to assist him. His report is rendered to the governor, who submits it to the legislature. The procedure has been resorted to scores of times for investigating the efficiency and honesty of governmental administration in New York.

What might be done along the above lines toward constructing a new instrument of government responsive to the problems canvassed in this book? As a practical matter, of course, it is highly likely that nothing will be done. In moments of crisis the responsible officials are too interested; in moments of tranquility they are not interested enough. Indeed, we have something more than intuition to go on in suggesting that remedial action is unlikely. In 1950, in the midst of controversy about Congressional investigations, Senators Thomas of Utah and Ives of New York introduced a bill to authorize the establishment of "Congressional investigating commissions" to be constituted upon concurrent resolution of both Houses of Congress. Each such commission would consist of seven members—two senators appointed by the President of the Senate, two representatives appointed by the Speaker of the House, and three persons appointed jointly by the President of the Senate and the Speaker of the House from a panel of thirty persons in private life available to serve on such a commission, the panel to be appointed by the President of the United States and confirmed by the Senate. There are many questionable features in this plan, but surely it deserved serious consideration. It got none. Whether such a plan would receive consideration today is doubtful.

The factor that has as a practical matter militated against the enactment of reforms in the field of official fact-finding is also the factor that poses the greatest obstacle to successful adaptation of the British experience to American needs: the difference between the Parliamentary system and our own. In Great Britain there is little conflict between the legislative and executive branches of the Government, since the executive is simply the functioning voice of the majority party in Parliament. This makes it materially easier for the British to assign delicate problems of fact-finding to a Tribunal of Inquiry or a Royal Commission, even when the investigation may yield results embarrassing to the Government. The nature of the problem becomes apparent when we ask what provision could be made in the United States for setting up such tribunals and appointing their members. In the American context, these problems pose formidable theoretical difficulties, to say nothing of what may be insurmountable practical obstacles.

There is no dodging the issue by confining the solution to the executive or the legislative branch alone. It seems highly unrealistic to suppose that a special tribunal established on Congressional initiative and appointed by Congress would ever be efficacious, although such a solution might stand a relatively good chance of Congressional approval. A purely Congressional tribunal would, indeed, only intensify the conflict between the two branches when the matter under inquiry involved the conduct of officials within the executive branch. It might be expected to provoke many invocations of "executive privilege" as a bar to inquiry. On the surface, a proposal to set up such tribunals wholly by executive action might have more appeal, but that too would be unworkable. Without Congressional action, such tribunals could not be given any of the powers necessary for adequate performance of their job: they could not, for example, even be empowered to take testimony under oath, let alone to compel the attendance of witnesses. They could, in short, function like a Royal Commission (if the President could scrape up the money) but not like a Tribunal of Inquiry. That would not be good enough. Congress and the President would have to cooperate.

The two major problems that would have to be faced in framing federal legislation authorizing the creation of an adequate instrument of inquiry modeled on the British experience are, first, who shall determine when a tribunal should be convened and, second, how and by whom shall the tribunal's members be appointed. The determination of necessity presents a range of possibilities: determination by the President alone; determination by the President subject to the approval (or disapproval) of one or both houses of Congress; determination by one or both houses of Congress subject to the approval (or disapproval) of the President; determination by one or both houses alone; etc., etc. My preference would be for a system that permitted initiation by either branch subject to a reasonably speedy check by the other, on the view that both will always have an interest but that on any given occasion that interest may be less intense in one branch than in the other. Thus it might be provided that a tribunal could be convened either at the President's instance, subject to disapproval by either house within a fixed time (an arrangement analogous to the present provision for reorganization plans), or by resolution of either house subject to Presidential disapproval. In either event, the view of a simple majority of one house that a matter is (or is not) of sufficient importance to warrant creation of a tribunal ought to be enough.

The appointment problem is more complex. It has two aspects: who shall be eligible to serve and who shall make the appointments? On the issue of eligibility, the Thomas-Ives proposal provides an example of the struggle between principle and expediency that makes a satisfactory solution hard to come by. The proposal recognizes that persons from outside Congress should serve, but members of the Senate and House are included, presumably to soften Congressional resistance to the scheme. I think the concession is a fatal one. A Congressman is not less a Congressman because he serves on something called a commission or a tribunal rather than on something called a Congressional committee. The influences of politics and publicity will make themselves felt, whatever name is given to the forum. It is, in my view, no accident that the successful operation of the British models has involved reliance on persons drawn from outside Parliament. Of course, the same principle excludes politically appointed officers in the executive branch. And it is unlikely that adequate confidence could be reposed in a roster chosen from among those protected by Civil Service. That leaves, from official life, only the judges. Federal judges cannot be compelled to perform extrajudicial functions, and there is a body of informed opinion holding that they should not do so voluntarily. Yet their presence can add much, as it did in the Pearl Harbor inquiry undertaken by Mr. Justice Roberts, and I should not wish to see them excluded as a source of talent. The state judiciary provides another reservoir that should perhaps be available. But the backbone of a successfully functioning institution of this sort should be a roster of persons drawn from private life.

The idea of a standing panel contained in the Thomas-Ives proposal may be a useful one, although I doubt that thirty names would give a sufficient diversity of outlook and experience to meet the range of uses to which fact-finding tribunals might be put. A hundred or even two hundred eligibles, including such judges as are willing to serve, would be better.

The panel device would serve the additional function of giving the competing governmental interests an advance share in the appointment power. It might, for example, be provided that the President of the United States, the President Pro Tempore of the Senate and the Speaker of the House should each designate one-third of the total number of persons to serve on the panel from which members of tribunals would be drawn, all designations to be subject to Senatorial (or Congressional) approval. With that kind of screening device in operation, it might then be unobjectionable to provide for Presidential appointment to a tribunal, after one has been constituted, without requiring that the appointees be confirmed for service on the particular tribunal.* The President might be required to appoint members in equal numbers from each of the three groups of panel members—the Senate's, the House's, and his own. Thus the qualifications of appointees could be studied at leisure and without reference to the particular fact-finding job they might be asked to undertake. Then, as the actual need arose, a tribunal could be appointed without delay and without bickering about the suitability of its members. The members of the panel would be available for a fixed period of time, say four years, after which a new panel would be constituted.

This scheme for constituting a tribunal and appointing its members may seem complex, but assuredly some scheme of equal complexity would be required to minimize the frictions inherent in the American system of separated powers. Whether such a scheme would stand any chance of acceptance would depend in part on what powers it is proposed to give a fact-finding tribunal and on what its relation should be to other instruments of inquiry, especially Congressional investigating committees.

At first glance, it might seem wise to provide that once a fact-finding tribunal has been constituted, it should "occupy the field" to the exclusion of Congressional committee inquiries into the same subject matter. Experience suggests, however, that Congress would never agree to such a curtailment of its jurisdiction. And even if it did, the result would very likely be an unseemly race to get a legislative committee started on an investigation or, worse yet, a reluctance to approve any call for a fact-finding tribunal if any Congressional committee had an interest in the subject of the po-

---

* Lodging the appointive power in the Chief Justice, a superficially attractive solution, may raise constitutional problems.

tential inquiry. Better that there should be an occasional overlap. Indeed, it may be desirable to have some conflicts of jurisdiction at the start, if only to give the new instrument of inquiry an opportunity to demonstrate its utility. As instances multiply and a tradition establishes itself, a pattern of deference to the new device can be expected to develop in proportion to its success in discharging the distinctive function assigned to it. It would be wrong to try to build that pattern of deference into the system at the start; it cannot take root except in experience.

The *ad hoc* nature of these tribunals is essential. Each tribunal should be freshly constituted with new members and allowed to employ its own staff and, most important, its own counsel. Perhaps some continuity in staff personnel is inevitable, even desirable; but the members and the counsel should come from other callings and return to them after the tribunal has performed its appointed task. Otherwise, politics and publicity are bound to reappear as baneful and distracting influences.

The powers that such a tribunal should exercise have already been enumerated: ideally it should possess the power to subpoena witnesses and documents, to take testimony under oath, to compel testimony as to which the privilege against self-incrimination is invoked by granting immunity from criminal prosecution, and to obtain such material from the files of the FBI and other Government agencies as it may deem pertinent to the subject of inquiry and to the testimony of witnesses called before the tribunal. These last two powers—the immunity power and the power to invoke what I have referred to as the *Jencks* principle—are essential to the successful operation of fact-finding tribunals. These powers are also, as I have said before, capable of being used oppressively. There is no way to ensure that they will not be so used by these tribunals; we can only observe that the stimulus to oppressive use seems lacking in a system such as the one we have been considering.

The procedures of a fact-finding tribunal should not be prescribed by law, but should be molded to fit the exigencies of the particular occasion. Ordinarily, the counsel and staff should investigate and interview potential witnesses before their testimony is formally taken. In that way, situations that may call for use of the immunity power or the *Jencks* principle can be uncovered and dealt with deliberately rather than on the spur of the moment.

That, of course, will usually occur only where the tribunal is charged with looking into allegations of past misdeeds, as in the case of the British Tribunal of Inquiry, not where it seeks purely to gather information on a social problem, as in the case of a Royal Commission. It is in the first of these two roles that the proposed tribunal would find its greater use, I think, simply because it is that role in which our existing fact-finding institutions are most conspicuously deficient.

The tribunal should be allowed to hire experts to help in its work. If the subject of inquiry were, let us say, the allegation made by Senator McCarthy in 1950 that Communists had infiltrated the State Department and were, even then, occupying policy-making positions, consider how helpful it would be to have on hand a historian or political scientist at home in the factual setting of the problem. I do not think that this kind of need is satisfied by calling such persons as "expert witnesses." Rather, they should participate as members of the staff and advisers to the tribunal.

Since the only object of the tribunal is to find facts, since no sanctions will be or can be imposed as a consequence, the tribunal should not have to follow formal rules of evidence or observe niceties of internal divisions of function. It should have the power to hear witnesses in private and to publish as much or as little of the testimony so given as it sees fit to publish. It should, however, be required to accord witnesses the right to be assisted by counsel and to cross-examine adverse witnesses or, failing that, to be apprised of and given the chance to reply to any charges made by adverse witnesses. The tribunal's report, rendered as soon as careful study of the problem permitted, should be a public document and would undoubtedly receive extensive publicity. It is just as desirable that publicity be encouraged at the end as that it be discouraged during the process. Providing for controlled publicity of this sort is not an easy task in this country, as a matter either of constitutional law or of the practicabilities of control, but the effort should surely be made. The power to proceed in private, reinforced by the contempt power or by a criminal statute, should go a long way toward dealing with the problem of publicity.

It would be fanciful to speculate on the extent, if any, to which a new instrument of inquiry, fashioned along these lines, would have yielded more public enlightenment than the various proceedings we have analyzed in these pages. It would be even more fanciful to speculate on the extent, if any, to which public decorum would have been preserved and the rancors of the past fifteen years avoided. The extent to which changes in laws and in legal institutions result in changes in the way people behave is one of the ultimate imponderables.

The problem of Communist penetration in this country is now a stale one. It is in all likelihood too late to traverse again, even with greatly improved fact-finding processes, the ground that has been so unsatisfactorily covered in the past. Individual scholars must take over, as they are indeed now doing. But the problem of Communist penetration is not unique in its capacity to stir issues upon which there is a need for public enlightenment that cannot be satisfied by private efforts. Charges of corruption in government are always going to be with us; issues of public policy on which disinterested official scrutiny is needed constantly arise. Many such charges and many such issues can be dealt with satisfactorily enough by existing instruments of inquiry. But there will always be those that arouse too much controversy and that strike too deep to be handled as they are at present. When that happens, as it surely will again, we would be fortunate to have at the service of the body politic an instrument of inquiry that could enlist the best talents of our society in the aid of public enlightenment.

APPENDIXES

APPENDIXES

APPENDIX A

The "Government Witnesses" project conducted at the Stanford Law School was undertaken at the instance of the Fund for the Republic, Inc., which made a grant to Stanford University for the purpose. This volume is the principal result of the project. In the course of the work, a systematic analysis of all the testimony of the four witnesses selected for study—Chambers, Bentley, Budenz, and Lautner—was made. That analysis, a necessary bridge between the great mass of raw data and the studies presented in this volume, is contained in an Index-Digest of the testimony, which is not being published as part of this volume, but which this Appendix will briefly describe.

From the first, it was recognized that this project would require three preliminary stages of work: collection of the testimony of the witnesses, formulation of an analytical method, application of the analytical method to the data. As it turned out, problems encountered in the first stage had a marked effect on the next two. The task of assembling the record proved to be a formidable one. With the assistance of various bibliographical aids, notably the indexes published by the House Committee on Un-American Activities and the Senate Internal Security Subcommittee, and the Fund for the Republic's *Digest of the Public Record of Communism in the United States,* we compiled a list of proceedings in which the four witnesses had testified. This list was augmented by such ancillary materials as the published writings of the various witnesses.

The collection of this body of material occupied more time than we had originally supposed that it would. Some items proved difficult to obtain. Arrangements had to be made to reproduce the transcripts of hearings before the Subversive Activities Control Board and to microfilm the transcripts of Smith Act trials. When all the materials on which we could lay our hands had been assembled it turned out that we had more than 200,000 pages of testimony to examine.

Even before all the material was in, it became obvious that our original plan for analyzing it would have to be revised. We had supposed that once the material was in hand it could be dealt with by reading through the testimony of a particular witness or the testimony of several witnesses on a particular subject and then preparing and presenting an analysis of each such block of material. However, in sheer volume, in multiplicity of subjects and incidents, and in complexity of subject-matter there was clearly too much material to permit such treatment. If this material was to be examined for corroboration, contradiction, internal consistency, and gaps, some more systematic means of going about the process was needed. Although from the start much of the material we had collected seemed repetitious and cumulative, we did not think that we could conscientiously assume that to be the case. Consequently, we determined to devise a means for examining the entire body of testimony and simultaneously recording the results of the examination in usable form. Our problem was to do this without rivaling the bulk of the original material.

The result of our efforts was the Index-Digest of the testimony of our four witnesses. After a considerable amount of testimony had been read, and by a laborious process of trial and error, we developed an outline for classifying the testimony. This outline is described in detail in the Introduction to the Index-Digest, and the description will not be repeated here. The outline serves to chart the testimony of each witness with respect to his role in the Communist movement, and the substance of his testimony relating to persons, policies, and activities. Of particular interest is Topic 3, entitled *Individuals: Spectrum of Communist Allegiance*, which synopsizes the testimony of each witness with respect to the activities and degree of affiliation of all the persons whom he named as being involved in Communist activities. It is here, of course, that the most acute controversies have arisen. The Index-Digest under this heading shows concisely not only the identification of persons made by each witness but also all other evidence, adduced either in the instant proceeding or in another proceeding, bearing on the identification, including testimony, if any, by the accused. In order to facilitate reference to the Index-Digest we constructed an Index of Names, giving representative references to testimony regarding each of the persons named by the four primary witnesses. Some idea of the magnitude of this task, as well as of the task of building the Index-Digest itself, may be gained from the fact that this Index of Names contains over one thousand entries and approximately five thousand references.

The Index-Digest actually comprises separate digests of testimony taken on different occasions, linked together by their common organization under the outline previously described and by the Index of Names. Hence it affords the means of obtaining a summary of testimony in any one of several ways: all the testimony of a given witness on a particular occasion, all the testimony of a given witness on a particular subject, all the testimony of more than one witness on a particular subject, all the testimony relating to a particular witness.

We anticipate that the Index-Digest may be used with profit by scholars who seek to study the testimony of these witnesses as an important source of information about the nature and extent of Communist penetration in the United States. Our intention is to issue it separately in a small offset edition, within the year, and to make it available upon inquiry to interested persons.

APPENDIX B

This is a complete listing, by source, of the Congressional hearings, court trials, and SACB proceedings analyzed in the course of this study. Within each category, the proceedings are arranged alphabetically by the symbol in the left-hand margin, which identifies the source by an abbreviation of its title and, in the case of Congressional hearings, by the number of the Congress and Session in which the hearing took place. These symbols identify the sources listed in the Notes to Chapters 2, 3, 4, and 5.

I. CONGRESSIONAL HEARINGS

HOUSE UN-AMERICAN ACTIVITIES COMMITTEE

ABBREVIATION	HEARING
HUAC–A-Bomb (80:2)	*Communist Activities in Connection with the Atom Bomb* (1948)
HUAC–Albany (83:2)	*Communist Activities in the Albany, N. Y. Area* (1954)
HUAC–B&S (81:2)	*Testimony of Philip A. Bart (general manager of Freedom of the Press, publishers of the Daily Worker, official organ of the Communist Party) and Marcel Scherer (coordinator, New York Labor Conference for Peace, and formerly district representative of district 4, United Electrical, Radio and Machine Workers of America, CIO)* (1950)
HUAC–Balto (82:1)	*Communist Activities in the Defense Area of Baltimore* (1951)
HUAC–Bud (79:2)	*Investigation of Un-American Propaganda Activities in the United States (Louis F. Budenz)* (1946)

ABBREVIATION	HEARING
HUAC–Calif (83:2)	*Communist Activities in the State of California* (1954)
HUAC–Chi (82:2)	*Communist Activities in the Chicago Area* (1952)
HUAC–Cinci (81:2)	*Communist Activities in the Cincinnati, Ohio Area* (1950)
HUAC–Clubb (82:1)	*Testimony of Oliver Edmund Clubb* (1951)
HUAC–Columb (83:1)	*Communist Activities in the Columbus, Ohio Area* (1953)
HUAC–Dayton (83:2)	*Communist Activities in the Dayton, Ohio Area* (1954)
HUAC–Eis (80:1)	*Re Gerhart Eisler* (1947)
HUAC–Esp (80:2)	*Communist Espionage in the United States Government* (1948)
HUAC–Esp (81:1&2)	*Hearings Regarding Communist Espionage* (1949–50)
HUAC–Farm (82:1)	*Communist Activities Among Farm Groups* (1951)
HUAC–Hlywd (82:1)	*Communist Infiltration of Hollywood Motion-Picture Industry* (1951)
HUAC–Infil Govt (84:1&2)	*Investigation of Communist Infiltration of Government* (1955–56)
HUAC–J&L (80:1)	*Re Leon Josephson and Samuel Liptzen* (1947)
HUAC–JAFR (79:2)	*Investigation of the Joint Anti-Fascist Refugee Committee* (1946)
HUAC–LA (83:1)	*Communist Activities in the Los Angeles Area* (1953)
HUAC–Labor Unions (81:1&2)	*Communist Infiltration of Labor Unions* (1949–50)
HUAC–Legis (81:2)	H.R. 3903 and H.R. 7595, *Proposed Legislation to Outlaw Certain Un-American and Subversive Activities* (1950)
HUAC–Mass (82:1)	*Communist Activities in the State of Massachusetts* (1951)
HUAC–Meth Ed (83:1)	*Communist Methods of Infiltration (Education)* (1953)

ABBREVIATION	HEARING
HUAC–Meth Infil (82:2)	Methods of Communist Infiltration in the United States Government (1952)
HUAC–Mich (83:2)	Communist Activities in the State of Michigan (1954)
HUAC–Milwaukee (84:1)	Communist Activities in the Milwaukee, Wisconsin Area (1955)
HUAC–MPI (80:1)	Communist Infiltration of the Motion Picture Industry (1947)
HUAC–Newark (84:1)	Communist Activities in the Newark, N.J. Area (1955)
HUAC–NY Area (84:1)	Communist Activities, New York Area (1955)
HUAC–NYC (83:1)	Communist Activities in the New York City Area (1953)
HUAC–Pac NW (83:2)	Communist Activities in the Pacific Northwest Area (1954)
HUAC–Phila (82:2)	Communist Activities in the Philadelphia Area (1952)
HUAC–Press (82:2)	The Role of the Communist Press in the Communist Conspiracy (1952)
HUAC–Pub (83:2)	Communist Influence in the Field of Publications (March of Labor) (1954)
HUAC–Seattle (84:1)	Communist Activities in the Seattle, Washington Area (1955)
HUAC–SF (83:1)	Communist Activities in the San Francisco Area (1953)
HUAC–Trot (81:2)	American Aspects of the Assassination of Leon Trotsky (1950)
HUAC–USG (81:2)	Communism in the United States Government (1950)
HUAC–W Pa (81:2)	Exposé of the Communist Party of Western Pennsylvania (1950)

HOUSE COMMITTEE ON EDUCATION AND LABOR

HE&L–Fur (80:2)	Communist Infiltration into the Fur Industry (1948)
HE&L–GSI (80:2)	Investigation of the GSI Strike (1948)

ABBREVIATION	HEARING
HE&L–NLRA (80:1)	Amendments to the National Labor Relations Act (1947)
HE&L–NYDT (80:2)	Communism in the New York City Distributive Trades (1948)
HE&L–TU, 555 (80:2)	Investigation of Teachers Union, Local No. 555, UPWA–CIO (1948)
HE&L–UERMWA (80:2)	Investigation of Communist Infiltration of UERMWA (1948)

HOUSE SELECT COMMITTEE TO INVESTIGATE TAX-EXEMPT
FOUNDATIONS AND COMPARABLE ORGANIZATIONS

H–TEF (82:2)	Tax Exempt Foundations (1952)

SENATE SUBCOMMITTEE ON IMMIGRATION AND NATURALIZATION
OF THE COMMITTEE ON THE JUDICIARY

SI&N–Aliens (81:1)	Communist Activities Among Aliens and National Groups (1949)

SENATE INTERNAL SECURITY SUBCOMMITTEE
OF THE COMMITTEE ON THE JUDICIARY

SIS–DPOWA (82:2)	Subversive Control of Distributive, Processing and Office Workers of America (1952)
SIS–Ed Proc (82:2, 83:1)	Subversive Influence in the Educational Process (1952, 1953)
SIS–IPR (82:1,2)	Institute of Pacific Relations (1951, 1952)
SIS–ISGD (83:1,2)	Interlocking Subversion in Government Departments (1953, 1954)
SIS–Lab Orgs (83:1,2)	Subversive Influence in Certain Labor Organizations, on S. 23, S. 1254, S. 1606, Legislation designed to Curb Communist Penetration and Domination of Labor Organizations (1953, 1954)
SIS–Matusow (84:1)	Strategy and Tactics of World Communism; The Significance of the Matusow Case (1955)
SIS–Print (83:1)	Communist Underground Printing Facilities and Illegal Propaganda (1953)

ABBREVIATION	HEARING
SIS–Prop (83:2)	Communist Propaganda (1954)
SIS–Rec Esp (84:1)	Strategy and Tactics of World Communism, Recruiting for Espionage (1955)
SIS–SCEF (83:2)	Southern Conference Educational Fund, Inc. (1954)
SIS–Telegraph (82:1)	Subversive Infiltration in the Telegraph Industry (1951)
SIS–UERMWA (83:1)	Subversive Influence in the United Electrical, Radio, and Machine Workers of America, Pittsburgh and Erie, Pa. (1953)
SIS–UPWA (82:1)	Subversive Control of the United Public Workers of America (1951)
SIS–US-UN (82:2; 83:1)	Activities of the United States Citizens Employed by the United Nations (1952, 53)
SIS–WOR COMM (83:2)	Strategy and Tactics of World Communism (1954)

SENATE COMMITTEE ON FOREIGN RELATIONS

SFR–SDLI (81:2)	State Department Employee Loyalty Investigation (1950)

SENATE SUBCOMMITTEE ON INVESTIGATIONS OF THE COMMITTEE ON EXPENDITURES IN THE EXECUTIVE DEPARTMENTS

SEED–EP&L (80:2)	Export Policy and Loyalty (1948)

SENATE PERMANENT SUBCOMMITTEE ON INVESTIGATIONS OF THE COMMITTEE ON GOVERNMENT OPERATIONS

SGO–Army (83:1)	Communist Infiltration in the Army (1953)
SGO–Arm Civ (83:1)	Communist Infiltration Among Army Civilian Workers
SGO–ASC (83:1)	Army Signal Corps–Subversion and Espionage (1953)
SGO–Aust (83:1)	Austrian Incident (1953)
SGO–Cur Pl (83:1)	Transfer of Occupation Currency Plates—Espionage Phase (1953)

ABBREVIATION	HEARING
SGO–Defense (83:2)	*Subversion and Espionage in Defense Establishments and Industry* (1953, 1954)
SGO–GI (84:2)	*Communist Ownership of G.I. Schools* (1956)
SGO–SDIP (83:1)	*State Department Information Program—Information Centers* (1953)
SGO–Sec UN (83:1)	*Security—United Nations* (1953)
SGO–WHT (84:1)	*William H. Taylor, Treasury Dept.* (1953)

II. COURT TRIALS

Bary	*United States* v. *Bary* (Smith Act, Denver, 1955)
Dennis	*United States* v. *Dennis* (Smith Act, N.Y., 1949)
Flynn	*United States* v. *Flynn* (Smith Act, N.Y., 1952)
Forest	*United States* v. *Forest* (Smith Act, St. Louis, 1954)
Frankfeld	*United States* v. *Frankfeld* (Smith Act, Baltimore, 1952)
Fujimoto	*United States* v. *Fujimoto* (Smith Act, Hawaii, 1952)
Hiss I	*United States* v. *Hiss* (Perjury, N.Y., 1949)
Hiss II	*United States* v. *Hiss* (Perjury, N.Y., 1950)
Huff	*United States* v. *Huff* (Smith Act, Seattle, 1953)
Kuzma	*United States* v. *Kuzma* (Smith Act, Philadelphia, 1954)
Mesarosh	*United States* v. *Mesarosh* (Smith Act, Pittsburgh, 1953)
Remington I	*United States* v. *Remington* (Perjury, N.Y., 1951)
Rosenberg	*United States* v. *Julius and Ethel Rosenberg* (Espionage, N.Y., 1951)
Scales	*United States* v. *Scales* (Smith Act Membership Clause, North Carolina, 1955)

ABBREVIATION	HEARING
Schneiderman	*United States* v. *Schneiderman* (Smith Act, Los Angeles, 1952)
Silverman	*United States* v. *Silverman* (Smith Act, New Haven, 1955)
Trachtenberg	*United States* v. *Trachtenberg* (Smith Act, New York, 1956)
Wellman	*United States* v. *Wellman* (Smith Act, Detroit, 1953)

III. SUBVERSIVE ACTIVITIES CONTROL BOARD PROCEEDINGS

SACB–ACPF	*Brownell* v. *American Committee for the Protection of the Foreign Born* (1955)
SACB–APC	*Brownell* v. *American Peace Crusade* (1955)
SACB–CLS	*Brownell* v. *California Labor School, Inc.* (1955)
SACB–CPUSA	*Brownell* v. *Communist Party of the United States of America* (1951)
SACB–CRC	*Brownell* v. *Civil Rights Congress* (1954)
SACB–JSSS	*Brownell* v. *Jefferson School of Social Science* (1953)
SACB–LYL	*Brownell* v. *Labor Youth League* (1953)
SACB–NCASF	*Brownell* v. *National Council of American-Soviet Friendship* (1954)
SACB–UMDC	*Brownell* v. *United May Day Committee* (1955)
SACB–VALB	*Brownell* v. *Veterans of the Abraham Lincoln Brigade* (1954)
SACB–WPU	*Brownell* v. *Washington Pension Union* (1955)

IV. OTHER PROCEEDINGS

Dep–ETB I	*Deposition of Elizabeth Terrill Bentley taken at Opelousas, La., May 17, 1954 (in re William Henry Taylor* v. *Washington Daily News)*

ABBREVIATION	HEARING
Dep–ETB II	*Deposition of Elizabeth Terrill Bentley taken at Washington, D. C., July 26, 1954 (in re William Henry Taylor v. Washington Daily News)*
Dep–WC	*Deposition of Whittaker Chambers taken in re proposed libel suit* (1948)
FCC–Lamb	*In re Application of Dispatch, Inc., Erie, Pennsylvania. For Renewal of License of Television Station WICU* (1954)
NY Bd	*Inquiry by the Board of Regents Relative to Subversive Organizations Pursuant to Chapter 360 of the Laws of 1949 with regard to the Communist Party of the U.S.A.* (New York, 1952)
TH–Reinecke	*Dept. of Public Instruction v. Doctor John E. and Aiko T. Reinecke* (Territory of Hawaii, 1948)

NOTES

NOTES

These Notes are intended mainly to serve as guides to further references on some of the matters discussed in the text. In addition, the proceedings primarily relied on in each of the four studies comprising Chapters 2, 3, 4, and 5 are identified at the beginning of the Notes to each of those chapters by symbols designating the often cumbersome titles of the proceedings. These symbols, in turn, are identified in Appendix B, a complete list of the proceedings analyzed in the course of the project.

NOTES TO CHAPTER I

Pp. 1–6. The principal secondary source now available for information on Communism in American life is the series of volumes produced with the financial support of the Fund for the Republic, Inc. under the general editorship of Clinton Rossiter. Of the volumes so far published in this series the one that bears most directly on the subject matter of this book is Shannon, *The Decline of American Communism* (1959). For an excellent short account, see Howe and Coser, *The American Communist Party* (1957). Kempton, *Part of our Time; Some Ruins and Monuments of the Thirties* (1955) is a superb evocation of the setting in which Communism made and then lost friends in the labor movement and among intellectuals of the Left.

The Fund for the Republic has also sponsored the publication of a valuable compilation of references to the public record, *Digest of the Public Record of Communism in the United States* (1955), edited by Charles Corker. This work is an indispensable research tool for students of the subject.

Pp. 7–12. There is no good general work dealing on a comparative basis with the legal institutions of American society. Of the greatest value, although rather inaccessible in more senses than one, is Hart and Sacks, *The Legal Process*, published in 1958 in a mimeographed edition by the Harvard Law School. For a pioneering historical study, see Hurst, *The Growth of American Law* (1950). There has been no book so far on the use of the criminal process against Communists and Communist activities, although the subject is touched on in Kirchheimer, *Political Justice* (1961). On perjury generally, see Perkins, *Criminal Law* 382–396 (1957); American Law Institute, *Model Penal Code*, Tent. Draft, No. 6, 100–140 (1957). The Smith Act trials await impartial treatment. For a decidedly biased view, see Somerville, *The Communist Trials and the American Tradition* (1956). The constitutional issues, which lie outside the scope of this book, have been extensively canvassed in the legal literature. See 1949–1952 *Index to Legal Periodicals* 797. An account of the legal fortunes of the Government in prosecuting Smith Act cases will be found in the successive Annual Reports of the Attorney General of the United States under the heading "Internal Security."

Pp. 12–16. On administrative tribunals generally, see Davis, *Administrative Law and Government* (1960). On the McCarran Act, see Note, 51 Columbia Law Review 606 (1951). The history of the litigation involving the Communist Party is recounted in the Supreme Court's decision upholding the constitutionality of the registration provisions of the Act, *Communist Party of U.S.* v. *Subversive Activities Control Board*, 81 S. Ct. 1357 (1961).

Pp. 16–17. The literature on Congressional investigations is voluminous. The best historical account is Taylor, *Grand Inquest* (1955). A particularly valuable series of discussions is contained in the symposium *Congressional Investigations*, 18 University of Chicago Law Review 421 (1951). Carr, *The House Committee on Un-American Activities, 1945–1950* (1955) provides an illuminating case study. See also Barth, *Government by Investigation* (1955).

NOTES TO CHAPTER 2

SOURCES

HUAC–Esp. (80:2)	*Hiss* II	*SIS–IPR* (82:1&2)
Dep–WC	*HUAC–USG* (81:2)	*SIS–US–UN* (82:2)

P. 21. The Hiss case has evoked a considerable if not very satisfactory literature. Each of the protagonists has produced a book: Chambers, *Witness* (1952); Hiss, *In the Court of Public Opinion* (1957). Neither can be read uncritically. Cooke, *A Generation on Trial* (1950) is lively and readable but suffers from defects in analysis that are devastatingly summarized in a book review by Rebecca West, 18 University of Chicago Law Review 662 (1951). Jowitt, *The Strange Case of Alger Hiss* (1953) contains a keen analysis of the evidence but is marred by naive forays into psychological and sociological speculation. De Toledano and Lasky, *Seeds of Treason* (1950) is a brief for the prosecution; Cook, *The Unfinished Case of Alger Hiss* (1958) is a brief for the defense.

Pp. 25–41. The material on which this analysis is based is drawn primarily from affidavits submitted in connection with Alger Hiss's motion for new trial. These are contained in Appendix to Appellant's Brief on Appeal from Order Denying Motion for New Trial on Ground of Newly Discovered Evidence, *United States* v. *Hiss*, 201 F.2d 372 (C.A. 2 1953).

P. 49; The Immunity Act. The constitutionality of the provisions of the Immunity Act with respect to testimony before grand juries was upheld in *Ullmann* v. *United States*, 350 U.S. 422 (1956). There is, however, a technical question about the constitutionality of the provision relating to testimony before Congressional committees. Unlike the grand jury provision, the procedure for compelling testimony before a Congressional committee requires the "approval" of the U.S. district court for the district in which the hearing takes place. This provision is thought by some to impose a nonjudicial function on U.S. courts set up under Article III of the Constitution, which are incapable of exercising such functions. See Rogge, *The New Federal Immunity Act and the Judicial Function*, 45 California Law Review 109 (1957). Assuming that this kind of "approval" is indeed a "nonjudicial function," the argument overlooks the fact that the District Court for the District of Columbia is constitutionally capable of performing "nonjudicial" functions, that most Congressional hearings take place in the District, that Congress can see to it that litigation about the Immunity Act is confined to the District, and that it is unlikely that a witness, summoned to testify in the District, would have standing to attack the constitutionality of the statute as applied to courts outside the District. However that may be, whether because of constitutional doubts or for other reasons, it does not appear that a Congressional committee has ever resorted to the Immunity Act.

NOTES TO CHAPTER 3

SOURCES

SEED–EP&L (80:2)	*Remington I*	*SIS–ISGD* (83:1,2)
HUAC–Esp (80:2)	*SIS–IPR* (82:1&2)	*Dep–ETB* (1)
SI&N–Aliens (81:1)	*HUAC–Press* (82:2)	*Dep–ETB* (2)
HUAC–USG (81:2)	*SGO–Cur Pl* (83:1)	

P. 60; Characterization of "Out of Bondage." Miss Bentley's alleged characterization of her book as "fiction" is said to have been made during a deposition taken in connection with a libel action, *Taylor v. Washington Daily News*, C.A. No. 5394-53, District of Columbia. The asserted characterization is contained in an affidavit made by Byron N. Scott, Esq., counsel for Taylor, through whose courtesy copies of papers relating to Mr. Taylor's case were made available to me.

Pp. 75–102. There is little secondary literature on the Remington case. Cook, *The Remington Tragedy*, 185 The Nation 485 (1957), is a brief, unimpartial account of the affair. The reported decisions in the case include: 191 F.2d 246 (C.A. 2 1951), reversing the first conviction; 342 U.S. 895 (1951), denying the Government's motion for leave to apply for dismissal of the first indictment; 343 U.S. 907 (1953), denying Remington's petition for certiorari in which he attacked the original indictment; 208 F.2d 567 (C.A. 2 1953), affirming Remington's conviction at his second trial; 347 U.S. 913 (1954), denying certiorari to review that conviction.

P. 102; Harry Dexter White. Aside from the extended references in Chambers, *Witness*, the only secondary source on the White affair is *Harry D. White–Loyal American* (1956), by his brother, Nathan I. White.

Pp. 108–114. The literature on the Fifth Amendment and the inferences to be drawn from its invocation is large. Contrasting positions are set forth in Griswold, *The Fifth Amendment Today* (1955), and Hook, *Common Sense and the Fifth Amendment* (1957). Keen comment on the problem will be found in Lipson, Book Review, 10 Stanford Law Review 785 (1958).

Pp. 114–116. The William H. Taylor case is described in an article by his attorney, Byron N. Scott, *The Letter Nobody Wrote*, 184 The Nation 5 (1957).

NOTES TO CHAPTER 4

SOURCES

HUAC–Bud (79:2)	*Dennis*	*SIS–IPR* (82:1&2)
SEED–Ep&L (80:2)	*SI&N–Aliens* (81:1)	*H–TEF* (82:2)
HUAC–Esp (80:2)	*SFR–SDLI* (81:2)	*SACB–CPUSA*

Pp. 126–128; Senator McCarthy. For contrasting views on the activities of the late junior senator from Wisconsin, see Buckley and Bozell, *McCarthy and His Enemies* (1954); Rovere, *Senator Joe McCarthy* (1959).

P. 156; Lattimore's Testimony. Professor Lattimore's book *Ordeal by Slander* (1950) is an interesting and effective recapitulation of the case up to and including his exoneration by the Tydings Committee. It does not cover the far more stringent "ordeal" to which he was later subjected during the IPR Hearings and during the subsequent period in which he was under indictment for perjury.

Pp. 164–171; Alsop. After his tempestuous appearance before the Subcommittee, Mr. Alsop published an article, *The Strange Case of Louis Budenz*, The Atlantic Monthly, April 1952, p. 29, which is a lucid if not entirely impartial account of the affair.

NOTES TO CHAPTER 5

SOURCES

SACB–CPUSA	*Flynn*	*Forest*
Frankfeld	*Fujimoto*	*Kuzma*
Schneiderman	*NY Bd*	*Silverman*

NOTES TO CHAPTER 6

P. 231; The Immunity Act. See Notes to Chapter 2, p. 49.

P. 233; The Jencks Principle. The Supreme Court decision is *Jencks* v. *U.S.* 353 U.S. 657 (1957), reversing the conviction of a labor union official for filing a false non-Communist affidavit, on the ground that statements given to the FBI by two government witnesses should have been made available to the defendant for use in cross-examining the witnesses (who happened to be undercover agents for the FBI). After this decision Congress promptly passed the so-called "Jencks" Act, 18 U.S.C. §3500, limiting the circumstances under which statements made to government agents by government witnesses are required to be produced for inspection by criminal defendants. Some of the difficulties inherent in the statute are exposed in later decisions, *Palermo* v. *U.S.* 360 U.S. 343 (1959); *Rosenberg* v. *U.S.,* 360 U.S. 367 (1959).

Pp. 234–236. For an authoritative description of the British experience, see Finer, *The British System,* in the symposium *Congressional Investigations,* 18 University of Chicago Law Review 521 (1951). Another article in the same symposium, Rogers, *The Problem and Its Solution* (*id.* at 464), describes the functioning of Tribunals of Inquiry as well as of the New York Moreland Commissions and suggests in general terms the adaptation of these devices to aid in discharging the Congressional investigative function. Professor Rogers's proposal, when originally made in 1950, contributed to the formulation of the Thomas-Ives bill (*id.* at 476). Another suggestion for a new instrument of inquiry based on the British experience is advanced in Barth, *Government by Investigation* 211–15 (1955).

INDEX

INDEX

Abt, John, 43f, 58, 64, 105, 109
Adler, Solomon, 57, 61
Administrative hearing, 3, 13–16, 230–31, 262. *See also* McCarran Act; Subversive Activities Control Board
"Aesopian" theory, 12, 193, 214
Ageloff, Sylvia, 123
Agricultural Adjustment Administration, 44–45
Alsop, Joseph, 164, 166, 175, 264; quoted, 167–71
Amerasia, 130, 155–56
American Communist Party. *See* Communist Party of the U.S.
American League Against War and Fascism, 53
American Workers' Party, 121
Auto Workers Union, 179, 202

Baker, Rudy, 188
"Baltimore Documents," 26, 26n, 29–40 *passim*
Barnes, Joe, 135
Bart, Philip A., 252
Bayer, Teddy, 196
Bebrits, Louis, 186
Benjamin, Robert, 25
Bentley, Elizabeth Terrill (52–120): and Remington case, 17–18, 75–102, 228; appearance before HUAC, 18, 47, 59–71, 91, 115, 227; her life, 52–56; *Out of Bondage*, 55, 59–60, 84, 263; her espionage contacts, 57–58; and William H. Taylor, 57, 60–62, 114–16, 258f; testimony quoted, 61–71 *passim*, 92–101 *passim;* and FBI, 68–75, 96–102, 234; corroboration of her testimony, 102–14; contradic-

tions of her story, 114–17; gaps in the record, 117–20
Berle, Adolf A., 43
Black, Hugo L., 13
Board of Economic Warfare, 57
Boucot, Joseph R., 45–46
Brandt, Joe, 194
Brockwood Labor College, 121
Brodsky, Carl, 196
Brothman, Abraham, 91, 113f
Browder, Earl: meeting with Foster re Lattimore, 4, 129, 131f, 146, 153f, 156; and Bentley, 56, 59–60, 118; and Budenz, 122, 160; before Tydings Committee, 152–54; testimony quoted 152–54; and Communist Political Assoc., 181; criticisms of his policies, 186, 188–89, 190, 207; and Comintern, 195f
Brown, F., 54
Brownell, Herbert, 71–75 *passim*, 91, 235, 258; quoted, 110
Brunini, John, 85–90, 88n–89n
Budenz, Louis (121–177): as expert on Communism, 5–6, 18–19, 223–24; "Aesopian" theory, 12, 214; his definition of Communist, 19, 175–77, 224; and Bentley, 99–100, 102, 105; his life, 121–24; and Tydings Committee, 125, 128–58, 174–75, 224, 228; and IPR hearings, 125–26, 158–72, 175; testimony quoted, 128–44 *passim*, 159–166 *passim*; mentioned, 4, 225, 234, 252
Burke, Edmund, 220
Bykov, Boris, 46

CIO Political Action Committee (PAC), 64, 64n

Calomiris, Angelo, 193
Carpenter, The, 121
Carr, Sam, 187
Catlett, Perry, 27, 30, 38
Chambers, Whittaker (21–51): charges against Hiss, 9, 21–24, 22n–23n; forged typewriter theory, 17, 25–41, 50, 115; disagreements with Hiss, 25n, 75–76; libel suit against, 37–38, 259; unresolved questions in testimony, 42–51; *Witness,* 43, 45f, 262; and Bentley, 52, 60, 105, 117, 120; vindication of, 83, 221; and White, 103–4, 222
Chanler, William, 90–102; quoted, 92–101 *passim*
Chennault, Clair, 164, 166, 169–70
Chiang Kai-shek, 130, 141, 164–65, 169
Childs, Morris, 131
Civil Rights Congress, 195, 258
Civil Service Commission, 108
Coe, Frank, 57, 62–63, 68, 110, 112, 114
Collier's, 134, 136, 175
Collins, Eileen H., 85–86
Collins, Henry H., 43f
Columbia Spectator, 54
Commerce Dept., 58
Committee for a Democratic Far Eastern Policy, 147
Committee on Immigration, 95
Communist, 196
Communist Information Bureau (Cominform), 196, 204
Communist International (Comintern), 122, 195f, 202, 214
Communist Party, The: A Manual on Organization, 186
Communist Political Assoc., 181, 190
Communist Party of the U.S.: and SACB, 2, 13, 183; Marxism-Leninism, 6, 11, 186–90 *passim,* 197–98, 199f, 218–19; and Smith Act, 8–13 *passim;* Ware Cell, 43–45; relation to Russia, 52, 195–97, 204; control Commission of, 54; underground organization, 191–92; and Communist Parties of other nations, 197; objectives, 198, 202, 214; and "Exceptionalism," 198; mentioned, 5, 65, 130. *See also* Political Bureau

Communist Workers' School, 53–54
Conference for Progressive Labor Action, 121
Congressional investigation, 1–5 *passim,* 226, 244–45; techniques of, 16–17, 19; advantages and disadvantages of, 227–30; and Immunity Act, 233, 263; listed, by source, 252–57; mentioned, 8, 50n. *See also* House Un-American Activities Committee; House Committees; Senate Committees; Senate Internal Security Subcommittee
Cooke, Alistair, 75
Court trial, 2, 7–8, 21, 48, 230; perjury trials, 8–10, 86, 226; Smith Act indictments, 10–13, 204–17, 250, 262; Remington case, 74–102; listed, by source, 257–58
Crouch, Paul, 202, 203
Currie, Lauchlin, 57, 66–67, 114

Daily Worker: and Budenz, 18, 122ff, 128, 145, 153, 159f; and Bentley, 78; and Lattimore, 140–41; and Browder, 154; and Trachtenberg, 161; and Lautner, 182, 194, 196; and Duclos letter, 206–7
Dennis, Eugene, 190, 205; *U.S. v.,* 11–13, 181–82, 193, 215, 257
Departmental Committee (British), 238f
Devin-Adair, 84–85
Dies Committee, 199
Dimitrov, Georgi, 122
Dodd, Dr. Bella V., 145–47, 157, 160; testimony quoted, 145–47
Donegan, Thomas J., 87–90; testimony quoted, 88n–89n
Douglas, William O., 13
Duclos, Jacques, 188; letter by, 188, 202, 204, 206

Early, Steve, 66
Ehrlich, Evelyn, 28–33 *passim,* 36f
Eisler, Gerhardt (alias Edwards), 195, 202f, 205, 253
Engels, Friedrich, 122
Espionage Acts of 1917 and 1918, 10
Fansler, Thomas, 27, 32f, 35f, 50
Farm Security Administration, 57
Federal Bureau of Investigation: agents in Communist Party, 15,

147, 204; and Bentley, 18, 56, 68–75, 81, 91, 96–102, 113, 118–19; and Hiss typewriter, 36; and Silvermaster ring, 72, 109; and White, 104; and Budenz, 124, 134, 139, 175; and Lattimore, 127–28; and Lautner, 182–83, 193, 209–10; and Jencks principle, 233f, 245, 265

Federal Criminal Code, 8

Feehan, Ramos C., 26

Ferguson, Homer, quoted, 94, 159, 165f

Field, Frederick Vanderbilt, 129–34 *passim*, 146f, 154–57, 161; quoted, 155–56

Fifth Amendment, 45, 47, 49, 109–12, 155, 264

Finer, Herman, quoted, 236

Finnish-Russian War, 142

Finnish Committee, 142

Fitzgerald, Edward, 58, 109

Flynn, Elizabeth Gurley, 179–80, 181f, 188, 218; *U.S.* v., 193, 199–200, 204–12 *passim*, 217, 257

Foley Square trial, 8

Ford, James, 188

Foreign Agents Registration Act, 195

Foreign Economic Admin., 58

Forest, U.S. v., 206–7, 214, 257

Fortas, Abe, 134–35

Foster, William Z., 188–91, 195, 207ff

Foundations of Leninism, 200, 211

Frankfeld (Baltimore) case, 210, 217, 257

Frankfurter, Felix, 80

Franklin, Francis, 188

Freedom of the Press, Inc., 122f, 252

Friends of the Soviet Union, 196

Fuhr, Mrs. Lee, 53

Fujimoto, U.S. v., 200, 210ff, 257

Fund for the Republic, Inc., 249, 261

Garrity, Devin, 84

GPU, 98f

Glasser, Harold, 58, 109f

Goddard, Henry W., 25n

Gold, Bela, 57, 63, 114

Gold, Sonia, 57, 114

Golos, Jacob, 62, 113, 123, 222; and Bentley, 54–56, 61, 76ff, 91–94, 105f

Gouzenko spy case, 187

Grand jury, 8–9, 56, 232; and Remington, 76, 79, 84–90; and Immunity Act, 50n

Green, Gil, 195, 203

Green, Theodore F., quoted, 129, 136f, 141–2

Gregg, Joseph, 58

Gromov, Anatol, 56, 69–75, 102

Gyetvai, John, 186f

Halperin, Maurice, 58, 109f

Hand, Learned, quoted, 87–89

Hanson, Haldore, 175

Harlan, John Marshall, quoted, 193

Hathaway, Clarence, 122

Hebert, Paul M., quoted, 65, 70–71

Heller, Peter, 73–74, 98–102 *passim*

Hickenlooper, Bourke B., 133, 149; quoted, 146–47

Hillman, Sidney, 64n

Hiss, Alger, 42, 75–76, 129, 221–22; court trials of, 8–9, 21–24, 22n–23n, 257; forged typewriter theory, 17, 24–41, 115; *In the Court of Public Opinion*, 23–25, 42, 262; grounds for new trial, 24–25, 25n, 262–63; libel action against Chambers, 37–38; Ware Cell, 43–45; at Smithtown, 45–46, 50; gift of rug, 46–48, 50–51; and Timothy Hobson, 48, 51

Hiss, Priscilla (Mrs. Alger), 26, 45–46, 50–51

"Hiss Standards," 26, 29–31, 33f, 39f

History of the Communist Party of the Soviet Union, The, 196, 210

Hobson, Timothy, 48, 51

Hoover Commission of 1947–49, 240

Hoover, Herbert, 55

Hoover, J. Edgar, 72, 119, 127; and Bentley, 69, 73, 109, 112–13; quoted, 72, 112

House Committee on Education and Labor, 254–55

House Committee on Tax-Exempt Foundations (Cox Comm.), 176, 255

House Un-American Activities Committee, 43, 47f, 79, 129, 249; and Bentley, 18, 60–71, 91, 115, 227–28; hearings listed, 252–54

Huber, John, 147–52, 156

Hudson, Roy, 180, 188
Hughes, Charles Evans, 240
Hungarian Bureau, 179, 207
Hungarian National Training School, 186, 188, 214

Immigration and Naturalization Service, 2
Immunity Act, 49f, 118, 263, 265; use of, 112, 231–33
In the Court of Public Opinion, 23–25, 42, 262
Inslerman, Felix, 47
Institute of Pacific Relations, 58, 129, 152–55 *passim*, 158; IPR hearings, 44, 72, 125–26, 158–75, 249, 255, 264; *Pacific Affairs*, 129, 173
Internal Security Act. *See* McCarran Act

Jacson, Frank, 123
Jaffe, Philip, 130
Jefferson School of Social Science, 203, 207, 258
Jencks principle (*U.S. v. Jencks*) 233–34, 245, 265
Jessup, Philip, 155
Johnson, Howard, 194
Johnson, Manning, 203
Johnstone, Jack, 188
Joint Anti-Fascist Refugee Committee, 78, 253
Joseph, Bella, 58
Joseph, J. Julius, 58, 109
Justice, Dept. of, 11, 13, 20, 216–17

Kaplan, Irving, 57–58, 110
Kerley, Larry E., 151, 156; quoted, 147–48
Kling, Jack, 194, 196
Kornfeder, Joseph, 202
Kramer, Charles, 43f, 58, 104f, 109
Kun, Bela, 178
Kunming, cables, 164f, 169f
Kuzma, U.S. v., 201, 211, 257

Labor Age, 121
Labor Youth League, 258
Landy, Avro, 180, 188
Lane, Chester, 25–29, 32–38, 41, 50
Lattimore, Owen: and Budenz, 19, 125–26, 127, 224; and Tydings

Comm., 127–58, 174f; and Communist line in China, 134–36, 139–43 *passim*, 152, 155f; *Situation in Asia*, 140–43 *passim*, 264; and Wallace mission, 162–69; and IPR hearings, 172–74
Lautner, John (178–220): "Aesopian" theory 12; as Communist functionary, 19–20, 185–98; his life, 178–83, 198; quoted, 181, 189f, 195, 208–13 *passim*; reliability of his testimony, 183–85, 201–6, 217–20, 224–25; cross-examinations of, 199–201; inconsistencies in testimony, 206–16; and FBI, 209–10; motives for falsification, 216–17
Lee, Duncan, 58, 105ff, 114f, 117, 223
Lenin, V. I. (Nikolai), 122, 185, 187
Lieber, Maxim, 45–46, 50
Lippmann, Walter, 58, 117, 229–30
Little Lenin Library, 191, 212
Lodge, Henry Cabot, Jr., quoted, 132–33
Loyalty Board, 78, 81
Loyalty proceeding, 81–82
Loyalty Review Board, 78, 81, 84
Lynskey, George J., 237

McCarran Act, 14–16, 220, 231, 262
McCarran Committee. *See* Senate Internal Security Subcommittee
McCarran, Patrick A., 5, 126, 159, 172
McCarthy, Elizabeth, 28, 31–32, 36f
McCarthy, Joseph R., 139, 264; Communists in State Dept., 125–28, 157, 246; and Huber, 148f, 152
McCormick Act, 122–23
McIntyre, Marvin, 66
McMahon, Brien, 149–51, 153–54
Magdoff, Harry, 58, 62, 109
Majer, Gus, 186
Marini, Feruccio, 54
Markward, Mary Stalcup, 204
Marshall Plan, 142f, 176
Marx, Karl, 122
Marx-Engels-Lenin Institute, 161
Marxism-Leninism. *See under* Communist Party of U.S.
Massing, Hede, 4, 41
Matthews, J. B., 151

Matusow, 203, 255
Medina, Harold R., 12
Meyer, Frank S., 203
Midwest Daily Record, 122
Miller, Robert, 58, 105–7, 114f, 223
Mindel, Jacob "Pop," 187–8, 190
Minor, Bob, 180, 195
Moreau, Alberto, 191
Moreland Act, 240–41
Moreland Commission, 265
Morgan, Edward P., 131, 135, 157; quoted, 135–44 *passim*, 147–53 *passim*
Morris, Robert, 148, 158, 162; quoted, 149–52, 159–66 *passim*
Mosely, Dr. Philip, 202
Mundt, Karl E., 68
Murphy, Frank, 208
Murray, Edith, 25n
Muste, A. J., 121

NKVD, 54
National Labor Relations Act, 255
National Trade Union Commission, 123
Nationality Groups Commission, 207
New Masses, 76
N. Y. Journal American, 147
N. Y. Labor Conference for Peace, 252
N. Y. State Board of Regents, 183, 187, 200–1, 210, 212–13, 217, 259
N. Y. State Trade Union Comm., 123
New York World-Telegram, 52, 76, 84
Noonan, Gregory, 79
Norman, Bob, 191
Norman, Daniel P., 32–33, 36f
North, Joe, 76ff
North Carolina Progressive Party, 117–18
Nowell, William Odell, 202

Office of the Coordinator of Inter-American Affairs (CIAA), 58, 105
Office of Strategic Services (OSS), 58, 106, 126
Ordeal by Slander, 264
Out of Bondage, 55, 59–60, 84, 263

PM, 77f, 77n
Pacific Affairs, 129, 173
Park, Willard Z., 58

Parris, Leonard, 134, 136–37; quoted, 135
People's Front, 122
Pepper, Claude D., 62
Perjury trial. *See under* Court trial.
Perlo group, 58, 64, 105, 117
Perlo, Victor, 43f, 58, 62, 104f, 109f
Peters, J., 43f, 122, 186f; his *Manual*, 202
Political Affairs, 196
Political Bureau (Politburo) of the Communist Party of the U.S.: onionskin documents, 130–31, 144f, 153, 160; and Budenz, 122f, 128–133 *passim*, 160; and Wallace mission, 163, 166f
Pressman, Lee, 25n, 43–45
Price, Mary, 58, 106, 117–18
Price, Mildred, 58, 117
Profintern 196, 202
Progressive Citizens of America, 64, 64n

Rankin, John E., quoted, 64–67 *passim*
Rajk, Laszlo, 180, 182, 193
Redmont, Bernard, 58, 105ff, 114–15, 223
Remington, Ann Moos (Mrs. Wm.), 76, 79, 81, 87–93, 103, 105
Remington, William, 8–9, 18, 76–84, 223, 227–28, 263–64; first perjury trial, 52, 73f, 90–02, 257; first indictment, 84–90; and Mrs. Remington's testimony, 102–3; mentioned, 58, 106, 222
Reynolds, John Hazard, 56
Roberts, Owen J., 243
Rogers, William P., quoted, 78
Roosevelt, Franklin D., 164, 170, 207
Rosen, William, 47
Rosenberg, Allen, 58, 109
Rosenberg, Ethel, 257
Rosenberg, Julius, 113–14, 257
Royal Commission of Inquiry, 237–42 *passim*, 246
Russo-Finnish War, 142

Santa (Santo), John, 186
Saypol, Irving, 90–102; quoted, 93, 99–101

Schapiro, Meyer, 46–47, 51
Schneiderman, William, *U.S.* v., 207–8, 215–17, 258
Schraffts' meeting, 76f, 91–93
Scott, Byron N., Esq., 263
Sefa, Leyla, 85–86
Semonofsky, Ben, 196
Senate Committee on Expenditures, Investigations Subcommittee, 76–79, 81, 91–92, 94, 256
Senate Committee on Foreign Relations, 125f, 157, 256. *See also* Tydings Committee
Senate Committee on Government Operations, Investigations Permanent Subcommittee, 256
Senate Committee on the Judiciary, 125–26, 162, 255. *See also* Senate Internal Security Subcommittee
Senate Internal Security Subcommittee (IPR hearings), 44, 72, 125–26, 158–75, 249, 255, 264
Sheen, Fulton J., 124
Shelhorse, Mildred, 93
Silverman, Abraham George, 46–47, 58, 62ff, 66, 109f; *U.S.* v., 187, 209f, 214, 217, 258
Silvermaster, Helen, 58, 61ff, 104, 118, 223
Silvermaster, Nathan Gregory, 57, 66, 72f, 104, 108ff, 223
Silvermaster ring, 57–63 *passim*, 66, 73f, 103, 109, 115
Simon, Hal, 181, 191
Simon, Moses, 194
Siskind, George, 187
Situation in Asia, 140–43 *passim*, 264
Smith Act, 2, 6, 8, 14, 220, 230; indictments, 10–13, 204–17, 250, 262
Smith, H. Alexander, quoted, 163, 167f, 171
Sokolsky, George, 151
Sourwine, Jay, quoted, 162f, 167–68
Soviet Russia 6, 46, 52
Soviet Russia Today, 196
Stachel, Jack, 122, 128–32 *passim*, 138, 144f, 162–63, 207
Stalin, 122f, 140, 187, 211, 213
State, Dept. of, 125–26
State Dept. Employee Loyalty Investigation. *See* Tydings Committee

Statute of limitations, 8–9
Stilwell, Joseph W., 164–70 *passim*
Stripling, Robert E., 61–64; quoted, 61–64, 70
Subversive Activities Control Board, 2, 15, 231, 249–50, 258; and Lautner, 183, 195–97, 202–4, 206, 209f, 217; proceedings against Communist Party, 202ff, 213f; proceedings against Jefferson School of Social Science, 207
Supreme Court, 13–16 *passim*, 26, 49, 80, 203f, 207–8

Tennessee Valley Authority, 79, 82
Tenney, Helen, 58
Thomas, John W., 241; quoted, 65–66, 71
Thomas-Ives bill, 243, 265
Thompson, Bob, 181, 191, 194
Trachtenberg, Alexander, 122, 161, 194; *U.S.* v., 258
Trade Union Unity League, 196, 202
Treasury Dept., 57f, 61, 103f, 115f
Tribunal of Inquiry, 236–37, 241f, 246, 265
Tribunals of Inquiry (Evidence) Act, 238f
Trotsky, Leon, 55, 123, 254; Trotskyites, 121, 123
Truman, Harry S., 15, 71, 119, 235
Twilight of World Capitalism, The, 205, 209
Tydings Committee: and Browder, 118, 152–54; and Budenz, 125f, 128–44, 224, 228; and Lattimore, 125f, 156, 264; formation of, 126–27; appearances before, 128–56; criticisms of, 156–58; compared to IPR hearings, 158–60; conclusions of, 174–75
Tydings, Millard E., 5, 125–26, 158; quoted, 127, 129, 132–33, 137–41 *passim*, 144, 148–51, 155–56
Tytell, Martin, 26–30, 37

Uj Elore, 186
Ullmann, William Ludwig, 116, 118, 123, 223; v. *U.S.*, 49, 232, 262; and Bentley, 57, 61, 66, 112; use of Fifth Amendment, 109f
United Electrical, Radio and Machine

Workers of America, CIO, 249, 255, 256
United Mine Workers, 215
U.S. Court of Appeals, 26, 79–80, 82, 86–87
U.S. Service and Shipping Corporation, 56, 72

Vaughan, Harry H., 72
Veterans of the Abraham Lincoln Brigade, 2, 258
Vincent, John Carter, 162–72 *passim*

Wadleigh, Henry Julian, 47
Wallace, Henry, 64, 64n; mission to China, 130, 162–72, 175
War Production Board, 58, 76
Ware Cell, 43–45
Wedemeyer, Albert Coady, 164ff, 169f

Weil, Ruby, 123
Weinstock, Louis, 186, 193–94
Wellman, Solly, 194, 258
Weyl, Nathaniel, 4, 40f, 44–45, 105
Wheeler, Donald, 58, 109
White, Harry Dexter, 47, 71–72, 116, 222, 235, 264; and Bentley, 57, 62, 71–73, 103–4, 114
Williamson, John, 188, 189, 203, 206f
Witness, 43, 45f, 262
Witt, Nathan, 43f
Wolfenden, Sir John, 239; report, 239–40
Woodstock Co., 27, 35f
Workers' School, 123
World-Telegram, 143
World Tourists, 54f

Yates v. *U.S.*, 13
Young Communist League, 80f, 83, 188, 203